Western Man and the Mo[dern World]

Industrialism, Imperialism, and War

About the Series:

Western Man and the Modern World is a series of 5 separate books, each covering one aspect or period of World History.

A *Teaching Resource Book* accompanies the texts with a large selection of readings and exercises.

A *Sound-filmstrip* series is also available.
The texts are:
- I *Origins of Western Civilization*
- II *Rivalry, Reason, and Revolution*
- III *Industrialism, Imperialism, and War*
- IV *The Western World Today*
- V *Africa, Latin America, and The East*

About the Author:

Leonard James, the author of the 5 texts, received his B.A. and Diploma in Education from the University of Bristol, England. As Frances Riggs Fellow he received his M.A. in History and Political Science from the University of Michigan. He was Chairman of the Social Studies Committee of the Secondary Education Board and President of New England History Teachers' Association; Chairman of Department of History, Cecil F. B. Bancroft Foundation, and also on the Independence Foundation at Phillips Academy, Andover, Mass. He is the author of *Following the Frontier: American Transportation in the Nineteenth Century*, (Harcourt Brace) for young readers, and of *The Supreme Court in American Life*, and *American Foreign Policy* (Scott Foresman).

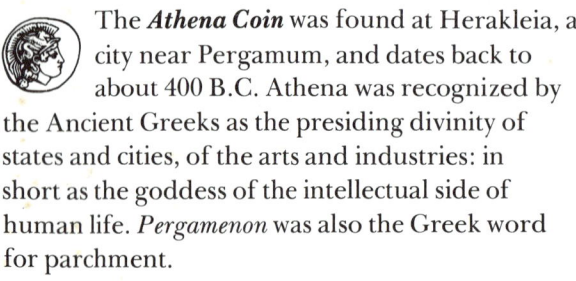

The **Athena Coin** was found at Herakleia, a city near Pergamum, and dates back to about 400 B.C. Athena was recognized by the Ancient Greeks as the presiding divinity of states and cities, of the arts and industries: in short as the goddess of the intellectual side of human life. *Pergamenon* was also the Greek word for parchment.

Western Man and the Modern World: III

Industrialism, Imperialism, and War

by **Leonard F. James**

Content Editor	Jean P. KixMiller, *New Trier Township High School*
Project Co-ordinator	John R. L. Dent, *Pergamon Press Inc.*
Maps	David Cox & Jill Thompson, *Pergamon Cartographic Dept.*
Picture Research	Sandi Hughes-Jones and John Dent
Typography	Carl F. Zahn

Pergamon Press Inc. New York Oxford Toronto Sydney Frankfurt

Copyright © 1973. Pergamon Press Inc.

Pergamon Press Inc.
Maxwell House, Fairview Park, Elmsford, N.Y. 10523

Pergamon Press, Ltd.
Headington Hill Hall, Oxford

Pergamon of Canada, Ltd.
207 Queen's Quay West, Toronto 117, Ontario

Pergamon Press (Aust.) Pty. Ltd.
Rushcutters Bay, Sydney, N.S.W.

Pergamon Press GmbH
Frankfurt-am-Main, W. Germany

All Rights Reserved. No part of this publication may be reproduced, stored in a retrieval system or transmitted in any form, or by any means, electronic, mechanical, photo-copying, recording or otherwise, without prior permission of Pergamon Press Inc.

Library of Congress Cataloging in Publication Data

James, Leonard Frank.
    Industrialism, imperialism, and war.

    (His Western man and the modern world, # 3)
    SUMMARY: One in a five volume series on the history of Western civilization, this volume traces that history from 1760 to 1925.
    1. History, Modern--19th century. 2. History, Modern--18th century. 3. European War, 1914–1918.
[1. History, Modern--19th century. 2. History, Modern--18th century. 3. European War, 1914–1918]
I. Title.
CB245.J34 vol. 3 [D358.5] 910'.03' 1812s [909'.09'81207]
ISBN 0-08-017202-4   72-10951
ISBN 0-08-017203-2 (pbk)

First Printing March 1973

Second Printing November 1973

Third Printing April 1977

Printed in the United States of America

To my wife
Maja
for her cheerful encouragement

Contents

1 Industrialization and its Consequences — 1

1. The Industrial Revolution, 3
2. The Agricultural Revolution, 6
3. Effects of the Industrial Revolution, 8
4. Defenders of Laissez-Faire, 9
5. Critics of Laissez-Faire, 12
6. "Scientific" Socialism of Karl Marx, 17
7. The Second Industrial Revolution, 22

2 The German Empire and Italian Unity — 27

1. The Unification of Germany, 1848–1870, 29
2. Domestic Problems and Solutions, 1870–1890, 33
3. Foreign Affairs of the German Empire, 1870–1890, 36
4. The Unification of Italy, 1815–1871, 37

3 The Growth of Democracy in Great Britain, France, and the United States — 45

Great Britain, 47–56
1. Parliamentary Reform, 47
2. Improvement of Working Conditions, 50
3. Later Parliamentary Reform, 52
4. Social Security, 55

France, 56–60
5. The Second Empire, 56
6. The Third Republic, 58
7. Crises of the Third Republic, 59

United States, 60–65
8. Agitation for Reforms, 60
9. Political and Social Reforms, 63

4 The British Empire and Commonwealth — 67

1. Canada, 69
2. Australia and New Zealand, 72
3. Ireland, 76
4. South Africa, 80
5. The British Commonwealth and Empire, 83

5 Nineteenth Century Imperialism — 87

1. Motives for Imperialism, 89
2. The Opening of China, 91
3. Japan Westernizes and Expands, 95
4. Reaction to the Partitioning of China, 98
5. Imperialism in Southeast Asia, 102
6. Imperialism in Africa, 105

6 The United States: Industrial Nation and World Power — 113

1. The Growth of Corporations and Railroads, *115*
2. Regulation of Railroads and Corporations, *116*
3. Attempts of Labor to Organize, *118*
4. The Agrarian Revolt, *120*
5. The Progressive Movement, *121*
6. The Emergence of the United States as a World Power, *124*

7 Background and Origins of World War I

1. The Rival Alliances, *133*
2. Tensions between Alliances, *137*
3. Responsibility for the War? *142*

8 World War I — 147

1. German Preparations for War, *149*
2. The Germans Halted, *150*
3. Stalemate on the Western Front, *154*
4. The United States Enters the War, *157*
5. Peace Proposals and the Armistice, *160*

9 The Search for Peace through Collective Security — 167

1. The Paris Peace Conference, *169*
2. Terms of the Versailles Treaty and Other Treaties, *170*
3. German Acceptance of the Treaty of Versailles, *177*
4. Evaluation of the Treaty of Versailles, *178*
5. The League of Nations, *180*
6. Collective Security v. The Alliance System, *183*

Glossary — 189

General Index — 193

Map Index — 197

Maps and Diagrams

Maps

Unification of Germany: Prussia, 1866	*31*
Unification of Germany: North German Confederation, 1867	*31*
Unification of Germany: The German Empire, 1871	*33*
Italy after the Congress of Vienna	*38*
Unification of Italy, 1859–1871	*41*
Reform of Parliament	*48*
Immigration, 1830–1910	*60*
Canada, 1791–1912	*71*
Australia and New Zealand	*75*
Ireland	*76*
South Africa	*81*
British Empire and Commonwealth, 1922	*84*
Imperialism in the Far East: 1842–1914	*94*
British India	*103*
Africa in 19th Century	*108*
United States, Growth of Railroads	*116*
United States and the Caribbean	*125*
European Alliance System to 1914	*138*
Schlieffen Plan	*149*
World War I, 1914	*150*
Sea Power	*153*
World War I, 1915	*155*
World War I, 1916–1918	*158*
World War I, Allied Victory	*161*
Europe after Treaty of Versailles	*171*
Ethnic and Linguistic, 1914	*174*
Distribution of German Colonies	*181*
League of Nations and the Mandates	*182*

Diagrams

The House of Lords	*54*
Immigration (U.S.) 1830–1910	*60*

Art in Color

Between Pages	*88 and 89*

Introduction

The themes of this book all connect in logical order. *Industrialism* changed the whole economic and social structure of Western man's life. *Imperialism* grew because of the need of Western nations to control the areas of the world that provided the raw materials needed in new industry. *War* became world wide as nations sought to protect their industrial and imperial interests.

None of these themes is one of which Western man is any longer proud. However, the late 20th century has now seen the first major efforts to counteract the problems that these three themes produced. This volume is an essential starting point for an understanding of modern events and movements.

Acknowledgments

The author's thanks go to Barbara McDonnell, Director of the Oliver Wendell Holmes Library, Phillips Academy, for her professional assistance. Thanks are also due Jean KixMiller, teacher of history in Winnetka, for her editorial comments and suggestions; to John Dent, co-ordinator of the project, who in addition to producing the filmstrips to complement the text, kept a tight rein on all in the enterprise, made many a valuable suggestion, and gathered up the many loose ends of getting a book to press; and to Sara Lofving, copy editor.

L. F. J.

1

Industrialization and its Consequences

The Industrial Revolution
The Agricultural Revolution
Effects of the Industrial Revolution
Defenders of Laissez-Faire
Critics of Laissez-Faire
"Scientific" Socialism of Karl Marx
The Second Industrial Revolution

The Industrial Revolution, which changed much of Western society from an agricultural to an industrial economy, commenced in England where increasing demands for woolen cloth accelerated inventions in textile machinery. The use of mechanical power to process large quantities of raw materials created the factory with its machines, source of power, labor to tend the machines, and the necessary capital.

The need to transport raw materials to factories, and finished products to market accelerated the construction of roads, railroads, and shipping. Concentrations of population in manufacturing centers revolutionized methods of raising food, and created problems not experienced by agricultural communities: police and fire protection, sanitation regulations, health precautions, education, and unemployment.

The new factory owners and businessmen demanded freedom of action and denounced government intervention in business. Critics of the new individualism charged business with lack of responsibility for the community, and demanded government intervention.

Karl Marx used contemporary conditions to argue that social revolution was inevitable because free enterprise doomed itself to competitive self-destruction. The Marxian doctrine of state ownership of all means of production and distribution was to become the political and economic ideology of Soviet Russia and other Communist countries.

Terms

1. Industrial Revolution
2. Flying Shuttle
3. Spinning Jenny
4. Cotton Gin
5. Agricultural Revolution
6. Enclosures
7. Domestic System
8. Factory System
9. Industrial Capitalist
10. Laissez-faire
11. Economist
12. *Wealth of Nations*
13. *Principles of Political Economy*
14. *Principles of Population*
15. Iron Law of Wages
16. National Minimum
17. Utopian
18. Socialist
19. Phalanx
20. New Harmony
21. Co-operatives
22. "Scientific" Socialism
23. *Communist Manifesto*
24. *Das Kapital*
25. Dialectical Materialism
26. Thesis, Antithesis, Synthesis
27. Economic Determinism
28. Class Struggle
29. Dictatorship of the Proletariat
30. Workingmen's Internationals
31. Communist International (Comintern)
32. Christian Socialists
33. Fabian Socialists
34. Second Industrial Revolution

People

35. John Kay
36. James Hargreaves
37. Richard Arkwright
38. Eli Whitney
39. Solomon de Caus
40. Thomas Savery
41. Thomas Newcomen
42. James Watt
43. Jethro Tull
44. "Turnip" Townshend
45. Robert Bakewell
46. Arthur Young
47. Adam Smith
48. John Stuart Mill
49. Thomas Malthus
50. David Ricardo
51. Gracchus Babeuf
52. Charles Fourier
53. Robert Owen
54. Karl Marx
55. Friedrich Engels
56. Georg Hegel
57. Henry Bessemer

Events

1712 Thomas Newcomen: steam pump
1733 John Kay: flying shuttle
1765 James Hargreaves: spinning machine
1776 James Watt: steam engine
       Adam Smith: *Wealth of Nations*
1793 Eli Whitney: cotton gin
1798 Thomas Malthus: *Principles of Population*
1826 Robert Owen: New Harmony founded
1838 John Stuart Mill: *Principles of Political Economy*
       Karl Marx: *The Communist Manifesto*
1864 First International Workingmen's Association
1889 Second International
1919 Third (Communist) International

1. The Industrial Revolution

Definition of the Term

The term "Industrial Revolution" is used to explain the mechanical inventions and the use of power that changed western Europe from an agricultural to an industrial society. These changes began about 1750 and have continued ever since then, with the first great acceleration in the 19th century, sometimes called the Second Industrial Revolution. Not only did machines replace hand tools, and steam power replace human energy, during the First Industrial Revolution, but agricultural techniques were greatly improved to provide food for growing populations and concentrations of factory workers.

The term "revolution" usually refers to a sudden and violent change in society, such as the American or the French Revolution. The Industrial Revolution was neither sudden nor violent, and although it occurred over a long period of time it drastically changed the lives of the people in every country which became industrialized. From the middle of the 18th century through the early years of the 19th century, the development of textile machinery and the steam engine proceeded so rapidly that their greatly increased production of manufactured goods and their effects upon the living and working conditions of so many people could certainly be regarded as "revolutionary."

Perhaps the great change can be appreciated if we turn back to the 18th century and see how people lived then. Most people were peasants depending upon farm production and a little extra handwork such as spinning and weaving. Industry was still in the handicraft stage; roads in most countries were generally no better than those upon which the Roman legions had marched across Europe; and transportation was limited to wagons, stage-coaches, and sailing ships. It is an interesting fact that so little technical advance had been made over the previous 300 years that the naval ships which Admiral Nelson commanded at the Battle of Trafalgar in 1805 had no greater cannon-range than the ships commanded by Sir Francis Drake against the Spanish Armada in 1588.

London and Paris, the largest cities in Europe, were not much larger than ancient Rome. They were capital cities but not the industrial centers they were later to become. Large populations could not live together in the early 18th century because there was no work for large groups, and transportation was inadequate to bring in the great quantities of food needed for large urban areas. Yet by the end of the 19th century England, and, to a lesser degree, Germany, France, and Belgium had changed rapidly into industrial nations with great numbers of their people working in factories and others busy transporting manufactured goods to the far corners of the world.

Reasons for the Industrial Revolution

Man has always been able to use nature for his own purposes. History has seen him taming rivers, growing food, using metals, and in other ways making life easier and better for himself. And yet for many centuries he had done little more than use his own energy and that of animals to do the necessary work. Of course, he used wind and streams to run simple tools such as windmills and flour mills. But these forces were natural ones, and man was still to a large degree dependent upon nature. Handicraft methods depended upon a tool, which was simply the extension of an arm. A workman's strength, skill, and intelligence in the use of tools determined the production of goods.

Even a cotton gin turned by hand, or a series of spinning wheels joined together and turned by a crank were tools. The machine on the other hand, did not depend upon a workman's strength and skill but upon power to run it, whatever the source of power. A machine was simply fed and kept in working order by a workman, and it often replaced one or more workers.

In the 17th and 18th centuries England had a large trade with other countries in woolen cloth, but all the processes of turning raw wool into cloth were done by hand. Growing demand at home and abroad, and the great number of people engaged in home spinning and weaving encouraged men to invent improved techniques in both these occupations. For decades one weaver could use the work of four spinners, because hand spinning was so slow and tedious a process. The fluffed-up fibers had to be "drawn out" into a continuous loose thread and then twisted by a spinning wheel run by a foot pedal, and finally wound onto a bobbin or spool.

The bottleneck in weaving was getting the threads separated and a cross-thread put between them. On the hand loom alternate threads were raised and lowered in the form of a "shed" or angle. The weaver then reached to his right and threw a shuttle across the loom to his left. He then "beat" that thread tightly against the previous one, changed the warp threads by a foot pedal reversing their position, then reached to his left and threw the shuttle back to his right. The width of the cloth was limited by a man's reach to left and right, although two men could work a wider loom together.

Inventions in Textile Machinery

The first important textile invention was the "flying shuttle," invented by John Kay in 1733, who devised a pulley system. The weaver pulled a rope which caused a hammer at the right to hit the shuttle across the loom to his left. He then used the foot-pedal to reverse the position of the warp, pulled a rope at his left, which

The Flying Shuttle Loom. The shuttle was "thrown" horizontally — the threads were raised by the foot pedals.

knocked the shuttle back to the right. This invention so speeded up the weaving process that either the number of spinners had to be increased or the spinning process be much improved.

James Hargreaves in 1765 patented the "spinning jenny" or spinning machine which was a box frame with a row of spindles that were turned by a hand crank, and could spin eight or more threads at a time. Richard Arkwright improved upon this by adapting the spinning-machine to water-power to drive a hundred spindles. Once hand labor for spinning was replaced by water-powered machines, a textile manufacturer needed centrally-located buildings containing large and expensive machines. In this way the factory was born, with a large labor force necessary to tend the machines.

As demand for cheap cotton cloth increased, so did the demand for raw cotton. In 1793 Eli

The Spinning Jenny

Whitney in the United States invented the cotton gin or engine, a simple machine which could clean raw cotton by separating the seeds from the fibers much faster than could be done by hand cleaning. His invention made possible the profitable growth of short-staple cotton which had previously been so expensive to clean by hand that it was uneconomical to grow. So great was the demand for raw cotton in England that between 1793 and 1801 its production in the United States increased from 2,000,000 pounds to 85,000,000 pounds.

The Steam Engine

The use of steam was known to the ancient Greeks because evidence shows that Hero of Alexandria constructed a device on which a ball was made to rotate by the use of steam. But almost no attention was paid to the possible uses of steam until the 17th century, when the French experimenter Solomon de Caus (1576–1630) discovered that if a tank filled with steam were closed, and the steam condensed, then a sufficient vacuum would be created to move a simple piston. Around 1700 A.D. Thomas

Eli Whitney's Cotton Gin

Savery devised a simple steam engine based on the principle of "the power of suction induced by steam." A friend told him of an incident which proved this. He had ordered a flask of wine, drunk the wine, and flung the empty flask on a fire. As he stood washing his hands in a bowl of water he noticed steam in the flask. He picked it off the fire, plunged the mouth into the bowl of water and saw water driven up into the flask by pressure of the outside air.

Savery used this principle in devising an engine to pump water from a depth of 62 feet. But this device was not practicable for pumping water out of coal mines until Thomas Newcomen (1663–1729) improved it by using a piston. His improvements and the wide use of his engines justified his title of "father of the steam engine." Actually Newcomen's engine was expensive to run because fuel wastage was close to 99 percent. One critic remarked that it took an iron ore mine to build a Newcomen engine and a coal mine to run it.

James Watt (1736–1819) not only improved its efficiency and lowered its cost but also adapted the simple reciprocating, up and down, movement to rotary motion to turn a wheel. This development opened up the use of steam to drive a locomotive and turn paddle wheels. Transportation was soon radically changed from wagons and stage-coaches to steam locomotives and steam ships. Rails could be laid anywhere in the country to connect ports to mines and cities, and speed up the movement of raw materials and manufactured goods in greater amounts.

Coal, Iron, and Machine Tools

The invention of machines and the need for more efficient power than water power made coal-mining a source of new wealth for England. The annual production of 2,000,000 tons in 1700 increased to over 60,000,000 tons by 1850, and this resulted in necessary improvement in coal-mining, the draining of mines, and better transportation facilities. As more ore was mined and smelted by the old technique of burning it with charcoal, which is wood cooked in an oven to burn off impurities, the forests of England became depleted and the price of charcoal rose to almost prohibitive levels. Then coal was used as a substitute for charcoal. But natural coal had so many impurities that the iron was practically useless until the gas was burned off and other impurities cooked out. Coke was then used to cast iron for pots and cannons, and for pig iron to be hammered into wrought iron. Iron was later processed into steel by re-melting it in a crucible and adding pure carbon.

Later developments in coal, iron, and steel became the basis of the economic system of Britain, Germany, and Belgium. Great Britain had two advantages in the industrial age. Her invention of textile machinery gave her textile products a leading position in the world market, and by mid-19th century she had opened more than two-thirds of the world's productive coal mines. Coal was essential both to provide the heat necessary to smelt iron ore and also to boil water in the steam engine.

2. The Agricultural Revolution

Need for Improved Methods

As late as 1700 the methods of producing food were much the same as they had been for the past several centuries. The land was farmed under the three-field system and in open strips. Agricultural instruments were crude, and there was almost no attempt to study agriculture or apply scientific methods to food-raising and animal-breeding. Because the population had increased only very slowly during the previous

Watt's Steam Engine

three centuries there was scarcely any increased demand for food, and therefore little need to improve.

By the end of the 18th century, however, factories were starting up in England on a fairly large scale, roads and transport had improved, and demand for food was growing for a population now increased by 70 percent to 10,000,000 people. England could import some food from Russia and France, but she preferred to depend upon her own resources. The Napoleonic Wars proved the danger of depending upon European nations for vital supplies. The New World could supply some foods, but the vast wheat-growing areas had not yet opened up. England had the alternatives of starvation, dependence upon other nations, or new methods.

The Enclosure Movement
The open-field system of little cultivable strips separated by uncultivated strips was wasteful. Not only did a farmer produce relatively little but he was unable to experiment, and the improvement of stock-breeding was impracticable when animals grazed upon common land open to all. These conditions were in part remedied in the 16th century when many villages accepted the enclosing of fields. Scattered strips were replaced by compact sections and fenced or hedged in. Farmers experimented, crops increased and farming villages became more prosperous. But one kind of enclosure brought bitter protest and serious hardship. The demand for English woolen cloth made sheep-rearing more profitable than produce-growing. Landlords enclosed farms into large sheep-runs, gave former serfs and peasants their freedom, and hired back a few sheep herders.

In the late 18th century the demand for food grew so great that the government passed several thousand enclosure acts. The 19th century was the age of the large farm and the comparatively wealthy farmer willing to experiment and increase his production. The agricultural revolution was essentially an increase in production and efficiency. Both these were influenced by the growth of population, improved methods of transportation with subsequently wider markets.

Improved Farming Methods
Jethro Tull (1674–1741) proved that seed sown in rows instead of by random hand-scattering produced better crops. He invented a simple mechanical drill for the purpose, and kept the spaces between rows free of choking weeds. Not until the latter part of the 18th century did enclosures make his technique profitable.

Lord Townshend (1670–1738) adopted Tull's deep-plowing, sowing, drills and hoeing, and proved the value of crop rotation. Instead of leaving one of every three fields fallow or idle each year, he rotated the grain crops with turnips and clover. Nicknamed "Turnip Townshend" for his enthusiasm for turnip-growing, he performed a great service in proving that turnips could be used as winter fodder for cattle, whose feeding in winter had been so serious a problem that only breeding cattle could be kept throughout the winter months.

Robert Bakewell (1725–1795) contributed to the scientific breeding of live-stock. Sheep had long been raised mainly for their wool, cattle for milk, and oxen for the plow. Bakewell experimented with breeding in order to increase the nation's meat supply. Cattle and particularly sheep were increased in size and quality, so that in time England's meat production tripled.

Arthur Young (1741–1820) performed a great service for farming by writing voluminously, and very profitably for himself, on farming; he also lectured across the country, and finally persuaded the British government to set up the

Board of Agriculture which published farming information gathered from all parts of the nation.

3. Effects of the Industrial Revolution

The Factory System
The factory is the symbol of industrialization because the factory demanded heavy machines, a large labor supply, a source of power, and large amounts of capital. The factory system radically changed methods of production from the old domestic or "putting-out" system to that of centralized working places. By the old domestic system the local merchant brought raw material to peasants who processed it into the finished article and were paid for the work. Markets were uncertain and generally expanded only slowly, capital was scarce, and peasants did the work in their spare time. Textile machines and improved transportation methods made it more efficient and profitable to bring workers from their homes to factories, where they became full-time workers.

Power Looms in a Factory

The Industrial Capitalists
The domestic system was run by individual merchants, each with his own supply of raw material, and his regular peasant-workers. The merchants were the middlemen between hand-loom and the market-place.

The organizing and operating of factories became the occupation of experts and men who now invested money in the large enterprises. Under the factory system a business was run on the capitalist method of investment for private profit. The owners of the company owned buildings, machines, raw materials, hired the workers, and found markets for their products. The investor or lender of money expected payment for his investment in the form of a dividend. Savings were re-invested in expanded factories, until little businesses and factories became large, impersonal operations with vast capital.

Problems Created by the Factory System
The first obvious effect of the factory system was the concentration of people into what soon became factory towns. This urbanization, or growth of industrial towns, introduced problems that had not previously existed. Under the domestic system the peasant was not completely dependent upon the extra work. He could always grow his own food, and he had a place to live. As a factory worker he was entirely dependent upon his job for food and rent. If he became unemployed, then he had to depend upon local charity, for he rarely earned enough to put any money aside for bad times. There were no such methods of dealing with unemployment as unemployment insurance or public works, as governments provide today.

Modern society usually sets up requirements on such issues as minimum wages, maximum hours, conditions of work, child labor, unemployment, and care for dependents. But

Children at Work

throughout the 19th century little was done by any government authority, except in Germany, to remedy long hours, low wages, and conditions which were frequently intolerable. Some of the reasons for this state of affairs will be examined in the section discussing *laissez-faire* and its defenders. Economists of the day had not yet realized that the wealth of a country is determined in large part by full employment, and that unemployment removes buying-power, in the form of wages, from a large segment of the population, with the possibility of increasingly severe unemployment and loss of buying-power.

Other problems of urbanization are still evident in society today. Rules about sanitation, housing standards, education, police and fire protection are among the many needs that cannot be performed by individuals today, but must be carried out by the government of the community.

4. Defenders of Laissez-Faire

Early Economic Practices
Although man struggled during six thousand years of recorded history to survive and improve his conditions, no economist appeared upon the scene to guide him. Soldiers, politicians, historians, statesmen, artists, and others all recorded man's life, in ancient times, defended it and attempted to explain it, but no one during those thousands of years tried to show men or nations how to make a better day-to-day living. This curious fact has a simple explanation. Men had for centuries lived either by careful tradition, handed down from one generation to another, or else under authoritarian governments. Most men lived as men had always lived, working the land, growing and producing enough, on land that was bought and sold as it is today, but which was often part of someone else's estate to which the ordinary peasant was usually bound, and on which he worked to live.

Change came very gradually as trading between communities developed, but even then man was not a free agent to buy and sell as he wanted. In the Middle Ages no one could trade in a town unless he was a member of the town guild or was allowed to do so by the town authorities. The guild laid down rigid rules of production, buying, and selling. Towns usually specified, for example, the quality of thread used and the precise number of threads for each yard of cloth. Work after dark was usually prohibited because goods made by candlelight could be of poor quality. Even quantity was regulated so that no man might get an advantage over another. There were severe rules against what we would regard today as normal business methods and the use of initiative and hard work. Practices such as "regrating," "forestalling," and "engrossing" were severely punished. Regrating was selling at a higher price than one paid without adding to the value of the goods. Forestalling was simply "getting the jump" on other merchants by going out to buy up goods before they came on the open market. Engrossing was what today we call "cornering the market," or trying to buy up all the available supply of goods. The idea of making a profit, at least any profit more than that specified by the guild, was regarded not only as unethical but illegal and punishable. For centuries the medieval Church and governments denounced usury, or the lending of money for interest. It was not only a crime for which a man could be punished but also a sin for which he could be excommunicated by the Church. It is interesting to note that in China also the local guilds laid down similar rules, because if competition were permitted, then someone might have "an empty rice bowl," as the Chinese picturesquely put it, and become a burden upon the community.

The citizens of Bristol, England, were emphatic in their opinion of a forestaller, "a manifest oppressor of the poor, and a public enemy of the community . . . making gain, oppressing his poorer neighbors . . . and so by fraudulent art or craft (meaning trickiness) he misleads the town and country."

In a society where tradition or strict rules regulated the life of people there was no place for an economist, a man who attempted to discover the underlying rules for the better production, consumption, and distribution of goods for the general benefit. During the 16th and 17th centuries, as we have seen, many nations believed in the economic practice called mercantilism, a system by which the government protected a nation's interests by prohibiting foreigners from trading and shipping. But this was not a system devised to encourage increased sales. It was supposed to protect the wealth of a nation. The people of the day failed to realize that trade could be partly determined by the price and attractiveness of goods as well as by need. Thinkers in the 18th century began to question this system as the Industrial Revolution developed.

Why was there no economist until the 18th century? Basically because there was no system which today we call the "market" or the "exchange" system, in which everyone acts freely for personal gain. If everyone did just as he wished, and not according to tradition or by orders of a local or central body, would all the necessary jobs get done? The economist asked this question and attempted to analyze how a person's or a nation's best interests could be served. For example, would a nation benefit most by free exchange of goods with another nation, or should there be a limit on foreign imports, so that native workmen would not be undersold by cheaper foreign goods and perhaps be thrown out of work? With the development of the factory system which employed hundreds and thousands of workers and produced increasing quantities of goods, men realized that techniques and methods of production and selling were necessary.

Economists by no means thought alike. Some defended and some attacked the capitalist system based upon private gain. Some wanted government regulation, while others demanded complete freedom from government interference. The group which opposed government interference, such as minimum wages, maximum hours, conditions of labor, and the like, believed in laissez-faire, literally to leave a person alone to do as he pleases, more briefly "hands off" in the sense of no regulations on production and distribution, and no limits on foreign imports or foreign shipping.

Supporters of Laissez-Faire

Adam Smith (1723–1790) in 1776 published one of the famous books of the world, *The Wealth of Nations*. Its full title, "An Inquiry into the Nature and Causes of the Wealth of Nations," clearly suggests that the author was attempting to draw up rules for a nation's economic operations. Adam Smith wrote his book before the Industrial Revolution had come into full operation, but he knew that more goods were already being produced more rapidly because men seldom made an entire item but performed one part of the whole process. This "division of labor" was the difference between early capitalism before the factory system and modern capitalism.

Smith opposed the regulations of mercantilism and favored laissez-faire, because he thought that free competition and private gain together would benefit the nation. The important economic purpose of a nation, according to Smith, was to produce "consumable" or usable goods. People would want to buy as cheaply as they could and sell as dearly as possible. If a man wanted to sell, then he must either undersell his competitor or make a better article for the money. This would lead to competition which would work for the benefit of all because it would provide more jobs. If there were no restrictions, then everybody would be free to make a profit, and this would stimulate production. Smith thought that certain "natural" laws of supply and demand would always operate in a society. He was the first man to advocate unlimited initiative and free competition.

The industrialists liked this because they would not be bound by any restrictions. They could justifiably, under this theory, pay the lowest wage possible, work their employees long hours, avoid using costly safety devices on machines, and make as large a profit as possible. Adam Smith wrote before Newcomen developed the steam engine and Watt adapted its use to driving wheels. As could be expected, once the factory system developed in the 19th century, other economists supported Smith's laissez-faire doctrine.

Thomas Malthus (1766–1834) published a book in 1798 which, in essence, excused anyone from any obligation to raise living standards for the workers. Population, he wrote in his famous *Principles of Population*, always tends to outrun food supply. In any given period, say a hundred years, population increases by geometric progression at the rate of 2, 4, 8, 16, 32, while food increases by arithmetic progression 2, 4, 6, 8, 10.

This, said Malthus, was a simple law of nature, and any attempt to remedy the situation by paying higher wages and improving conditions for the workers would only increase both population and misery. Higher wages would result in large families, which would mean too many people, with less food to share among them. Malthus opposed paying higher wages, giving any public assistance or even private charity. Supporters of laissez-faire heartily agreed with Malthus that nothing should be done to alter the situation. As a result, real reform was delayed for several decades.

David Ricardo (1772–1823) had several ideas on economics, but the one for which he is remembered best is his "iron law of wages." He believed that wages should be left to free competition between worker and employer, and that any deliberate attempt to pay high wages would simply attract more people to that industry, with the result that families would get larger, and by the iron law of economics wages would be forced down again by competition for jobs. This "brazen law of wages" was, in the words of Thomas Carlyle, "false, heretical, and damnable." This is the basic issue on which capitalism has been attacked by socialists and communists alike ever since, even though such an "iron law" is not necessarily operative today.

John Stuart Mill (1806–1876) had a childhood which is such an extraordinary account of a young man's upbringing that he deserves to be known for more than his economic ideas. At the age of seven he had read most of the dialogues of Plato, in Greek. By the time he was twelve he had read a great part of the writings of fifteen Latin authors, poets, and historians, and in the next three years mastered algebra, geometry, and calculus. Not until the age of 42 did he write his *Principles of Political Economy*, taking only six weeks to complete the long work.

While Mill supported laissez-faire and also Jeremy Bentham's ideas of utilitarianism, he shocked some liberals by saying that social and economic injustice could be remedied by redistributing wealth through income and inheritance taxes. If people thought wealth was unfairly divided, said Mill, then they could soon solve that problem by changing the laws. Mill said that there was no one and final "correct" distribution of wealth. Since men made laws, then they should decide how wealth should be shared. Mill in effect said that there was no fixed law which determined what wages and profits should be.

5. Critics of Laissez-Faire

Inequities of the Factory System

There were many ill-effects of the factory system, not the least being the long hours, low wages, and poor conditions of work. But these were not simply products of industrialization, because many of them existed under the domestic system in which craftsmen worked at home on their own hand equipment. Wages were low then, conditions were desperately bad, and the use of child labor was a common practice. Those were the days of "infant slavery," wrote one man who saw children of five years old doing such simple tasks as they could handle. Their "employers" were their own parents who could get a few pennies from the work of their children's labor, and were often the harshest of taskmasters. Unemployment was a serious problem in the days of the domestic system because towns and local governments would not allow unemployed people to come into their communities and become a burden. Apprenticeship laws were rigid and prevented a man who could find no work in his own trade from shifting to another. Even a specialist in textile work, such as a weaver, might not be permitted to work at another specialty operation in the same trade.

Many of these conditions increased in industrial society because more people were employed in industry, and because a factory worker living in a town had no other resources to fall back upon, as did a man living in the countryside.

Another factor which increased the problem of inequities of the factory system was that inventions developed rapidly just at the time when government believed in the doctrine of laissez-faire and did almost nothing to ameliorate social and economic ills. Accepting the doctrines of Adam Smith, Malthus, Ricardo and others, the government was convinced that it should not interfere with business in any way, not even to insist upon adequate safeguards on dangerous machines, much less make rules about wages and hours.

The opponents of laissez-faire became more insistent. What is the final test of economic progress, they asked, if it is not the condition of the people who make up the country? If mechanization simply degrades people and forces them into increasingly poor conditions, what is progress? Some people claimed that the success of businessmen would be beneficial to all because the wealth of the country increased. Others insisted that although a few people became wealthy, it might be at the expense of the many.

One employer of labor expressed his feelings when he compared the domestic system with the factory system. Under the domestic system there was usually a personal relationship between

The English Industrial Landscape. A contemporary drawing of the area around Wolverhampton.

master and workman, but under the factory system "we simply employ thousands; we do not know their faces; they are 'hands' to us, they are not men; there is no sort of mutual sympathy, and that is the top and bottom of all the mischief."

Critics of laissez-faire argued that to ignore the health and happiness of the community would defeat the very purpose which increased production was supposed to achieve. With reluctance the English parliament had to admit that it could not afford to ignore the health and well-being of the citizens who might be called upon to defend the nation. In 1832 a Parliamentary Committee was appointed, under the chairmanship of Michael Sadler, to investigate the abuses of child labor in English factories.

The Sadler Report exposed almost unbelievable conditions in factories. One boy of 10 years of age began work at 5 o'clock in the morning, worked until noon, and was then allowed 40 minutes for his first meal since 5 o'clock, and then worked on until night. A girl in the same mill worked from 5 o'clock in the morning until

11 o'clock at night, with 40 minutes allowed for a meal once during that long day of 18 hours!

A young man of 20 years of age testified that he worked for 34 hours straight.

"I went to work at 5 o'clock on a Monday morning and had half an hour at breakfast, and half an hour at drinking (in Yorkshire this term meant afternoon refreshment); then went on till nine on Monday evening, and then stopped half an hour; then went on to twelve at midnight, and stopped an hour; then went on to half-past four on Tuesday morning, and stopped half an hour; then went on again from five to eight, and stopped half an hour; then went on till twelve, and stopped an hour; then went on again from one to five, and stopped half an hour; then went on again to 9 o'clock at night, when we went home."*

He continued throughout the week along the same general lines, and put in a work week of 108 hours from Monday at 5 o'clock in the morning until Saturday at 5 o'clock in the evening.

Machines were not provided with safeguards, and consequently accidents were common. One factory worker testified before the Sadler Committee on such conditions.

"A boy was brought in about 5 or 6 o'clock in the evening from a mill; he had got catched with the shaft, and he had both his thighs broke, and from his knee to his hip the flesh was ripped up the same as if it had been cut by a knife, his head was bruised, his eyes were nearly torn out, and his arms broken. His sister, who ran to pull him off, got both her arms broke and her head bruised, and she is bruised all over her body.

---

*Quotations come from: Great Britain, *Sessional Papers*, 1833, vol. 123, cd. 706, pp. 5–11; 158–164; 428–430; 598–602. (As used in Knoles and Snyder, eds., *Readings in Western Civilization*, New York, Lippincott, 1954, pp. 565–586.)

The boy died last Thursday night but one, about 8 o'clock; I do not know whether the girl is dead, but she was not expected to live."

The Committee then called in a medical doctor, who stated that it was his firm conviction that twelve hours a day in the factory was too long, that a person needed at least eight hours sleep, and no more than eight hours of factory labor. The doctor had spent some time practicing his profession on the slave plantations in the West Indies. The Committee asked:

"It appears in evidence before this Committee, that the labour in mills and factories undergone by children and young persons of both sexes, is rarely less than fourteen hours a day, including the time allowed for meals; and that in many instances it greatly exceeds that term, and extends sometimes to eighteen or twenty hours, or upwards; during your residence in the West Indies, was there any system of labor imposed upon any of the children and young persons at all equal to that?"

"Never in the slightest degree approaching to it."

"It is in evidence that the children and young persons employed in factories have often to be roused from their lethargy induced by exertions too long continued, and to be stimulated to their labor by constant whippings, beatings, or other means of a like nature; are the children of the slaves in the West Indies more hardly worked or more cruelly treated than this state of things implies?"

"In the colony of which I have spoken, I never saw nor heard of such inhumanity."

In part as a result of this Report, both parties in Parliament worked toward regulating conditions of work. As a consequence of the Sadler Report, the Factory Act was passed in 1833, and this piece of legislation marked the end of unrestricted laissez-faire in England. In time, increasing restrictions upon working conditions led to the completely new idea of a *national minimum*, a level of existence and income below which no person should be allowed to drop.

Whether this was regarded as good economic sense because people could buy more goods and so help the nation's economy, whether it simply made for a healthier and stronger nation, whether it meant more votes for the party in power, or whether it was plain humanitarianism, the idea of a national minimum became a belief of social morality and obligation.

The critics of laissez-faire can be divided into the "New Liberals," the Utopian Socialists, and the so-called Scientific Socialists. The "New Liberals" were men from both political parties who supported Acts which improved working conditions and wages, who favored the existence of trade unions, and advocated the extension of voting rights to workingmen.

The Utopians were those people who generally supported a gradual liberalizing of the capitalist system to one of socialism, a Utopian or ideal society in which all the means of production and distribution would be owned by the State, run for the benefit of all, and not for private profit. The Utopians believed that the industrialists would voluntarily reform the capitalist system toward socialism.

The Scientific Socialists are typified by Karl Marx, who attempted to prove, at least to the satisfaction of himself and his followers, that socialism or state-owned businesses would inevitably replace an industrial free enterprise system, regardless of whether or not men wished that to happen. According to Marx, this change was historically predictable and "scientifically" provable. Marx did not believe that the capitalists would voluntarily reform themselves.

The Roots of Socialism in the French Revolution

When the Directory government in France took over in 1795 it introduced a period in which most of the ideals of the French Revolution were ignored. The Directors were politicians, and they and their banker and merchant friends speculated in confiscated estates, inflated the currency, and in general served their own private interests. During the severe winter of 1795–1796 French people died from hunger and cold in the streets of Paris.

In 1793 a Frenchman who called himself Gracchus Babeuf, an ardent supporter of the Revolution and its ideals, was appointed to a minor position in the Bureau of Subsistence of the Paris Commune. What he found in the accounts led him to believe that government officials were deliberately creating a scarcity of foodstuffs in the city in order to make money on rising prices. He arranged to have a commission of investigation appointed, but it was suppressed by the authorities, and Babeuf himself was charged with fraud in his earlier position. He started a newspaper in which he denounced the constitution of 1795 for its very limited voting rights, but this was also suppressed, and Babeuf and his followers jailed. As soon as he was freed he organized the Society of Equals which went underground when it was suppressed, and plotted a revolution against the government. So effective was the group that even government troops in Paris were infected with its ideas, and had to be disbanded.

Babeuf was arrested, taken to prison in a cage, and there tried by a court which he knew had already decided to execute him. In his defense he argued that the real question before the court was not whether he was guilty of a conspiracy against the government, but whether he was advocating ideas against the interests of the dominant ruling class. Before he died on the guillotine, with 30 of his followers, in May 1797, he wrote to a friend, "I believe that in some future day men will give thought again to the means of procuring for the human race the happiness which we have proposed for it." This purpose was the motivation of the Utopian Socialists. Babeuf was less a Utopian and more a Communist reformer, for he and his small group, the Conspiracy of Equals, advocated the overthrow of the government and the substitution of a dictatorial system, which he chose to call "democratic."

The Utopian Socialists

The Comte de Saint-Simon (1760–1825) went out to America from France in 1778, fought in five campaigns of the Revolutionary War, was decorated with the Order of Cincinnatus, and became a firm supporter of the ideals of democracy. Back in France, he supported the French Revolution, and over the next two decades observed that despite the ideals of Liberty and Equality, society still suffered from poverty. The former authority of Church and aristocratic social system had gone, and the factory system was gradually replacing them, but the mechanical inventions which were expected to aid humanity were failing to do so, and people were still miserable.

Saint-Simon's utopian idea was summed up in words he addressed to the Holy Alliance, "Unite in the name of Christianity and learn to accomplish the duties which Christianity imposes on the powerful . . . to better as rapidly as possible the lot of the very poor."

Charles Fourier (1772–1837) was an advocate of communal settlements, or phalanxes as he called them, which would achieve the objectives of socialism. In Lyon, France, he had seen the lives of the people steadily worsened by the conditions and wages of the textile mills, and had later in Marseille watched the owners of a business throw into the river a consignment of rice which they had allowed to rot in order to keep up the price in a city of desperately hungry people.

He wished to set up small self-sufficient communities, dependent upon private capital but with the proceeds to be divided among the people with a basic minimum for everybody, and the remainder to be divided into four-twelfths for capital, three-twelfths for talent and skills, and five-twelfths for labor. Unpleasant jobs would be paid at a higher rate than agreeable ones, and since there would be something for everyone in the community, all should be satisfied.

Fourier was, to say the least, an eccentric who could visualize a society in which everyone liked to work, and who could precisely determine that there would be 2,985,984 phalanxes in the world once his ideas had encircled the globe. Fourier was by no means the only eccentric, since there were over forty phalanxes in the United States, with the Trumbull Phalanx in Ohio, the North American Phalanx in New Jersey, and New Icaria, Brook Farm, and Oneida in other states. Although none of these succeeded against the hard facts of reality and human nature, Fourier must be credited with pointing out the harshness of the new industrial society. Fourier and others like him were looking at the conditions they saw around them, and saying, in effect, if this is capitalism, then it must be replaced with something better.

Robert Owen (1771–1858). Up into the hills of Scotland, a day's stagecoach journey from Glasgow, more than 20,000 people journeyed between the years 1815 to 1825 to visit a remarkable industrial community of two-roomed houses, factories where no children under 10 were allowed to work, and where a school was provided for the young children. What amazed such distinguished visitors as Prince Maximilian of Austria, and the Grand Duke who would be

Czar Nicholas I of Russia, was that the town of New Lanark made a good profit. Robert Owen was literally a self-made man, with a supreme confidence in himself, and an ability to match it. He set out not simply to make money but to prove that it could be done in pleasant conditions which could provide the workers with happy surroundings. He paid his workers higher wages than other employers did, provided them with the unheard-of comfort of *two* rooms, worked them for shorter hours, looked after them during depressions, and put all the proceeds of his business back into the community after paying himself and his partners a fixed amount. Since he could do this, he wondered why all society could not operate along similar lines.

Owen hoped to persuade the government and the public to set up an experimental Village of Cooperation in which some thousand people would form a self-sufficient farm and factory community. But *planned* economic societies were not popular in the days of laissez-faire and Owen's scheme had no chance of success in England. So he sold out his New Lanark business and decided to build such a community in the United States where political liberty was already well-established. He spent the greater part of his fortune in the purchase of 30,000 acres on the banks of the Wabash River in Indiana, set up the community of New Harmony in 1826 and went back to England.

Regrettably Owen's ideals were not matched by the planning ability of those he attempted to help, and within three years New Harmony was a total failure, and Owen sold the property. He made other attempts in England and Ireland but sank so much money into the projects that his sons had to support him. His real achievement was his encouragement of co-operative stores.

Workingmen bought goods at wholesale, sold to themselves at close to cost, and after paying rent and salaries and putting enough aside for expansion, paid a dividend to the buyers in proportion to the amount each had spent. Owen had little real interest in these consumers' co-operatives, but they were one of his few real achievements in attempting to relieve the brutality of the industrialism of his day.

6. "Scientific" Socialism of Karl Marx

In 1848, the year of revolutions, in England a pamphlet appeared with these opening words,

Robert Owen. This title page from one of his pamphlets gives an idea of his objectives.

"A specter is haunting Europe—the specter of Communism." This is the opening sentence of the *Communist Manifesto*, a call to industrial workers of all nations to rally together to improve their conditions. The pamphlet finished with, "Workers of the world unite, you have nothing to lose but your chains!"

Karl Marx (1818–1883), the author of this work, was born and educated in Germany where he studied history and philosophy for his degree of doctor of philosophy, and was greatly influenced by the German philosopher Hegel who believed that history was a series of conflicts. The traditional, established order, said Hegel, is challenged by a new idea or movement, and is changed to a new order, which is in turn challenged and changed.

Karl Marx lived during the years of great industrial change, and saw that the industrial system had profoundly affected men's lives, had sometimes brutalized them. In 1844 he was living in Paris, where for the first time he met another German, Friedrich Engels, who was manager of a family factory in Manchester, England. In his travels around England, Engels had seen and written much about the desperate

Karl Marx

Friedrich Engels

conditions of workers in the typical English factory. The people lived in wretched one-room hovels, filthy with vermin, underfed, undernourished, simply existing. Women and children were employed in coal mines, crawling on their hands and knees, with chains around their waist and between their legs, hauling loaded coal cars. Factory life was equally horrible, with long working hours, poor conditions, and miserable wages. These experiences confirmed Engels and Marx in their criticisms of capitalism, but instead of simply condemning it, they set out to prove that a socialist society was inevitable. Marx was only one of a number of revolutionaries and of a number of prophets of future socialism, and he would probably have remained historically unimportant and unknown had it not been for his dialectical materialistic theory of history, and his analysis of capitalist society.

Marx and Engels believed that the development of the free-enterprise, capitalist society must inevitably lead to the collapse of the entire capitalist system and its replacement by a socialist society. This Marx set out to prove in a monumental work titled *Das Kapital*, which was eighteen years in the writing. Begun in 1851, the first volume appeared in 1867, and after his death in 1883 the remaining three volumes were published in sequence until 1910. Marx did not simply denounce the capitalism he saw around him, but with cold logic he examined an ideal capitalist society. If that could be shown to be doomed to failure, then certainly contemporary capitalism, with its many obvious faults, would be certain to collapse. Unlike the intellectual ideals of the Utopian Socialists, the Marxian doctrine was supposedly scientific, and was based upon three doctrines: (1) dialectical materialism and economic determinism, or the economic interpretation of history, (2) the class struggle, (3) the historic inevitability of communism.

Dialectical Materialism and Economic Determinism

Marx believed that economic conditions changed history. Hegel, the German philosopher, had taught that change in historical periods did not happen by chance but according to a pattern. This pattern he called *dialectical*, by which he meant a logical progression. The term had nothing to do with dialect but comes from a Greek word meaning a way of reaching a conclusion by argument.

The dialectic pattern was a struggle between one group which owned the means of production, such as the feudal landowner (the *thesis*), and a new group such as the commercial class struggling for power (the *anti-thesis* or *antithesis*), which led to a new economic society (the *synthesis*). So, logically or dialectically, a change occurred because of the struggle between two groups. Hegel applied his theory to ideas, but Marx turned the theory to work on economic or "materialistic" developments, and used the term *economic determinism*, because the change happened inevitably, according to Marx, and was therefore "determined." Nothing that men could do would prevent the change.

The Economic Interpretation of History

Marxian belief in economic conditions as the greatest factors in bringing about changes in history was based upon the fact that people have always been concerned primarily with producing goods. But *how* goods are produced, and *who* owns the means of production are the most important factors which have affected history from earliest times. Government, explained Marx, always represented the owning class, which passed laws in its own interests, and always operated the law for its own purposes. Political, intellectual, or religious causes of change in history were subordinate to economic or material factors, he said. For example, the Reformation was primarily caused by economic factors rather than religious or political reasons, insisted Marx.

The Class Struggle

That class which did not own the means of production, and believed that it was not getting a fair share of the income, was constantly in conflict with the class which did own the property—raw materials, factories, and capital. Marx believed that the *owning* class had a firm grip upon the whole economy of the country and ruled the rest of the people who were dependent upon the owners for their livelihood. The workers would attempt not only to take over all businesses but also take over the government and run it in their own interests.

The Historic Inevitability of Communism: The Marxist Doctrine

History, said Marx, is the record of class struggle, whether the society was a slave one in which slaves struggled against slaveowners, or a feudal society in which peasants opposed landlords, or an industrial society in which workers struggled against the owners of capital or means of production.

Only when the people, that is the state, controlled the means of production, would the class struggle cease. This last struggle was inevitable, predicted Marx, because capitalism would bring it about by the way it operated. Factory owners would compete with each other at home and in foreign markets, and then cut costs and reduce wages in order to exist competitively. The workers would become increasingly poor until they revolted against conditions. Then they would take over the factories, establish a *dictatorship of the proletariat* or workers, and crush all opposition and middle-class ideas. When only one class remained, the working class, there would be no need for further dictation, since there would no longer be classes struggling for power. This final struggle would result in a classless society where no man would exploit another, or use another man's labor for personal private gain.

Although Marx believed this revolution was historically inevitable, it could be hastened if the workers united for organized and, if necessary, violent action. Marx did not believe that his objectives could be attained through political action to get representation in a parliament, or through trade unions to get better wages and working conditions. The capitalist class, he said, could not afford and were not willing to pay better wages or improve working conditions.

Criticism of Marxist Theories

First, Marx expected that workers of all nations would realize that all capitalists were their enemies, and would work together, even against their own governments. But World War I proved that workers had strong nationalistic feelings and were ready to defend their own nations. Second, capitalism was prepared to make concessions when obliged to, and as a result workers became more interested in sharing in the rewards and gains of the free-enterprise system. Third, workers generally preferred to use political parties and trade unions to gain reforms rather than use revolutionary techniques. Fourth, Marx underestimated or ignored incentive as a great force in human relationships. Rewards for better work or greater effort can be an incentive to spur men on. Without such incentives, men may see no purpose in greater effort "for the state." Fifth, there can never be a "classless" society. Even if private ownership were to be eliminated, there would be other "status" symbols, power positions, or incentives. The opportunity for a better job, a better apartment, the chance to buy a car, or to be a white-collar worker carrying a briefcase instead of a blue-collar worker driving a bus are all incentives which can build up class distinction. Recent Russian history indicates that peasants produce larger crops if they are allowed to keep for themselves a proportion of what they grow. In any society few men continue to work hard unless they receive a reward for greater effort.

The Contribution of Karl Marx

Marx made a significant contribution by pointing out what *could* happen in an industrial society where workers were exploited, and in which those who had laissez-faire ideas regarded workers simply as factory "hands" whose living conditions were of no concern whatever to employers or government.

Marx performed the service of showing that there were grave injustices which men would not suffer indefinitely; he obliged men to understand the needs of an industrial society and to attempt to improve it. He also caused historians to become much more aware of economic factors in history. Marx predicted that only in an advanced industrial society like England would communism be successful. Historically he was proved to be wrong because two agrarian countries, Russia and China, were the two large nations to become communistic. It is of interest to note that Marx made no attempt to describe or explain the operation of the communistic society which he predicted. This was the "Utopian" part of Marx's non-Utopian theories.

The Internationals

The First International. Marx wanted to organize workers of every country and of every brand of radical belief to work toward the classless society. In 1864 the *First International Workingmen's Association* met in London. At first it attracted 7,000,000 members from all over the world, but mostly from the European continent where it earned the reputation of having influenced a wave of strikes. It was not a tough, organized group of communists, but only a motley collection of rather moderate socialists who did not approve of revolutionary theories. Its last meeting was in New York City in 1874, and it ended in failure partly because of Marx's intolerance of any ideas but his own.

Another reason for failure was its part in the armed rebellion of the Paris Commune of 1871 against the democratically elected National Assembly of France. Marx praised its action as a stage in international class war. Many followers were frightened away or left because they objected to its violence.

The Second International. This was a much more organized and dedicated group, consisting mainly of Marxian socialists. Founded in 1889 with the same purpose as the First International, it had only moderate success because workingmen's conditions were improving through labor unions, beneficial legislation by government, and because real wages, the buying power, were steadily increasing. By 1914 the working classes were no longer revolutionary, and when war broke out in 1914 the Second International collapsed. The workers supported their own countries and simply did not regard themselves as "workers of the world" to be organized against the capitalist system.

The Third International. This grew out of what was supposed to be the first post-war meeting in Switzerland in 1919 of the Second International. When the more radical delegates demanded "revolution as in Russia," where the communist government had already taken over all industry from its private owners, the majority of delegates denounced them. The minority left the meeting and went to Moscow where the Communist Party took over and planned to use the Third International, soon to be known as the Communist International, abbreviated to *Comintern*, to organize revolutions in other countries, and to discredit the moderate socialists. Parties joining the Comintern were required to drop the old-fashioned name "socialist" and call themselves Communist.

Moderate Socialist Reformers

In England, where the workers were benefitting from legislative reforms, the *Christian Socialists* were English reformers drawn from the clergy, who believed that the Church should help to remedy injustices by supporting reform measures and thus were, in a sense, successors of the Utopian Socialists. They depended rather upon private philanthropy than on state aid.

The Catholic response to Marxism was the organization of Christian or Social Democracy, but it lacked real force because Pope Pius IX was uncompromisingly against democratic governments and trade unions, on the grounds that the papacy and the Catholic Church should not become involved with liberalism.

The most effective group in England was the *Fabian Society of Socialists* which took its name from Fabius Cunctator, or Delayer, the Roman general who had overcome Hannibal's invasion of Italy by a policy of attrition or constant wearing-down of his enemy. Such well-known people as H. G. Wells and Bernard Shaw were members of the group which believed that there was no class conflict and therefore no necessity for revolution. They believed that political parties elected to power in Parliament would accomplish needed reforms, and claimed that these gradual reforms would in time bring about a socialist state. This prophecy has come partly true in Great Britain where, by the 1960's, two socialist governments were elected to power and experimented with several kinds of welfare and state ownership of some industries. The Fabians were willing, as are all socialists, to allow opposition political parties to function in a democratic country along with their own socialist party.

This is the main difference between socialists and communists. Although their ultimate goals, state ownership of the means of production and distribution, are similar, their means of achieving those goals, democratic versus revolutionary methods, are very dissimilar. Some observers believe that the recent disagreement between Russian and Chinese communists is over this same difference. The Chinese have accused the Russians of "revising" their communist practices and of becoming too moderate or "revisionist," rather than remaining revolutionary and "scientific" in practice.

7. The Second Industrial Revolution

The First Industrial Revolution, the Age of Coal and Cotton, that began in the 18th century, had a tremendous effect upon the economic and social life of many European countries. And yet, until well past the middle of the 19th century the chief sources of power were water and steam. The Second Industrial Revolution, the Age of Steel, is the period from 1870 to 1914 when the contemporary world began to take shape.

The Progress of Technology

The most revolutionary change of the second half of the 19th century was the new process of making steel cheaply and easily. Once this could be accomplished, the potential of industrial development was almost limitless. The discovery of cheap steel production was almost accidental, and did not occur because there was any general demand for steel. During the early months of the Crimean War, the English engineer Henry Bessemer developed a heavy elongated projectile which would rotate on its axis like a football in flight. Bessemer could not interest the British War Office in his invention, but the French tested the projectile at Vincennes, and the commandant of the fort raised the question which set Bessemer experimenting, "Was it possible to make guns that could take such a heavy projectile?" Bessemer determined to develop a superior cast-iron that could do the job. In two years he invented his converter.

The problem that Bessemer faced was the removal of carbon, silicon, and other impurities from ordinary pig-iron and cast-iron. He built an open-end container or converter with a double bottom pierced by holes through which jets of air could be forced into the molten iron. Oxygen combined with the impurities and burned them off. Then the proper amount of carbon was added to the "clean" molten iron to give it the hardness of steel.

Later developments in the production of cheap steel by Siemens and others introduced the Second Industrial Revolution because steel could be used with greater efficiency for every means of transportation, for the modernization of factories, and for increased efficiency of warships and weapons. The easy availability of steel meant that rails could now be rolled to replace the old iron rails. Locomotives were improved and could haul greater loads at higher speeds than before and open up larger markets.

The building of railroads increased rapidly after 1870 because the railroad became not only the symbol of economic power but was also a necessity for economic growth. Bridges were built with larger spans and for greater loads, farm implements were improved, and armor plate and guns provided greater effectiveness for navies and armies. Steel played a very important part in the development of merchant marines. Until almost the turn of the century the great majority of ships were wooden and

"S.S. Great Britain." This ship was raised in 1969 from the sea bed off the Falkland Islands where she had lain submerged and brought back to Bristol, England. Here she passes under Clifton Suspension Bridge another remarkable construction of her designer, Brunel.

were necessarily limited to about 300 feet in length. Although the first iron ship for the transatlantic service, the *Great Britain*, was built in the 1840's, an iron ship was the exception rather than the rule until late into the century. When it finally was developed, its increased efficiency proved its value. An iron ship did not become water-logged, it weighed about half that of wooden ship of equal capacity, and its length was limited only by the strength of its engines and the ports that could accommodate it.

The Steam Engine and its Successors

The compound steam engine was another significant development because it used steam twice by the addition of a second cylinder which received steam from the first or high-pressure cylinder, and so saved the waste of steam. When this engine was used on ships it cut down fuel bills, gave more mileage for each ton of coal, and left more space available for cargo. In the late 19th century Diesel invented an engine which used oil as fuel and gave even greater operating efficiency.

Another great invention was the internal or gasoline combustion engine, first developed in 1876 by Otto, a German engineer, and then improved upon by Daimler, who in 1883 brought out a high-speed gasoline engine to be used in small boats and vehicles. The light gasoline engine was not only useful for "horseless carriages" but also for flying machines. Five years after the famous flight at Kitty Hawk by the Wright brothers a Wright machine flew 45 miles in a little over an hour, and a year later, in 1909, Bleriot startled the world by flying across the English Channel.

Until about 1914 coal was still used essentially for the production of steel, and the coal-producing areas of the world were the sources of great wealth. But already electricity was competing with coal as power, and by 1920 electricity produced by water-power was in use in factories and for transportation.

This rapid rise of economic power in the 20th century resulted in drastic changes in the organization of a nation's economy. The relatively smaller business organizations of mid-century were not large enough to meet the increased costs and the large markets of later years. Large businesses employing thousands of people replaced smaller companies and created the need for new occupations of clerical help, technicians, and sales forces. An inevitable change in society was the accelerated rise of trade unions and the growing participation of working people in politics, and the necessity of granting concessions in wages and working conditions.

Review Questions

Sections 1 and 2
1. In what ways did the expression, "Necessity is the Mother of Invention" apply to the Industrial Revolution?
2. Why was the term "revolution" a correct one to explain agricultural changes?

Section 3
3. Why was the term "factory system" not appropriate for business methods before the Industrial Revolution?
4. In what areas of town life did industrialization create problems not faced by farm workers?

Section 4
5. If mercantilist practices were at one time regarded as necessary, why did some economists criticize them in the 19th century?
6. Explain the laissez-faire ideas concerning (a) a nation's wealth, (b) population and food, (c) wages. Which of these do you think applies today, and which do not? Why?

Section 5
7. For what reasons did the British government change from its support of laissez-faire to support factory regulations?
8. Explain how Saint-Simon, Fourier, and Robert Owen differed in their beliefs in socialism. Which do you think came nearest to being the most practical? Why?

Section 6
9. Why did Marx label his socialist beliefs "scientific"? Do you think he was correct or not? Why?
10. What did Marx mean by "economic interpretation of history"? How did economic change work, according to Marx?
11. Why is Marx's claim of the "inevitability of communism" by no means necessarily true?
12. Did Marx make any contribution whatever to society, or were his writings a complete waste of time?

Section 7
13. What were the basic differences between the Second and the First Industrial Revolutions? Give some examples.

2

The German Empire and Italian Unity

The Unification of Germany, 1848–1870

Domestic Problems and Solutions, 1870–1890

Foreign Affairs of the German Empire, 1870–1890

The Unification of Italy, 1815–1871

While some European nations were becoming more democratic during the 19th century, two large areas of the Continent had yet to become unified. The German Confederation of 39 states created by the Congress of Vienna was without a central government and was therefore subject to outside influence and interference. Italy was still the "geographical expression" that it had been for centuries, divided among a number of independent states and possessions of foreign powers, without any semblance of national unity.

In Prussia the Chancellor, Otto von Bismarck, determined to use any means, including "blood and iron" if necessary, to weld the Germans into a nation. He deliberately initiated wars against the Danes, the Austrians, and the French as a means of creating a spirit of nationalism among the several German states. By the end of the 19th century the German Empire was a force to be reckoned with in European politics.

Popular sentiment in the Italian peninsula against foreign domination was welded into a powerful force through the efforts of several patriots who contributed political and military leadership. Even though Italy was officially a unified kingdom in 1861, it had achieved little more than physical unity by the beginning of the 20th century, for it still lacked a deep sense of nationalism and an effective government.

Terms

1. German Confederation
2. Frankfurt Assembly
3. Realpolitik
4. Augsleich
5. North German Confederation
6. Ems Dispatch
7. Deutsches Reich
8. Social Democratic Party (Progressive)
9. National Liberal Party (Moderate)
10. Catholic Center Party
11. Kulturkampf
12. The Black and the Red
13. Dreikaiserbund
14. Carbonari
15. Risorgimento

People

16. Frederick William
17. Otto von Bismarck
18. William I
19. Guiseppe Mazzini
20. Guiseppe Garibaldi
21. Camillo di Cavour
22. Victor Emmanuel II

Places

23. Denmark
24. Schleswig
25. Holstein
26. Sadowa
27. Hungary
28. Austria
29. North German Confederation
30. Metz
31. Sedan
32. Paris
33. Sardinia-Piedmont
34. Lombardy
35. Venetia
36. Tuscany
37. Parma
38. Modena
39. Papal States
40. Kingdom of the Two Sicilies
41. Savoy and Nice

Events

1862	Bismarck appointed Minister-President	1882	Triple Alliance
1864	War with Denmark		
1865	Seven Weeks' War with Austria	1848	Constitution for Piedmont
1867	Augsleich: Austria-Hungary	1854–56	Crimean War
1867	North German Confederation	1861	Kingdom of Italy
1870–71	Franco-Prussian War	1871	Italian Unification
1879	Dual Alliance		

1. The Unification of Germany, 1848–1870

"Blood and Iron" or Realpolitik

The German Confederation created at the Congress of Vienna was a region which was for many years the victim of outside interference and internal conflicts. The Frankfurt Assembly of 1848 attempted to unite the German people into a centralized federal government by offering the leadership to Frederick William IV of Prussia. His refusal of the offer doomed the immediate chance for unity because Prussian leadership was necessary for success. Yet by 1871 the German states were united in the German Empire, an achievement which was essentially the work of one man, Count Otto von Bismarck. He was a Prussian "Junker" or landed gentleman whose family had shared in local government for five hundred years. An autocratic, extremely conservative aristocrat, suspicious of all liberal ideas, he nevertheless was to succeed in uniting Germany, a feat which the Liberals of 1848 had been unable to accomplish.

Bismarck was so severe a critic of the 1848 revolution that Frederick William dared not give him ministerial office because Bismarck believed so strongly in force as the means to an objective. Nevertheless, Frederick's own conviction that Prussia must become the leader in any attempt at German unification, and that Prussia must take the leadership away from Austria, persuaded him to appoint Bismarck as the Prussian representative to the Diet of the German Confederation in 1851.

Bismarck understood that Austria would fight every move toward German unification, and so he flung down a challenge which typified him. When an Austrian representative at the Confederation Diet received him in shirtsleeves, Bismarck promptly took off his own jacket. Traditionally the Austrian delegate was the only member permitted to smoke, as a sign of honor. Bismarck took his seat and immediately lit up a cigar. He also proceeded to defeat every Austrian attempt to break up the Zollverein, which was the first essential step toward German unity.

The accession to the Prussian throne of William I (1861–1888) coincided with the beginnings of Italian unity, with the defeat of Austrian armies in Italy. William I appointed two military leaders, Moltke and Roon, who

Otto von Bismarck

quickly decided that the Prussian army must be reorganized and greatly expanded. The liberals in the Prussian Parliament opposed the necessary expenditure, not so much because they objected to a large army, but because they wished to show their power of control over the King and his ministers.

In 1862 Bismarck, serving as ambassador to Paris, was summoned home and appointed Minister-President and Foreign Minister of Prussia. He then seemed to go out of his way to affront the Liberals by saying that great issues would not be decided by resolutions of majorities, but by "blood and iron." This attitude was a practical one based on Bismarck's contention that people approved of success, whatever the method. This was the beginning of *Realpolitik*, a policy formed by considering the practical, not the ideal, and supported by might. "Realities" included national ambitions and armies.

Bismarck's first move was to crush Liberal opposition to the army expenditure by sidestepping parliamentary control of the budget. Since the representatives would not vote the necessary funds for an army, Bismarck persuaded the King to increase import taxes for that purpose. Freedom of the press was restricted, Liberals were put out of office, and Bismarck gambled that a strong foreign policy which gave leadership to Prussia would eventually overcome opposition. He carried out this purpose so successfully that by 1870 his position of leadership was virtually unchallenged. His methods were to eliminate Austria as a contender for leadership in Germany, and to prevent France and Russia from interfering in German affairs.

War with Denmark, 1864

In Denmark the Liberal party forced the King to centralize the nation and to incorporate into Denmark the formerly semi-independent and German-speaking Duchies of Schleswig and Holstein, the narrow strip between Germany and Denmark. How could Bismarck take advantage of the situation in such a way that the Duchies would become Prussian territory? First he "neutralized" Russia by securing her gratitude in helping to put down a revolt in the Russian province of Poland. He then obtained Austria's agreement to a joint Austro-Prussian solution to the Schleswig-Holstein question.

When Denmark refused his suggestion to refer the problem to a European congress, he sent in Austrian and Prussian troops. Very astutely Bismarck proposed that Austria should administer Holstein, the southern duchy, and Prussia the northern duchy of Schleswig. This "papering the cracks" would not last, because Bismarck knew that he could soon charge Austria with poor administration of Holstein.

The Austrian or Seven Weeks' War, 1866

Bismarck deliberately antagonized Austria by proposing a reform of the German Confederation which would exclude Austria. The reaction was what Bismarck anticipated. Austria proposed to all other members of the Diet that they attack Prussia. The war that Bismarck had deliberately instigated could now be called a defensive one, and he could claim justifiable attack upon Austria, a "defensive" attack.

One Prussian victory at Sadowa in Bohemia ended Austrian resistance, which collapsed before the new breech-loading needle-gun of the Prussian army. Bismarck showed his astute statesmanship by neither marching on to Vienna nor annexing a single piece of Austrian territory. All he demanded was that Austria return Venetia to Italy, a promise he had formerly made the Italians, and give Holstein to Prussia. German states which had supported Austria now paid for their temerity by being annexed to Prussia.

The Dual Monarchy in Austria

Austria actually benefited from defeat in the Seven Weeks' War, for she now decided that her main interest should be to run her own Empire effectively. Her people included several subject races, including the Magyars of Hungary who wanted some measure of self-government. In 1867 Austria gave Hungary a large measure of self-government under an agreement known as the *Augsleich*, or Compromise, which divided the Empire into two halves, Austria and Hungary.

The Austrian or northern part included Bohemia; Hungary, the southern part, included Transylvania and Slavic groups. The joint government or Dual Monarchy of Austria-Hungary controlled foreign and financial affairs, but left to each separate part its own parliament for internal affairs.

The North German Confederation, 1867

This new Confederation created by Bismarck gave Prussia the leadership because Austria was excluded from it. The King of Prussia added the title President of the Confederation, which had an Upper House to represent the federated states according to the size of each, and a Lower House based upon universal manhood suffrage. The rise of Prussia to leadership and the grant of voting rights won over Liberal support to Bismarck.

Still outside Prussian control were the two large German kingdoms of Bavaria and Württemberg, the Palatinate, and the Grand Duchy of Baden. Circumstances now played conveniently into Bismarck's hands and enabled him to gain the loyalty of the south German states by bringing about a war with France.

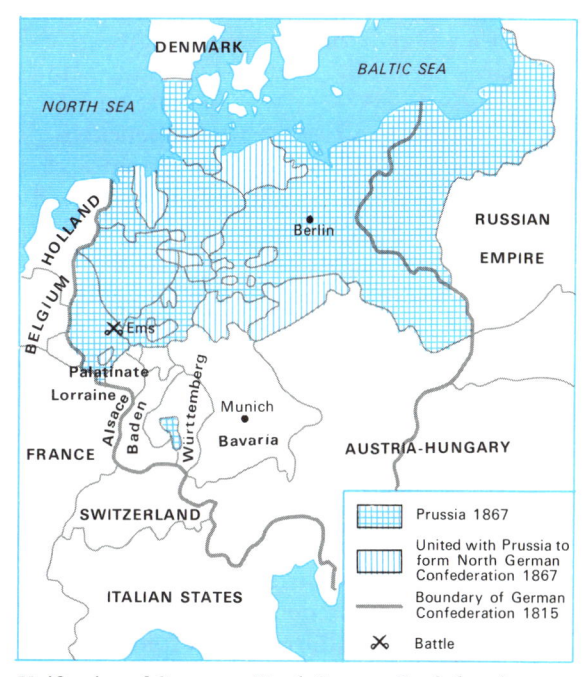

Unification of Germany: Prussia, 1866

Unification of Germany: North German Confederation, 1867

In 1870 the throne of Spain became vacant, and Bismarck deliberately encouraged Prince Leopold, a relative of the Prussian King, to offer his candidacy. Bismarck knew that France would fear German encirclement and would protest. Against their better judgment King William and the candidate allowed Bismarck to push the plan, and France reacted just as Bismarck had anticipated, demanding not only that the candidature be withdrawn but also that King William would agree not to authorize the candidature in the future.

The Ems Dispatch

In a personal interview at Ems with the French Ambassador Count Benedetti, the Prussian King agreed to the withdrawal of Leopold's immediate candidature but refused to make any guarantee about the future. William then played into Bismarck's hand by telegraphing the account of the interview and giving Bismarck permission to publish the statement in the newspapers. King William stated that he had decided "not to receive Count Benedetti again, but only to have him informed through an aide-de-camp, that his Majesty had received from the Prince confirmation of the news which Benedetti had received from Paris (of the Prince's withdrawal), and had nothing further to say to the ambassador."

Bismarck deliberately changed this into less diplomatic language to make it appear that the ambassador had insulted William, who had in turn severely snubbed the ambassador. The Frenchman was said to have "demanded" that William would never give his consent, and William was supposed to have decided "not to receive the ambassador again."

Immediately upon publication of the Ems Dispatch on July 14 the people of Berlin demanded war, and the people of France insisted that their "honor" be vindicated! And this ridiculous exchange of words and fancied insults was cause for the misery of war.

The Franco-Prussian War, 1870

Bismarck persuaded King William to mobilize the Prussian army. The next day France retaliated, and four days later declared war on Prussia. After a few minor successes the French suffered a crushing defeat with the Prussian occupation of Alsace and Lorraine and the surrender of the main French army at Metz. The Emperor Napoleon III wanted to fall back with his remaining troops to Paris, but his wife the Empress Eugenie, who boastfully called it

The Franco-Prussian War, 1870. Paris under siege.

"my war," forbade him to take this humiliating step with its probable consequence of the loss of the throne. On September 3, after a crushing French defeat at Sedan, the Assembly in Paris received a dispatch reading, "The army of Chalons has surrendered; I myself am a prisoner. Napoleon."

The reign of Napoleon III had opened in revolution, and now ended in revolution. Parisians stormed into the Assembly denouncing the Empire and demanding another republic. While Napoleon went on to Prussia as William's prisoner, the new republic fought on for four bitter, hungry months of resistance in Paris. Finally, after every animal in Paris had been eaten, including cats and rats and even the elephant in the zoo, the French army laid down its arms, and the Prussians marched down the streets of Paris.

Meanwhile a temporary Government of National Defense at Bordeaux attempted to raise an army to relieve the siege of Paris. Once the capital had fallen, a new National Assembly was elected to negotiate peace terms with Prussia. The negotiators met at Versailles for preliminary details, and signed the final terms at Frankfurt in 1871. The Germans demanded a staggering indemnity of $1,000,000,000, the cession to Prussia of Alsace and most of Lorraine, and occupation by Prussian forces of French fortresses until the indemnity was paid.

Not content with the injury of taking Alsace and Lorraine, the Prussians added the insult of crowning their King as Emperor of the Germans in the famous Hall of Mirrors at Versailles, where French kings had lived. So the Confederation of North Germany became the *Deutsches Reich*, the German Empire, a title which could permit the kings of Bavaria and Württemberg to accept the leadership of the German Emperor.

From that date in 1871 France, which had

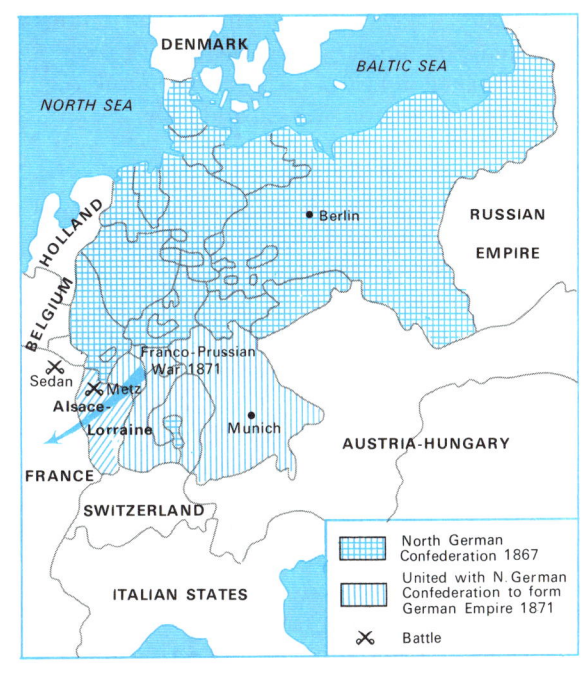

Unification of Germany: The German Empire, 1871

long been "the first state in Europe," was replaced by the German Empire for nearly half a century, until the tables were turned in 1919 when the peace delegates of the German Empire signed a humiliating peace in that same Hall of Mirrors at Versailles after World War I.

2. Domestic Problems and Solutions, 1870–1890

The Age of Bismarck, 1871–1890

The years 1871–1890 are usually referred to as the Age of Bismarck because as Chancellor of the German Empire he so completely dominated the politics of the European continent. Germany became the center of a network of diplomatic understandings and alliances which succeeded in keeping peace among the nations. Germany occupied the very heart of Europe and initiated policies which were generally followed by Austria, Russia, and Italy.

The Government System

Bismarck's dominant position in the German Empire was largely the result of the method of government in Germany. The King of Prussia was hereditary German Emperor or Kaiser, and the German Empire was a federation somewhat like that of the United States, with state governments sharing power with the central government. However, Prussia dominated the Empire, with two-thirds of the population, control of the army, and the dominant voice in both legislative houses, the Bundesrat and the Reichstag.

The Bundesrat or Federal Council represented the constituent parts of the Empire, with representatives from 26 Kingdoms, Grand Duchies, Duchies, Principalities, Free Cities and the territory of Alsace-Lorraine.* The Reichstag or Parliament was chosen by universal manhood suffrage throughout the Empire. However, the real political power was in the hands of the Chancellor, who was appointed by the Kaiser and could hold power while he enjoyed the Emperor's support, even though the Reichstag might unanimously oppose the Chancellor. Bismarck controlled the Bundesrat, and because all ministers held office at his pleasure he controlled the government for the Kaiser.

Political Parties in Germany

The several political parties reflected the internal differences within the Empire. In one sense the German Empire of 1871 was a political revolution because it had become powerful at the expense of the kingdoms and states within the Empire. Hanover resented its annexation, the Poles disliked Prussian rule, Danes in Schleswig objected to being part of Germany, the people of Alsace-Lorraine accepted their separation from France only under bitter protest, and southern German Catholics did not like being absorbed into a Protestant state.

Bismarck was well aware of these internal dissensions, and was afraid that they could weaken a Germany already facing the antagonism of other powers, because she had suddenly become a power to be reckoned with in Europe.

Her large population was second only to Russia's, and although her army was smaller than Russia's it was far more efficient and was probably the strongest in Europe. Her enormous resources of coal and iron, her rapidly-growing transportation system, her chemical industries and first-class technical schools were already challenging Britain's industrial supremacy. Germany was strong enough to play the dominant role in the balance of power of international politics.

Bismarck realized that the German people must be united by the removal of causes of discontent, and that a forceful statesmanlike foreign policy was essential if Germany was not to be confronted with a great combination of Russia, Austria, France, and perhaps Great Britain who was for the moment absorbed in her trade and overseas enterprises.

The Progressive or Social Democrat Party of shopkeepers, artisans, merchants, and minor officials opposed the very limited powers of the Reichstag, and wanted much broader social reform. Its supporters were, at least on paper, followers of a modified Marxist program and did not believe in collaboration with what they called bourgeois measures. It grew from

---

*The 4 Kingdoms of Prussia, Bavaria, Saxony, Württemberg; 6 Grand Duchies; 5 Duchies; 7 Principalities; the 3 Free Cities of the Old Hanseatic days, Hamburg, Bremen, Lübeck; the territory of Alsace-Lorraine.

nothing in 1870 to the largest party by 1914, and drew its support from industrial workers and those who demanded a ministry responsible, or answerable for policy, to the Reichstag.

The Moderates or National Liberals started out as the heirs of the 1848 liberals, but they gradually came to support a strong executive, a strong army and navy, and the policies of Bismarck. They were industrialists and businessmen who supported whatever helped business, and government officials whose careers depended upon the growth of the German Empire. The Moderates were less concerned with political rights than with national unity.

The Conservatives were originally landowners, later joined by businessmen who accepted social security measures which helped to unite the nation behind the concept of a strong, industrialized Germany. In many respects similar to the Moderates, they were only more emphatically nationalist.

The Catholic Center Party grew out of opposition to Bismarck's *Kulturkampf* or "civilization struggle" against the influence of the Catholic Church in politics. Their strength came largely from Bavaria and the Rhineland, and their followers in general opposed a strong central government and hoped to protect their interests against predominant Protestant influence.

Of Bismarck's five-point program, we are concerned essentially with three: repression of Catholics and Social Democrats, social security, and foreign alliances in the interests of Germany.

The Kulturkampf

Bismarck realized that recent German successes were of concern to his neighbors, who might have cause to fear the efficient Prussian army. His goal was a period of peace in which to forge a new Germany into a strong unified nation, and he had no intention of permitting the Reichstag, the elective German Parliament, to regard him and his ministers as servants of the Reichstag.

The first part of his program was the *Kulturkampf* or "civilization struggle," a conflict with the Roman Catholic Church. In 1864 Pope Pius IX issued a document which denounced the idea of the supremacy of the State over the Church. Bismarck's opposition was not religious but political, because he foresaw the possibility that the Church position would interfere with his plans to centralize the government and nation.

Bismarck needed the support of a leading group in the Reichstag if he was to put through the reforms he planned. He relied upon the National Liberal Party at first, the party of anti-clerical business and professional men, and won their support in his fight against the "Blacks," the pro-Catholic Center Party which generally opposed federalism. Bismarck was using the National Liberals for his own purposes, just as they thought they were using Bismarck for their ends. They believed that Bismarck would set up a liberal parliamentary government, guarantee individual liberties, and support their liberal ideas. Bismarck expelled the Jesuits who had, he thought, too much power in German education, and limited religious offices in Germany to German-born citizens. The conflict ended when Bismarck decided that the Catholics were not a serious threat to German unity.

Bismarck then broke with the National Liberals, who opposed the dominance of Prussia in the German government, and had recently attacked his large army budget. He turned instead to the conservative group of Prussian landed aristocrats, the *Junkers*, to the industrialists, and even to the Catholic Center Party.

These groups believed, with Bismarck, that the Socialists, the "Reds," with their Marxist beliefs, were dangerous to Germany's unity.

Social Security Legislation

He now turned his opposition away from the "Black," the Catholic Church, and on to the "Red," the Socialists, whose program might become so Marxist as to support an international movement and thus weaken Germany. At first he used the repressive measures of banning their meetings and their publications. But this policy only drove them underground and made them even more dangerous. So he adopted the policy of removing their opposition by introducing a state system of contributory social security by which the employer, the employee, and the state contributed to sickness and accident insurance and old age pensions. This was the most progressive program of social insurance introduced by any government at that time. Although this was a great step forward, the Socialist Party increased its membership because nothing was done by the government to improve wages or factory conditions.

3. Foreign Affairs of the German Empire, 1870–1890

The Dreikaiserbund: Three Emperors' League

After the successful Franco-Prussian War, Germany played little part in foreign affairs until the Congress of Berlin in 1878, after the Russo-Turkish War. Bismarck presided at the Conference, where the powers of Europe deprived Russia of most of her gains in the Russo-Turkish War, because they wished to prevent the expansion of Russian influence westward.

One result of the Congress was to postpone Bismarck's plan for a permanent alliance among the emperors of Germany, Russia, and Austria, which he hoped might prevent the spread of radical ideas in Europe. Austria had signed an agreement with Russia early in 1877 to remain neutral in the event of war between Russia and Turkey. Austria was to occupy the Turkish provinces of Bosnia and Herzegovina, in the Balkans, when she saw fit. She wanted these as a protection against a probable Russian expansion in the Balkans. But as later events were to prove, Bosnia and Herzegovina became a basis of contention rather than security between Austria and Russia. An earlier Three Emperors' League of 1872 had agreed that the status quo in Europe should not be changed. The Russo-Turkish War of 1877–1878 led to the collapse of this alliance.

Bismarck was worried over two possibilities. Austria and Russia could come to blows, and France might take the opportunity to find an ally against Germany. So in 1881 he negotiated the secret League which provided generally that if any one of the three should go to war, the other two would remain neutral, and that no change in the boundaries of Turkey should take place without the consent of the three. The League was little more than a "negative" one, since it did not provide for common action among the three.

The Triple Alliance

One of the reasons for Russia's agreeing to the Three Emperors' League was Bismarck's negotiation in 1879 of the Dual Alliance between Germany and Austria. The Dual Alliance provided that the two nations would act together if either should be attacked by Russia, and that if Germany were attacked by France then Austria would agree to remain neutral. The Dual Alliance was actually an alliance to *prevent* war, and was the first *permanent* alliance in

European politics, for it was to last for nearly forty years.

Another reason for the Dual Alliance was to bring pressure upon Russia to join in the Three Emperors' League. The Dual Alliance was expanded into the Triple Alliance in 1882 when Italy joined Germany and Austria, not because she had common interests with them, but because she was infuriated when France took over Tunisia as a colony, a part of North Africa which Italy wanted. Bismarck had really engineered this situation, for he had let France know that he would have no objection to her taking Tunisia. He accomplished what he had set out to do, the isolation of France on the Continent, for even Italy was now her enemy.

4. The Unification of Italy, 1815–1871

At the Congress of Vienna, Metternich aptly referred to Italy as simply a "geographical expression," because in 1815 it was divided into seven separate areas each ruled by a foreign power or by an independent ruler.

Ever since the days of the Roman Empire, nearly 1,500 years earlier, Italy had remained disunited and had been repeatedly throughout history the battleground of foreign powers. For the previous 300 years it had been the target of French, Spanish, and Austrian attempts to control it, and finally between 1792 and 1801 it had succumbed to French domination, from the Alps to the toe of the peninsula. Napoleon divided the country by annexing Piedmont, Savoy, and Sardinia to France, setting up the northern Kingdom of Italy, made up of Lombardy, several duchies, and part of the Papal States, and the Kingdom of Naples ruled by his relatives.

Napoleonic rule eliminated special privileges and feudal obligations, introduced a centralized administration and the Code Napoléon which made all men equal before the law. French rule not only introduced new ideas but caused humiliation and resentment against the occupation by foreign troops.

At the Congress of Vienna, whatever advantages the French had brought to Italy were swept away when Austria recovered control of Italian territory and simply reverted back to the repressive days before 1792.

Italy after the Congress of Vienna

Of the four main areas into which the country was divided, only one was ruled by an Italian, the old reactionary Victor Emmanuel I, who so objected to everything French that he destroyed the parks and the gas-lights which the French had installed. Victor Emmanuel ruled over the Kingdom of Sardinia, which included that island, the coastal region of Piedmont including Genoa, and the mountainous French-inhabited region of Savoy. As an Italian he was the one man around whom the people of Italy could rally. The two wealthy areas of Lombardy, with Milan its capital, and Venetia with Venice as its chief port, were brought directly under Austrian rule. Here no freedom of speech or press was allowed, and hundreds of Italians were imprisoned for political activities.

In central Italy the small duchies of Tuscany, Parma, and Modena became independent under Austrian rulers who had little concern for the interests of the people. The Papal States were one of the worst-ruled sections of the country. Only two percent of the people could read, the clergy restricted all freedom of opinion, and liberal ideas were thoroughly suppressed. Farthest south was the Kingdom of the Two Sicilies, consisting of the island of Sicily and the lower Italian peninsula previously called Naples.

Italy after the Congress of Vienna

This was a poverty-stricken area, plagued with bandits, and ruled with brutality by Ferdinand I of the Spanish royal family.

Throughout the peninsula the Austrian police ferreted out all subversive plots and kept close watch upon all activities by having all Italian mail censored by Austrian officials.

The Italian secret societies of Napoleon's day grew in number and size, and agitated against Austrian rulers, who were thoroughly detested across the country. Unfortunately, opposition was not efficiently organized, and the leaders of revolutionary movements could not agree on the form that a united Italy should take. Some wanted a centralized monarchy, some a federal government, while others would consider nothing but a republic with an elected head. In 1820 revolts broke out in the Kingdom of the Two Sicilies when the ruler, Ferdinand I, a member of the Bourbon family, agreed to a constitution, swore to keep his promise with the oath, "If I lie, do thou at this moment annihilate me," and then promptly secured Austrian aid to put down the revolt. When revolt broke out also in the Papal States, the Pope sent for Austrian troops to suppress his subjects, and so ruled out the possibility that he might become the leader of Italian independence.

The Leaders of Italian Independence

Standing head and shoulders above the numerous supporters of Italian independence and unity were four men, Mazzini, Garibaldi, Count Cavour, and Victor Emmanuel II.

Guiseppe Mazzini was a northerner of middle-class birth, a member of the secret Carbonari, or "Charcoal Burners" Society, and the prophet of Italian unity. He always wore black as a sign of mourning for a "chained" Italy, was exiled after an unsuccessful revolt in Piedmont in 1830, went to France and there organized the Young Italy movement, an underground society. He was so successful that he became so politically embarrassing to France that he was exiled, went to Switzerland, and from there first encouraged Italians to revolt, to set up republics wherever possible, then ultimately win complete independence and become a united nation.

Guiseppe Garibaldi was the colorful tough soldier, the fierce patriot who favored a republic. He attempted to lead a rebellion in Savoy in 1833, failed hopelessly, was condemned to death but escaped to France, and then went on to South America. There he learned the science of guerrilla warfare while fighting for Uruguay, and wore the red shirt that was later to become the symbol of Garibaldi's Red Shirt volunteers in Italy.

Count Camillo di Cavour was the statesman from the kingdom of Piedmont–Sardinia, now called Piedmont. He and his King Victor

Mazzini

Garibaldi

Emmanuel II (1849–1878) were wise enough to realize that Piedmont must become a model state that would attract patriotic Italians to rally around it, and secondly that Italians would need foreign assistance to expel their foreign rulers.

Victor Emmanuel was a crude, vulgar person but an Italian patriot ready to encourage and follow a resolute leader. Cavour had studied in England and had learned to admire its parliamentary form of government. He was tough, shrewd, and opportunistic, certainly not liberal in the sense that Mazzini and Garibaldi were, but astute enough to understand that he and his King must be liberal enough to attract liberals but not so liberal that they would offend conservatives.

These two men set out to make the House of Savoy, which ruled the Kingdom of Piedmont, the leader of Italian unity.

The Revolts of 1848

As in other European countries, the year 1848 became significant in Italy for attempts to win freedom. In January the new foreign ruler, Ferdinand II, made concessions to popular demands in the Kingdom of the Two Sicilies. Two months later King Charles Albert of Piedmont issued a constitution for Piedmont. When Charles Albert's attempt to aid Lombardy in its revolution against Austria proved unsuccessful, he abdicated in favor of his son Victor Emmanuel II, who was destined to become the first ruler of a united Italy.

Victor Emmanuel gave full support to his

energetic Prime Minister Cavour who set out to make Piedmont a model state. Cavour was already known throughout Italy for the newspaper he had founded years earlier, *Il Risorgimento*, or Resurgence, a slogan which soon applied to the process of Italian unification – a resurgence or resurrection of the great past that Italy had once enjoyed. He transformed Piedmont into a modern state, negotiated trade agreements with other nations, built a Piedmont line of Atlantic mail ships, reorganized the Piedmont army, and introduced modern business and banking methods into the country.

The outbreak of the Crimean War in 1854 provided Cavour with the opportunity to carry out his second objective – to secure foreign assistance to expel foreign rulers from Italy. He sent 15,000 troops in support of Britain and France against Russia, in the hope that his plans for Italy's independence would be supported abroad. At the peace treaty convention after the war Cavour pointed out that Austria was the main cause of Italy's troubles. Although Piedmont was not awarded the neighboring Duchy of Parma that she wanted, the Italian issue had been brought to the attention of the European Powers at the conference table.

Napoleon III Assists Cavour

Cavour's intervention in the Crimean War won the admiration of Napoleon III of France. In 1858, in a secret agreement between the two men, France promised to "set Italy free from the Alps to the Adriatic," and in return Sardinia would give to France the adjoining province of Savoy and the city of Nice.

Cavour provoked Austria into declaring war on Piedmont, and Napoleon immediately joined in on Piedmont's side. The allies defeated Austrian troops rather indecisively at Solferino, but Napoleon decided at this point to pull out of the war. The French and Austrian emperors

Count Cavour

met, agreed to cede Lombardy to Piedmont, but planned to strengthen Austrian rule elsewhere in Italy. Very quickly after this was known, the inhabitants of Parma, Modena, Tuscany, and the northern part of the Papal States called Romagna, rebelled successfully against Austrian rule, and voted to join Piedmont. Cavour kept his part of the bargain with Napoleon, and gave Savoy and Nice to France, an action for which he was bitterly criticized by Italian nationalists. But Cavour was realist enough to understand that mercenary troops, which the French were, had to be paid off. He believed that Nice and Savoy were a small price in exchange for the real beginning of Italian unity.

The Kingdom of Italy, 1861

One of Cavour's bitterest critics was Guiseppe Garibaldi, a native of Nice. Upon the outbreak of war with Austria in 1859 he returned from South America to fight the Austrians. In 1860 a rebellion in the Kingdom of the Two Sicilies was put down with brutality and with the imprisonment of 20,000 Italians. Garibaldi gathered around him his famous Thousand Red Shirts at Genoa, and sailed for Marsala on the west coast of Sicily. By sheer chance his two little steamships arrived at the port just as a small squadron of the British fleet arrived there to enforce respect for British lives and property. But the local garrison, which could easily have repulsed Garibaldi's small force, assumed that Britain was giving aid to Garibaldi. With the help of natives, Garibaldi's little army defeated forces several times its size, captured the entire island of Sicily, sailed to the mainland and captured the city of Naples, and drove out the foreign ruler.

So great was Garibaldi's popularity that he could have been elected president of a republic of southern Italy, and would probably have received support for an attack on the Papal States. Cavour forestalled these possibilities by sending Piedmontese troops into the Papal States and persuading Garibaldi to step aside

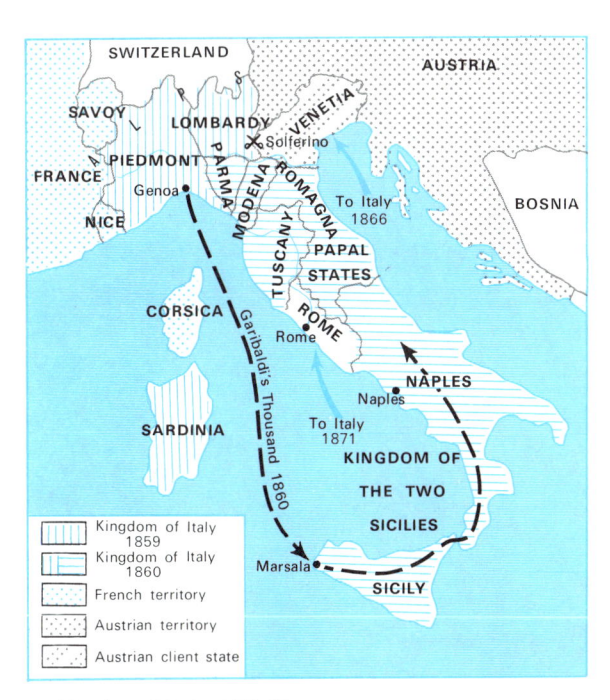

Unification of Italy, 1859–71

Italian Unity. Garibaldi, in this cartoon, suggests to Victor Emmanuel II that he use force to make the unification of Italy complete.

RIGHT LEG IN THE BOOT AT LAST.

GARIBALDI. "IF IT WON'T GO ON, SIRE, TRY A LITTLE MORE POWDER."

and recognize Victor Emmanuel II as ruler of the Two Sicilies. Cavour took possession of the Papal States in the name of the Kingdom of Piedmont, but made no attempt to include the city of Rome, which still remained as Papal territory. In 1860 the people of the Sicilies and the Papal States voted in a plebiscite to be annexed to Piedmont, and the "Kingdom of Italy" was officially proclaimed in March 1861.

Completion of Italian Unity, 1871

Two Italian areas were still not part of a united Italy, Venetia and the city of Rome. Italy's opportunity to acquire Venetia came in 1866 when Prussia went to war with Austria. Italy allied with Prussia, suffered defeat from the Austrian forces, but at the peace table was rewarded with Venetia surrendered by Austria under pressure from Prussia.

Four years later, when the Franco-Prussian War forced France to call back her troops protecting the Pope in Rome, Italy seized the opportunity to occupy Rome. Over the protest of the Pope, the city of Rome became the capital of a united Italy in 1871. The Pope did not accept this action, and until 1929 he and his successors chose to regard themselves as "prisoners" and refused to leave the Vatican. In that year an understanding was reached between Mussolini and the Pope, who acknowledged the situation that had existed since 1871.

Review Questions

Section 1
1. Through what domestic program did Bismarck help to unify Germany?
2. In what respects was Bismarck's foreign policy one of "blood and iron"?

Section 2
3. How did Bismarck attempt to use political parties to reduce the power of the Catholic Church in Germany?
4. By what means did Bismarck attempt to win the support of German workers? Why was he only partially successful?

Section 3
5. Was the Triple Alliance a defensive or an offensive alliance? Why?
6. In what way was the Triple Alliance a contradiction of the Three Emperors' League?

Section 4
7. Explain why Italy was no more than a "geographical expression" in the first half of the 19th century.
8. What was the contribution to the unification of Italy of each of the several Italian patriots?

3

The Growth of Democracy in Great Britain, France, and the United States

Great Britain
Parliamentary Reform
Improvement of Working Conditions
Later Parliamentary Reform
Social Security

France
The Second Empire
The Third Republic
Crises of the Third Republic

The United States
Agitation for Reforms
Political and Social Reforms

Industrialization in England helped to create a middle class of businessmen who demanded a voice in governments still dominated by landowners. Businessmen wanted cheap food and free trade for their products, while landowners wanted import duties on competitive foreign farm products.

By the Reform Act of 1832 the middle class shared power with the landowners and were able to enact legislation that suited their interests. In the following eighty years successive parliamentary reform measures extended the right to vote and widened membership in the House to include workingmen. Legislation reflected their interests, and during the 19th century and early 20th century England followed Germany's earlier lead of adopting social security measures.

In France political contests for power between monarchists and republicans kept the situation in a turmoil as the monarchy of 1830 was replaced by the Second Republic of 1848, which was in turn succeeded by the Second Empire of Napoleon III, from 1852 until 1870. Defeat in the Franco-Prussian War brought in the Third Republic, in the tradition of the Paris Commune of 1792. Although the Third Republic experienced severe domestic stresses, it was effectively in power by the end of the 19th century.

Industrialization in the United States led to demands for humanitarian reforms, better educational opportunities, improved working conditions, and the extension of voting rights to include women.

Terms

1. Rotten Borough
2. Pocket Borough
3. Reform Act of 1832
4. Corn Laws
5. People's Charter
6. Laissez-faire
7. Factory Act of 1833
8. Forster Education Act, 1870
9. Grand National Consolidated Trades Union
10. Trade Disputes Act, 1906
11. Budget of 1909
12. Parliament Act of 1911
13. Labour Party
14. Workmen's Compensation Act
15. Old Age Pensions Act
16. National Insurance Act
17. Second Empire
18. Franco-Prussian War
19. Third Republic
20. Paris Commune
21. New Harmony
22. American Colonization Society
23. *Uncle Tom's Cabin*
24. Australian Ballot
25. Direct Primary
26. Initiative
27. Referendum
28. Recall
29. Seventeenth Amendment
30. Nineteenth Amendment
31. *Hammer v. Dagenhart*
32. *West Coast Hotel v. Parrish*
33. Eighteenth Amendment

People

34. Chartists
35. Earl Grey
36. Duke of Wellington
37. Robert Owen
38. Benjamin Disraeli
39. William Gladstone
40. Louis-Napoleon
41. General Boulanger
42. Captain Dreyfus
43. Émile Zola
44. Mary Lyon
45. Lucretia Mott
46. Elizabeth Blackwell
47. William Lloyd Garrison
48. Harriet Tubman
49. Harriet Beecher Stowe
50. Horace Mann

Events

England

1832 Parliament Act: extension of the franchise
1833 Factory Act
1848 Repeal of the Corn Laws
1867 Parliament Act: further extension of franchise
1870 Forster Education Act
1875 Trade Unions legalized
1884 Parliament Act: virtually universal male suffrage
1906 Emergence of Labour Party
     Trades Disputes Act
     Workmen's Compensation Act
1908 Old Age Pensions Act
1911 National Insurance Act
     Parliament Act: power of House of Lords restricted
1918 Parliament Act: votes for women over thirty
1928 Parliament Act: votes for women over twenty-one
1946 Parliament Act: House of Lords restricted to one-year suspensive veto

France

1848 Second Republic
1852 Second Empire: Napoleon III
1870 Franco-Prussian War
     Collapse of Second Empire
     Paris Commune
1875 Third Republic
1887 Boulanger Affair
1894 Dreyfus Affair

United States

1822 Liberia established by American Colonization Society
1833 First admission of women to college: Oberlin
1840 First woman medical school graduate: Elizabeth Blackwell
1848 "Feminists" demand all rights and privileges
1852 Publication of *Uncle Tom's Cabin*
1920 Eighteenth Amendment: Prohibition
     Nineteenth Amendment: Women's Suffrage
1933 Twenty-Second Amendment: Prohibition repealed

Great Britain

1. Parliamentary Reform

Need for a Reform Bill

Parliament had won many rights in the 17th century but representation in the House of Commons was still limited to landowners. By the early decades of the 19th century England was well on the way to becoming an industrial nation. As a consequence, a new and important middle class of factory owners and businessmen demanded a share in government and the right to participate in legislation. The landlord group controlled parliaments, and could serve their own interests by excluding foreign cheap competitive products through high tariffs. But factory owners wanted cheap foreign wheat so that the wages of factory workers could be kept low. High food costs meant higher wages.

Another result of the Industrial Revolution was the rise of factory towns which had to be located near supplies of water power and coal. Towns in southern England which had been sending members to the House of Commons declined, and small towns in the north grew into large cities such as Birmingham, Sheffield, and Leeds. But southern towns, although declining in population and size, still sent members to Parliament representing the interests of the landowners, while the new industrial towns and middle-class were almost completely unrepresented. Many of the seats in the House of Commons were now known as "rotten boroughs" because they included so few voters that a wealthy person could easily buy their votes.

Some boroughs no longer had any population but still officially sent members to parliament. The owner of the land upon which a town formerly stood had the right to decide who should go to Parliament from that town. As a consequence, the borough was in one man's control, and was "in his pocket," which was the reason such a district was called a "pocket borough."

By 1830 many of the seats in the House of Commons were held by a few noble families. Parliament was no longer representative of 19th century England. Although there had been much talk in the 18th century about "parliamentary reform," it died down during the years of the French Revolution and the threat from Napoleon. But once the danger of French invasion had been removed, parliamentary reform became a political issue. The Conservative or Tory Party of landlords and country gentry did not favor extending the vote to more people, and certainly not to the workers. The Liberal or Whig Party, although led by some powerful noble families, was supported by the wealthy and increasingly important industrial class. The Whig Party supported limited parliamentary reform which would give the vote to the wealthy middle class, but certainly not to propertyless people.

A third group, known as Radicals, believed that government should serve the interests of all people, not just a particular group, and that every man should be able to participate in government. They demanded the vote for all adult males, and the payment of members of Parliament so that the ordinary man could afford to serve in Parliament.

The Reform Bill Forced through Parliament

In 1831 the Whig Party came into power and quickly passed a reform bill introduced by Earl Grey, the Prime Minister. Because the bill won a close majority, the Prime Minister decided to dissolve Parliament in the hopes that a new election would give him a larger majority. Earl Grey did win a majority and succeeded in getting another reform bill passed by a substantial majority. However, the House of Lords refused to pass the bill which had clearly been favored by the voters in the recent election. The unrepresentative House of Lords was clearly blocking the wishes of the elected House of Commons. In some towns protests against the House of Lords became riots in which property was destroyed. The Whig Party in the House of Commons passed another Reform Bill in 1832, but once again the Lords refused to pass such a bill. Lord Grey, the Prime Minister, resigned.

The King then called upon the Duke of Wellington, leader of the Tory or Conservative Party, to "form a government." However, his party was in the minority in the House of Commons and could not hope to get the support of the majority in Commons. Requests for money to pay for expenses of government would be refused by the Whig majority, so Wellington had to inform the King that Earl Grey must be asked to take over the government. Lord Grey then informed the King that he would do so on one condition only. The House of Lords must agree to pass the bill. Lord Grey could force the King's hand because he had the right to demand that the King "create" enough new peers or lords from the Liberal Party to outvote the Conservative members of the House of Lords. The threat to do this was sufficient, because the House of Lords did not want new upstart lords forced upon them. They gave way and passed the Reform Bill of 1832, which then became law once it received the King's signature.

The Reform Act of 1832

The Reform Act of 1832 (1) took away from 57 "rotten" and "pocket" boroughs their two members each, and from 30 other boroughs their one member each, (2) gave the suffrage, or right to vote, to "householders" who lived in

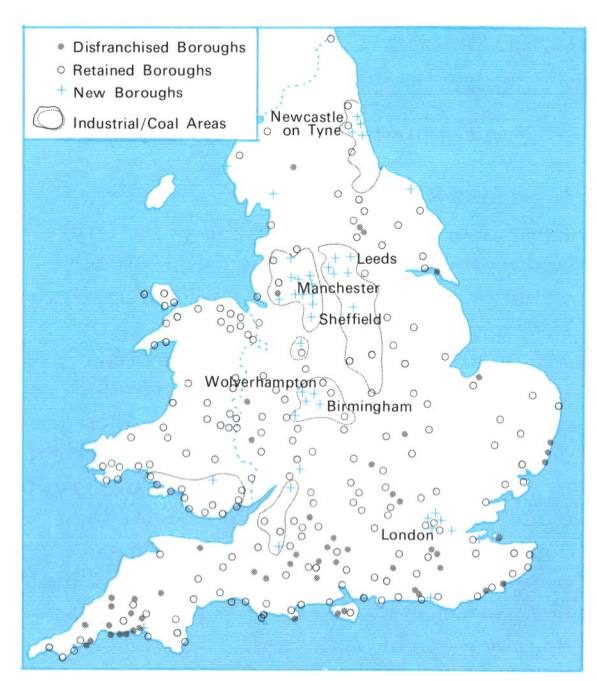

The Reform of Parliament. The 1832 Act caused new constituencies to be made in the industrial Midlands and North and the removal of rotten and pocket boroughs in the South.

houses worth a specific amount a year, which meant moderate-income farm owners and farm renters. Although the vote was not given to the mass of people, it was extended to the middle-class landowners and businessmen.

The Repeal of the Corn Laws

The newly-enfranchised middle-class businessmen now had the opportunity to enact laws in their own interest, and an important measure was the repeal of the so-called Corn Laws which placed heavy duties upon imported wheat and other food grains. The landowning majority in parliament had enacted the Corn Laws in order to protect their own crops against cheaper foreign wheat. Richard Cobden and John Bright, middle-class industrialists, organized the anti-Corn Law League in 1838 for the purpose of winning enough support to get the Corn Laws repealed, but their efforts were not successful until a severe potato-crop failure in Ireland in 1845 brought on a devastating famine in that country. Parliament was finally convinced that cheap food must be made available, and in 1848 it removed the duties on foreign foodstuffs. This action benefited not only the Irish who survived the famine but also the English industrialists who could claim the right to lower wages because food now cost less. It also benefited the lower classes, since they could also buy cheaper food.

The Chartists

The working class had not won the right to vote in 1832, and therefore could not send their own representatives to parliament. One group of workers, called the Chartists, agitated to get the vote and other rights for the workers. Another group believed that political methods would be useless, and that the better way to obtain results would be through trade unions which might be able to bargain with employers for higher wages and better working conditions.

The "People's Charter" was the program of the Chartists. It demanded legislation which would give the workingman not only the right to vote for representatives in parliament but also the opportunity for workingmen to become members of parliament themselves. The six reform proposals of the Chartists were: (1) the vote for all adult males, (2) equal voting districts to include adequate representation for new industrial towns, (3) the right for any man to be a member of Parliament, whether he owned property or not, (4) the secret ballot at elections in place of the "open" system of voting in which a man had to declare publicly to an official his choice of candidate, (5) the payment of members of Parliament, and (6) a newly-elected House of Commons each year.

These proposals were regarded as radical in the 1840's, although by 1911, when members of the House of Commons were first paid a salary, all the proposals except that of annually-elected parliaments had been adopted.

Chartists were generally unpopular because some advocated violence and antagonized the middle class whose support would be necessary for favorable legislation in Parliament. Some Chartists even suggested political rebellion. They circulated petitions at hundreds of mass meetings, organized riots, and even called a general strike which they hoped would cripple the country. What finally finished the Chartists as an effective group was partly the ridicule which they brought upon themselves, and partly a changing attitude among workers. In 1848 the Chartists collected a petition which they claimed contained over 5,000,000 signatures, although there were actually only some 2,000,000 on the petition. They hauled it across London in a carriage, presented it to Parliament, and awaited

Chartists. This cartoon shows the workers trying to force their petition into Parliament while on the right John Bull—the symbol of the ordinary Britisher—laughs.

results. Some of the signatures were so ludicrously bogus, such as "Pugnose," "Victoria Rex" (King Victoria), "Mr. Punch," that the public laughter which greeted the exposure helped to sink the Chartist movement, despite claims by the Chartists that their opponents had added the bogus names. By this time many workers believed that their best hopes lay in their own trade union organization outside parliament, and favorable middle-class support.

2. Improvement of Working Conditions

The Laissez-Faire Doctrine
During the 18th century the economic policy of the government began to change from the restrictions of the mercantile system to the doctrine of *laissez-faire*, or economic liberalism, literally "to leave alone to do," or simply "hands off." Government intervention of any sort in industry and commerce became increasingly unpopular, and businessmen demanded freedom from all restrictions. They claimed that government interference checked progress and expansion, and that the men who were engaged in business knew much more about it than did the government.

During the period of rapid development, government adopted the policy of non-interference, on the grounds that competition among businessmen would be beneficial to the country, and would be protection enough for workers and consumers. No government restrictions were to be placed on any business; chartered companies which had received special and sometimes monopolistic rights were no longer to enjoy these privileges; in 1848 Parliament refused to continue the Corn Laws and British farm products were now open to competition from foreign food grains. In 1849 the Navigation Acts, which had long closed to foreign ships the carrying trade to and from England, were repealed. Such trade was now open to ships of all nations. This was quickly followed by the repeal of protective tariffs because England had very little to fear from foreign competition, and wanted free and open markets for her goods in foreign countries.

Opposition to Laissez-Faire
Skilled handcraftsmen, faced with serious competition from machine-made goods, asked the government for protection of their crafts. Older industrial districts which were facing competition from new industrial towns rising on sites near the sources of raw materials or power for the new factories also wanted government assistance. Farmers who had for decades enjoyed a home market free from competition from abroad protested against the new policy of laissez-faire. Even some of the new manufacturers who had welcomed the repeal of the Corn Laws because of lower food prices now protested against competition from foreign manufactures.

An important group of people protesting against the policy of laissez-faire were reformers who had no personal interests to serve but were genuinely concerned about the plight of the workers. The reformers contended that the government had the obligation to protect the workers from economic exploitation, and should put a floor under wages and working conditions, and a ceiling on working hours and child labor. Economic progress of the nation, they said, must not take place at the expense of the workers, and there was no guarantee that the unrestricted interests of employers would necessarily benefit their workers. The reformers claimed that unrestricted competition could result in lower wages, longer hours, and unhealthy working conditions.

Factory Acts

Factory abuses were common because the laissez-faire theory permitted factory owners complete freedom in the handling of their workers. Women and children were used in mines, pauper children were apprenticed out to employers who paid them disgracefully low wages and worked them scandalously long hours. As early as 1784 the local officials of the town of Manchester refused to allow any children to work in the cotton mills, so bad were the conditions. Not unusually the hours of work for men, women and children lasted from 5 o'clock in the morning until 9 o'clock at night.

One of the first reformers was Robert Owen, the owner of cotton mills. He introduced the 10-hour day in his mills, refused to employ children, set up free schools for them, and encouraged his workers to set up co-operative stores which they owned and from which they could buy more cheaply than from private stores. Although Owen attempted to get factory legislation introduced into parliament, he was unsuccessful. It was William Ashley Cooper, better known in later years as Lord Shaftesbury, who was responsible for the first factory legislation. In 1833 he was asked to become chairman of a factory commission, and through his untiring efforts over a period of fifty years, he was responsible for a series of Factory and Mines Acts. The first effective Factory Act was that of 1833 which prohibited the employment of children under nine years of age, and limited the working day of children between the ages of 9 and 13 to nine hours. Young people between 13 and 16 were restricted to a 13-hour work-day.

When a bill was introduced into Parliament in 1844 limiting the work-day of women and children to ten hours, it was vigorously opposed, but was passed three years later. In a few years the working day was by law fixed between 6 a.m. and 6 p.m. or 7 a.m. to 7 p.m. Even some of the severest critics of factory legislation were in time convinced that the laws had not been disastrous to business. Not until 1867 were the principles of the Factory Acts, limited to cotton mills, extended to all factories and workshops. By the end of the century the minimum age limit for employment was 11 years, and all factories and mines were obliged to observe regulations regarding sanitation, safety precautions, and adequate ventilation.

Education

In 1840 a Commission on Education found that most children under fourteen were illiterate. The first government grant to education, a very modest sum of money, had been made in 1833, and under the Factory Act of that year all children employed in cotton mills were to spend two hours a day in school. But such schools as did exist were almost useless. The modern system of education began in 1870 with the Forster Education Act, partly because many workingmen had been given the right to vote, and partly because enlightened industrialists realized that educated people were more efficient workers. The 1870 Act made education compulsory, although parents were obliged to contribute to the cost. In 1891 education was made free, and within a few years was the responsibility of local governing bodies.

Trade Unions

The factory system was the cause of the rise of modern trade unions because the industrial population was divided between employers and employees. Early attempts of workers to organize for better working conditions and shorter hours were strenuously opposed by employers and the government, and in 1799 the Combination Act made illegal all combinations of workers, with a jail sentence for the criminal offense by a worker "who combined with any other to get an increase in wages or a decrease in hours," or who urged others to do so, or held meetings for such purposes.

Bad times led to the formation in 1834 of the Grand National Consolidated Trades Union, the G.N.C.T.U., whose aim became openly revolutionary through the strategy of overthrowing the existing system of government by means of a general strike of all workers in the country. Within a short time the organization numbered over half a million members. Opposed by government and press, it rapidly declined after the law courts showed that any agreements "in restraint of trade" were punishable. Six farm laborers who tried to organize a farm workers' union were sentenced to be transported to the convict settlement in Australia and serve seven years there, for daring to administer an oath of membership. Employers then obliged their employees, as a condition of employment, to swear that they were not members of the G.N.C.T.U. and did not intend to join.

More liberal unions, such as the Miners' Association and the Amalgamated Society of Engineers, accepted the existing system of government and concentrated upon trying to get increased wages and shorter hours for their members. In 1875 the first effective legislation was enacted, permitting unions to bargain collectively through designated workers representing the union and permitting them to strike.

However, unions received a severe setback in 1901 when the Railway Servants' Association was sued by the Taff Vale Railway Company for damages done during a strike. The House of Lords, sitting as the highest court of appeal, decided against the union on the grounds that damage done by any one member could render the entire union and its funds liable. Thus, a man could be paid by a company to join a union, and then be deliberately caught while causing damage to company property. Union funds were in great danger, as the $115,000 damages levied against the union indicated. Labor's greatest gain came with the Trades Disputes Act of 1906, the "Magna Carta of Trade Unionism" which protected union funds against any claim for damages.

3. Later Parliamentary Reform

Parliamentary Reform Acts, 1867–1946

Two outstanding men who were to dominate British politics for many years were Benjamin Disraeli and William Gladstone, the former to become leader of the Conservative Party, and Gladstone the leader of the Liberal Party. Disraeli, the son of a wealthy and cultured Jew, entered Parliament in 1837 at the age of 32, and deliberately attracted attention by adopting the extraordinary mannerisms, for those times, of green velvet trousers, lace-decorated jacket sleeves, and long, curled hair. By 1867 he was the accepted leader of the Conservative Party.

William Gladstone, son of a wealthy Liverpool businessman, was well educated and a conformist in dress and style. He went into Parliament in 1832 at the age of 23, was at first opposed to further parliamentary reform, but later supported it and became the leader of the Liberal Party.

In 1866 Gladstone proposed giving the vote to more men, but was defeated in the House of Commons by a combination of Conservatives and his own Liberals. Gladstone resigned as Prime Minister and was replaced by a Conservative government. The defeat of Gladstone's Reform Bill of 1866 aroused such great excitement in the country that parliamentary reform became a great cause.

Disraeli, although not prime minister, was leader of the Conservatives in the House of Commons, and decided to "take a leap in the dark" by supporting another Reform Bill and so win new supporters for his party. The Reform Act of 1867 was a combination of terms agreed upon by Gladstone and Disraeli, but actually carried through by the Conservative government. The new measure gave more representation to large industrial cities, and the vote to all city householders, to all men living in lodgings worth a certain yearly rental, and to many tenant farmers. Although it did not satisfy the old Chartist demand for universal adult male suffrage, it doubled the number of voters by adding another 1,000,000 men to the 1868 voting lists.

To the surprise of both parties, the workers voted for Liberal candidates in the election of 1868 and returned that party to power. Gladstone decided to "educate our masters," meaning that education must be provided for those whose votes would be deciding elections in the future. Elementary education was made compulsory, and in 1884 Gladstone helped to enact another Reform Act which gave the vote to all industrial workers in towns. This left out young men who lived at home, servants, and those who did not maintain separate households, but it did increase the voting list to include over four-fifths of all adult males. In 1918 the fourth Reform Act gave to these men and to women over 30 years of age the right to vote. Not until 1928 did the fifth Reform Act give the "Flapper Vote" to women when they reached the age of twenty-one.

Parliament Act, 1911

Although the Parliament Act had nothing to do with extending the vote, it was an important step in general parliamentary reform because it restricted the power of the hereditary, non-elective House of Lords in blocking legislation desired by the people.

Ever since 1885 there had been suggestions to "end or mend" the House of Lords, which was not responsible or answerable to anyone for the way it voted on any bill. The House of Commons, elected by millions of voters, was very sensitive to the wishes of the electorate. Yet the House of Lords, whose approval was necessary before a bill could become a law, had the power to veto a bill and prevent its passage indefinitely. There were no checks and balances on the Lords.

In 1907 a resolution of the House of Commons cast the shadow of the crisis which was to come to a head in 1909. "In order to give effect to the will of the people as expressed by their elected representatives it is necessary that the power of the other House (of Lords) be restricted . . . so that the final decision of the Commons shall prevail."

The Budget of 1909

When Herbert Asquith became Prime Minister in 1908 the government was in need of additional money to pay for the building of eight new battleships, for the recent Old Age Pensions Act, and plan for payments of other social security measures which the government intended to introduce in Parliament. Lloyd George, Chancellor of the Exchequer, and responsible for preparing and presenting to Parliament the annual budget of proposed income and outgo, included taxes that would make the rich contribute to the needs of the poor. His increased taxes on gasoline, automobiles, incomes and inheritance of property were generally regarded as necessary and acceptable. The proposal which met violent opposition was a tax on private land not used for agricultural purposes and a tax on unearned incomes, or "unearned increment," as it was called. This tax would be placed upon a man whose property, whether buildings or land, was increased in value simply because of its location in an expanding area and on which the owner had made no improvements.

This was a completely new use of the taxing power to "redistribute" national wealth.

Commons passed the bill but Lords rejected it. The Prime Minister called for a general election for all seats in Commons, with the 1909 budget as the main campaign issue. The Liberal Party won control of the House of Commons with the support of the Irish Nationalist Party and the Labour Party members. The new Commons promptly passed the bill, and the Lords, knowing that their power was in danger, decided to pass it to avoid further trouble. But the Lords were too late. The House of Commons, mindful of their right to initiate "money" bills and the traditional agreement of the Lords not to alter money bills, were determined to limit the power on all legislation, particularly those bills dealing with money, such as a budget.

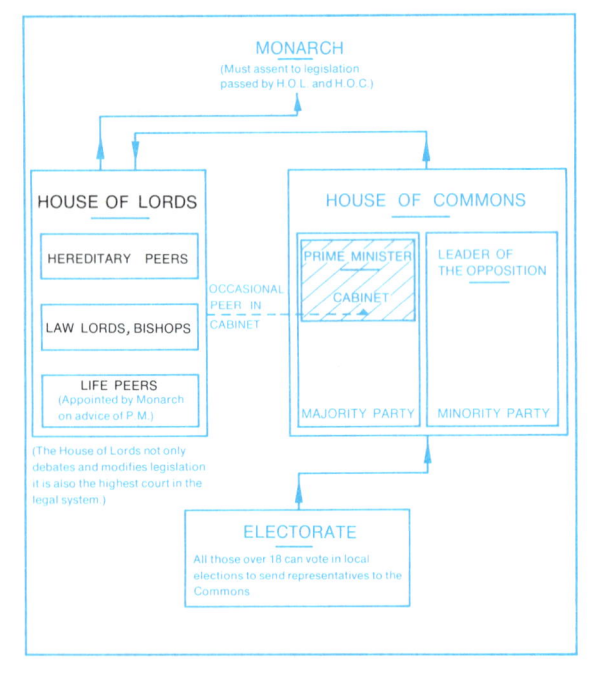

The House of Lords. This diagram shows the position of the House of Lords in the British Constitution.

The Parliament Bill introduced by the House of Commons proposed (1) that the Lords could not delay for more than one month any bill certified by the Speaker of the House of Commons to be a money bill, (2) any bill passed by the same House of Commons three successive times, with or without the agreement of the House of Lords, should become law provided that two years elapsed between the first and the third time the Bill was passed by Commons. This meant that the House of Lords would now have only a "suspensive" veto for two years, and could not prevent a bill from becoming law if the people of the nation wanted it.

After ten months of deadlock between the two Houses, the Prime Minister dissolved Parliament, and called for another election, with the main campaign issue this time the proposed Parliament Act.

Once again the strength of both parties in Commons remained the same, but the Liberals had a majority with the support of Labour and the Irish Nationalists. Again the Commons passed the Bill, and again the Lords set out to vote it down. But they had forgotten the right of the prime minister to ask the king to "create" enough new peers, or lords, to outvote those lords in opposition to the Parliament Bill.

Why would the king even consider such a request? Because the prime minister represents the majority in the House of Commons, and because the nation had just returned to Parliament members who were in favor of the Bill. The Lords were therefore thwarting the will of the people. Why could not the king pick from that majority party another prime minister, one who would simply drop the issue of the Parliament Bill? Because the Liberal Party, in favor of the Bill, would not work with such a man or vote him money to carry on the government. Then why should the king not avoid trouble by choosing a prime minister from the Conservative Party? Because it was the minority party, and each time it would attempt to bring in a bill to raise money, the majority party would vote it down, and the government would be unable to function.

When the Lords realized that the Liberal Prime Minister would present the king with a list of Liberal supporters to be given titles, to sit in the House of Lords and vote in favor of the Parliament Bill, they decided to keep their "club" select. Those against the Bill stayed away so that it could be passed.

In 1946 this process of limiting the House of Lords went one step farther by another Parliament Act which restricted the suspensive veto of the House of Lords to one year only. These two Acts were another method of democratizing Parliament.

4. Social Security

The political parties between them enacted during the 19th century parliamentary reform factory legislation, and legal recognition of trade unions. But one aspect of suggested reform they both resisted, and that was legislation to help those who suffered the "accidentals" of industrial life, such accidentals as old age, factory injury and sickness, and unemployment. Even though both political parties had to bid for working class votes after the 1884 Reform Act, they refused to support what they considered to be radical ideas. But the tide had set in strongly against laissez-faire, and further advances in social legislation were inevitable.

Appearance of the Labour Party

In 1906 a new election brought to power the Liberal Party, after ten years of Conservative government, with about 380 Liberal members out of a total of some 625 seats in the House of Commons. The very significant result of that election was the emergence of a new party, the Labour Party supported by trade unions, which were now actively involved in politics. This new situation resulted from a decision by the House of Lords, acting as the highest court of appeal, which made a union legally and collectively responsible for damage committed by any union member during a strike. Union leaders determined to form their own political party and get through parliament a law reversing this decision.

The importance of this small party of 29 members could not be overlooked by the Liberals, since they might need Labour support in the future. The new prime minister announced that his government would be concerned with "looking toward a greater equalization of wealth," and soon initiated a series of laws which were revolutionary in comparison with 19th century attitudes.

The Workmen's Compensation Act, 1906

In 1906 the Workmen's Compensation Act extended two earlier but quite limited Acts by making the employer liable for compensation in accidents and occupational diseases to workers earning less than $1,250 a year. A worker would receive about half his wages while unemployed because of such occupational injury or sickness, and in the event of death from his work, his dependents would receive a sum equal to three years' wages.

Old Age Pensions, 1908

For nearly two years the Old Age Pensions Bill was debated and finally passed, providing a sum between 25 cents and $1.25 a week to people over 70 whose income was less than $105 a year. The debate at times was heated because some members of Parliament feared that such a pension would be spent wastefully! One Labour member pointed out that "a man of seventy is going to cut a pretty shine on $1.25 a week," and others indicated that they could see little difference in principle in giving a substantial pension to a major-general and a small one to a laborer. Small though the pension was, it marked the beginning of a policy which was to be extended and increased over the years to come.

National Insurance Act, 1911

Between 1906 and 1909 a Parliamentary Committee made a study of incomes and related financial matters. Its forty volumes brought out statistics which in effect justified the proposed new legislation. In the population of about 44,000,000, one-eighth enjoyed 50 percent of the nation's income and wealth, while the remaining half of the wealth was divided among the other seven-eighths of the population. Very few adult workers earned more than $9 a week, while one-third earned no more than $6 a week. Therefore, most workers were unable to save money for emergencies. The majority of the Committee suggested better ways of looking after people who already were poor and in need of assistance. The minority proposed a bold program to remedy some of the causes of poverty, such as sickness and unemployment.

The government enacted appropriate legislation. By the Labour Exchanges Act of 1909 it established several hundred labor exchanges throughout the country to act as clearing-houses on information of jobs available throughout the nation. This would eliminate the sometimes fruitless searching for jobs by the unemployed.

In late 1911 the government passed what was probably the most important piece of social legislation. The National Insurance Act provided insurance against sickness and unemployment. Because poor people were unable to pay for medical attention, they were apt to become unemployed and unable to earn for their families. Sickness insurance was compulsory for all workers earning less than $800 a year. Employers, workers, and government contributed a small weekly sum. In the event of sickness the worker could receive medical attention and hospital care, and his family would receive a small weekly sum of money for their support. The unemployment section of the law was also contributory by employer, worker, and government, and provided the modest sum of $1 a week for a limited period, but not for unemployment caused by strikes or lock-outs. Such insurance was at first limited to the engineering and building trades, where unemployment was usually caused by seasonal work.

Workmen's compensation, old age pensions, and national insurance for sickness and unemployment were a break-through in the area of social legislation. Society had accepted the obligation of a minimum income for people who suffered from the accidentals of life through no fault of their own.

France

5. The Second Empire

Louis-Napoleon Bonaparte's father had been King of Holland when his son was born. When Napoleon's own son died in 1832 Louis-Napoleon took over as the head of the Bonaparte family, and twice tried, both times unsuccessfully, to seize power. The legend of Napoleonic glory still lingered on in France, and by 1848 a ground swell of near hero-worship stirred the people and resulted in overwhelming support for Louis-Napoleon as President of the Second Republic.

But discontent developed, and in 1850 the Assembly high-handedly kicked out 33 Socialist deputies, censored the press, prohibited public meetings, and deprived nearly one-third of the people of the right to vote, with the intention of silencing the Socialists, usually the poorest people. Louis-Napoleon then took advantage of the split between the conservative monarchists, of which both groups disliked Louis-Napoleon, but with one group supporting the old Bourbon line of kings who ruled immediately before and after the French Revolution, and the other group supporting the Orleanist line of Louis Philippe, ousted in 1848.

Coup d'État by Louis-Napoleon

Louis-Napoleon Bonaparte decided to win the support of the radicals by promising them to restore the vote. He then put in his own ministers to control the army and the police of France, and on December 2, 1851, the anniversary of Emperor Napoleon's defeat of the combined Austrian and Russian armies at Austerlitz, he suddenly dismissed the Assembly. He then proposed an extension of the term of the president of the French Republic from four to ten years, and replaced the Assembly with a complicated system of councils. Paris did not accept these changes peacefully, and before the fighting ended over 150 persons were killed in Paris, 100,000 persons were arrested throughout France and many were sent into exile. A short time later the voters elected Louis-Napoleon as president for ten years. One year later Louis-Napoleon announced the beginning of the Second Empire and assumed the title of Napoleon III, Emperor of the French.

France was now a dictatorship without any parliamentary government for the first time since 1815. The government consisted of a Council of State of experts who drafted legislation, and a Legislative Body elected by universal manhood suffrage. But the government selected each candidate for whom government officeholders must vote. Other candidates could stand for election but since they were not allowed to hold any political meetings, few were successful. The Legislative Body could only consider measures submitted to it by the Emperor. It could not initiate legislation, control either taxes or the army, and its members were not allowed to have their speeches published. The only newspapers permitted were those authorized by the government.

Napoleon III was ambitious to be known for his contribution to the economic development of France. The times were favorable because the rapid expansion of railroads in Europe, and the replacement of wooden sailing vessels by iron ships, kept French mines busy supplying raw materials. During these years of increasing

Louis-Napoleon III

wealth for France, trade unions won not only the right to exist but even the right to strike.

Involvement in Foreign Affairs

As a Napoleon, the Emperor felt himself obliged to engage in foreign affairs. When Russia invaded Turkey in 1853 Napoleon joined Britain in the Crimean War. The Treaty of Paris in 1856 momentarily halted Russia's advance into the Balkans. Napoleon's assistance to Count Cavour of Italy against Austria brought him military glory and the addition of Nice and Savoy to the territory of France. During this period France completed the conquest of Algeria and began its acquisition of a large portion of Indo-China.

To the east of France, Bismarck was setting out to build the German states into a unified country under the leadership of Prussia. In return for vague promises made by Bismarck that France might get the Rhine frontier, or Luxembourg, or part of Belgium, Napoleon III agreed not to interfere in any Austrian-Prussian war. After the Prussian victory over the Austrian army at Sadowa in 1866, Napoleon asked for compensation at the expense of Belgium.

Bismarck drew up an agreement supporting this French claim in return for French recognition of a federal union of German states. Bismarck then published this agreement with the deliberate and successful intention of causing France to lose friends. Then the Franco-Prussian War of 1870 was deliberately precipitated by Bismarck, but in such a way that France declared war on Prussia in July 1870 (*see* page 32). In September the Emperor Napoleon and the entire French army were captured at Sedan, and with this catastrophe the Second Empire fell. The republicans did not want to start a new regime under the cloud of such a humiliating defeat, and fought on for four more desperate months. Finally, France surrendered, paid a large indemnity of a billion dollars, and gave up Alsace and part of Lorraine to the new German Empire.

6. The Third Republic

The Paris Commune

The Third Republic replaced the Second Empire, but not until 1875 was it firmly established. Its first Assembly, which negotiated peace terms with Germany, was royalist. The Paris republicans, who had almost starved under the German siege of their city, refused to recognize the authority of the National Assembly administering France from Versailles. Republicans and radicals of every degree joined together to set up the Paris Commune or revolutionary city government, in the tradition of the 1792 Commune, to save the Republic from the royalists. The Communards wanted a republic

Paris Commune, 1871. A communard being led off by soldiers.

of France consisting of many little republics or communes. Karl Marx, author of the *Communist Manifesto*, welcomed the Commune as a pattern for future revolutions against the capitalist system. The Commune lasted from March to May 1871, and its supporters burned public buildings and killed hostages. In revenge the government killed 17,000 in cold blood after the fighting ceased, arrested thousands more, shot several thousands of those after drumhead courts-martial without a fair trial, and exiled over 7,000 to the French colony of New Caledonia in the Pacific Ocean. This vengeance was a poor omen for the future success of the Third Republic.

7. Crises of the Third Republic

In 1875 the various parties and factions agreed upon a republican form of government, with a president, a Senate elected by a complicated system of representation, and a Chamber of Deputies elected by universal male suffrage, with a cabinet headed by a premier.

France remained divided between the upper classes supported by the Catholic clergy and the professional army officers, and those who supported the republican form of government because it offered more individual opportunity than did monarchy. Two episodes endangered the Republic and showed that there was a deep division within the country, and that the republicans would have to defend their institutions resolutely.

The Boulanger Affair

Unfortunately, several republican politicians were discredited through using their offices for private gain. As in past times of crisis, people looked for the solution in a "Man on Horseback" who would turn out the politicians, sweep away the Republic as Louis-Napoleon had done in 1851, and let France be ruled by brave soldiers.

The man of the moment was General Boulanger, Minister of War, who gathered around himself not only monarchists and anti-republicans but also extreme radicals who wanted a war of revenge against Germany. On Bastille Day in 1887 Boulanger, in bright uniform and blond beard, and riding a black charger, caught the imagination of the crowd which almost seemed to think that the parade was in Boulanger's honor. The government immediately dropped him from his cabinet position, and appointed him to a military post away from Paris where he could do little harm. At the critical moment he lost his nerve, fled into exile across the frontier, and soon afterwards committed suicide.

The Dreyfus Affair

Further scandal shook the Republic, and the country soon became dangerously divided over a scandal which the army tried to cover up. In 1894 Captain Dreyfus, the first Jewish officer to be appointed to a post on the French General Staff, was accused of selling military secrets to the Germans. Disliked by fellow officers, he was found guilty by a military court, stripped of his commission, and sentenced to solitary confinement in the notorious Devil's Island penal settlement off the colony of French Guiana in South America.

The leakage of military secrets continued, and a gambling adventurer in the French army, a Major Esterhazy, was tried and acquitted, although evidence pointed strongly to his guilt. Anti-republicans, wishing to preserve the nation's confidence in the army and to discredit the republican government, refused to reopen the case until the French writer Émile Zola published in 1896 an open letter to the French President entitled *J'Accuse*, in which he attacked the military court-martial and accused the military of knowingly acquitting a guilty Major Esterhazy. So bitterly was France divided that Dreyfus became a symbol. The royalists, the Army, and the Church were generally anti-Dreyfus, while republicans and intellectuals were pro-Dreyfus. The case was reopened in 1899, but although Esterhazy had admitted his guilt, feelings ran so high that once again Dreyfus was found guilty. Fortunately, the President of France pardoned him, but not until 1906 was Dreyfus declared completely innocent and fully exonerated. This final verdict asserted the power of civil government over the army, and the power of the Republic over monarchists and anti-republicans. A further result of the Dreyfus affair was a great wave of sentiment against the Catholic Church, which had sided with the army. In 1905 an act was passed which ended the Concordat between Napoleon Bonaparte and the Church in 1801. Henceforth the French government ceased to pay the salaries of the clergy of any faith, and all Church property was officially taken over by the State, with agreements that the State would permit its use by the Church.

The Third Republic continued to show two serious weaknesses. It did not keep up with the industrial advances of other nations, and its governments suffered from the fifty changes of ministries that occurred during the 43 years up to 1914. Nevertheless, when World War I broke out in August 1914, the French Republic received the support of its people.

The United States

8. Agitation for Reforms

The decades of the 1830's and 1840's were a period when a number of reforms were attempted. Some were unsuccessful but others played an important role in establishing democratic freedoms. One reason for reformist movements during this period was the emphasis placed upon the individual in the era of Jacksonian democracy. When Andrew Jackson was elected in 1828 half of the states had adopted manhood suffrage. The last state to require land ownership in order to vote was North Carolina, and she dropped it in 1856. Because of the right to vote, more men took an interest in politics, became more aware of social and economic conditions, and realized that they could do something to remedy them. Two significant institutions that created increasing problems for the United States were the rise of factories in the North, and the system of slavery passionately defended by the South.

Factories and Immigration

In the early 19th century laborers worked a twelve- to fifteen-hour day in poorly-ventilated

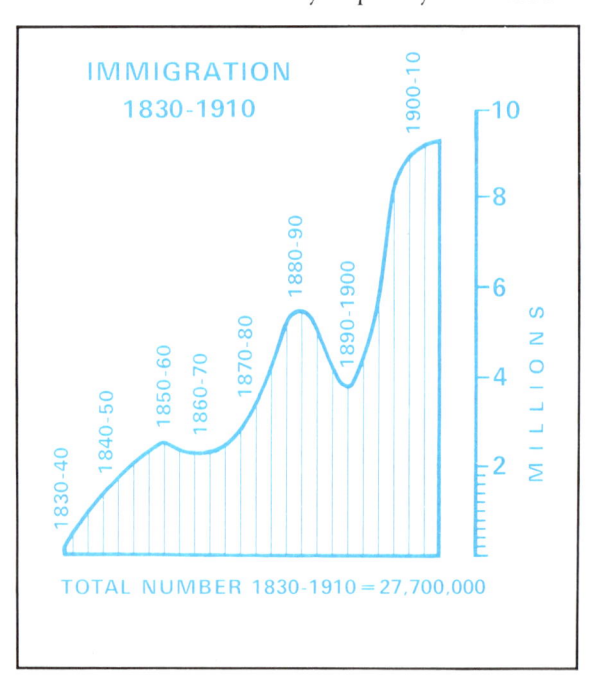

IMMIGRATION 1830-1910

TOTAL NUMBER 1830-1910 = 27,700,000

mills. The New England cotton mills employed women and children and made no provision for even the most elementary education. The flood of immigrants that came into the United States caused a worsening of conditions in factories, and led to attempts by labor to organize and demand better wages, hours, and working conditions. Between 1790 and 1830 a total of only 400,000 immigrants entered the country, but between 1830 and 1860 the tide rose to 2,500,000. By mid-century immigrants were half of the population of New York City and outnumbered the native-born in Chicago and St. Louis. Native workers feared for their standard of living because immigrants were desperate and ready to work for lower wages.

Utopian Communities

Some people decided to leave the regular pattern of factory and town life to set up communities where people would work for the common good. Of more than forty such communities, few lasted more than a short time, and all eventually failed. One of the better-known was the community of New Harmony, Indiana, set up in 1825 by the British industrialist Robert Owen, who had built schools for the children of his workers in his own factory town of New Lanark, Scotland. Membership in the New Harmony community would be voluntary, and people would work together for the common good. Robert Owen, a believer in socialism, expected such communities to multiply across the country until they eventually replaced private industry. Owen provided the land and advertised for members. Farmers, factory workers, and middle class reformers flocked to New Harmony, but very soon it suffered the fate of other communities that refused to accept the fact that centralized control was necessary for economic success. The members could not agree on how to govern themselves, and the

Immigrants. All immigrants had to undergo medical and educational tests before being admitted.

majority disliked the idea that members could take what they wanted from the common pool of goods regardless of how effectively each man worked. In two years Robert Owen and his son abandoned the community to its own devices, and a year later the co-operative enterprise was deserted.

Agitation for Emancipation of Women and Slaves

At mid-century no woman could vote, and once she was married she could not own any property, even that which she might have when she married. Not until 1833, when Oberlin College Institute admitted women, would any college or university admit women. Thus occupations that required higher learning were closed to women up to that time. Mary Lyon was instrumental in founding in 1836 Mount Holyoke Seminary, later rechartered as the first American college for women. Another "first" was the granting in 1840 of a medical degree by the Geneva Medical School to Elizabeth Blackwell, the first woman in the United States to receive one. She later opened the New York Infirmary and College for Women as the first hospital to be staffed by women.

The next demand was "Votes for Women," when Lucretia Mott and Elizabeth Stanton opened the first women's-rights convention in Seneca Falls in New York in 1848. These "feminists" demanded that women be given "all rights and privileges which belong to them as citizens of the United States," but not until the turn of the century did women have any success.

Protests against slavery had been expressed as early as 1688 by a religious group in Germantown, Pennsylvania. Anti-slavery societies gained support and momentum in the 1700's and early 1800's, and several colonization societies were organized to remove Negroes to Africa. The largest was the American Colonization Society, which established Liberia on the west coast of Africa in 1822, with its capital of Monrovia named in honor of President Monroe. But so few free Negroes wished to go that during the first ten years of its founding only 1,200 people left for Liberia.

The invention of textile machinery and the consequent vastly-increased demand for cotton beginning in the early 1800's led to agitation for immediate and uncompensated abolition of slavery, strenuously supported by William Lloyd Garrison in his paper *The Liberator*. Thomas Dwight organized the American Anti-Slavery Society, and Frederick Douglass, a former slave, began his own abolitionist newspaper, *The Northern Star*. Anti-slavery sympathizers organized the so-called "underground railroad" along which fugitive slaves were helped to escape to freedom to the North and to Canada. One such escape route was through Maryland and Delaware to Pennsylvania; another went through Tennessee and Kentucky to southern Ohio; and the third went from St. Louis up the Mississippi River to Kansas and Iowa. An outstanding Negro underground railroad worker was Harriet Tubman, who escaped from slavery and, although she had a reward of $40,000 on her head, she returned nineteen times to the South to lead 300 slaves to freedom.

Harriet Beecher Stowe who wrote *Uncle Tom's Cabin* and published it in 1852 was famous for her contribution in exposing the inhumanity of slavery. In one year it sold over 1,200,000 copies in the United States, and was translated into more than twenty languages, and had great success as a play in northern theaters. The great gains for anti-slavery were the Thirteenth, Fourteenth, and Fifteenth Amendments.

Education

One of the early steps in establishing free education was in 1821 when Boston set up the first public secondary school, followed a few years later by an act of the Massachusetts legislature requiring every large town to establish a secondary school. Pennsylvania was the first state outside New England to establish free public schools. A noted educational pioneer was Horace Mann, first secretary of the Massachusetts Board of Education, who in 1839 established the first "normal school," or teacher-training school in the country. Other states followed, and although these schools were only poorly supported with money, they were an essential step toward the profession of trained teachers.

9. Political and Social Reforms

In 1888 Massachusetts introduced the Australian ballot containing the full list of candidates, which was distributed to voters only in the polling booth, where they could register their vote in secret instead of announcing it in public to an official, as had previously been done.

Political reformers sought reforms through state legislation, believing that the *direct primary* was the effective method of giving people the opportunity to select independent and able candidates, instead of being restricted to candidates chosen by party machines. In a closed or direct primary the voters cast their vote for whichever candidate they prefer, regardless of party. Three other important reforms were the *initiative* which allowed the voters to propose legislation to be brought before a legislature, the *referendum* which provided the voters with the right to accept or reject measures enacted by legislatures, and the *recall* which gave the voters the right to remove unsatisfactory officials before their term of office expired.

The Seventeenth Amendment, ratified in 1913, took from state legislatures and gave to the voters the right of electing United States senators.

In the later years of the 19th century two separate women's groups, the American Woman Suffrage Movement and the National Woman Suffrage Association, campaigned to win for women the right to vote. In the election of 1912 Teddy Roosevelt endorsed women's suffrage, but the other two candidates, Taft and Wilson, evaded the issue. By 1914 eleven states had granted women the vote, but not until 1919 did Congress, by a narrow majority, initiate the

Women's Emancipation. A march through New York City, 1918.

measure which was ratified in 1920 as the Nineteenth Amendment, which gave women the right to vote.

Attempts to Regulate Working Conditions

The progressives were successful in securing social legislation in the great majority of states. By 1914 most states had set a minimum age, usually 14, for child labor. Unfortunately, the United States Supreme Court declared unconstitutional federal and state legislation intended to restrict the hours and conditions of work of women and children. The federal Keating-Owen Act of 1916 prohibited the shipment between states of products made by child labor, designated generally as under 14 years of age. In the *Hammer v. Dagenhart* decision in 1918 the

United States Supreme Court invalidated the act on the grounds that the federal government was interfering with the rights of states to regulate working conditions within their borders. Then when several states did enact laws regulating working conditions for women, the Supreme Court declared such acts unconstitutional because they denied women the right to bargain freely with their employers. The Court argued that since women had won rights of equality, especially the right to vote, they should not be restricted in making their own contracts with their employers. This decision was given in 1923 in *Adkins v. Children's Hospital*, and not until 1937 did the Supreme Court reverse this decision, and in *West Coast Hotel Company v. Parrish* recognize the right of states to regulate hours and conditions of work for women.

By 1920 most states had adopted accident insurance schemes which gave compensation to workers suffering accidents while on the job. Previously, the worker had to appear in court if he hoped to collect compensation for such injury. By 1930 the great majority of states had also adopted measures to provide aid to widows with dependent children, and to old and to destitute people.

Temperance and Prohibition

Early 19th century visitors to the United States commented on American drinking habits and the varieties of liquor available. Whisky was so cheap that it became almost a universal drink, served with and without meals in taverns and country inns. Attacks on heavy drinking began among preachers and reformers, and in 1833 the hundreds of temperance societies sent delegates to a national conference at Philadelphia, out of which grew the American Temperance Union. By 1840 the "teetotalers," insisting on complete abstinence from drinking, had taken over the movement. After the Civil War the Prohibition Party unsuccessfully ran on its first national ticket in 1872.

A new organization, the Women's Christian Temperance Union, became much more militant, especially with a new recruit from Kansas, the six-foot, 175-pound Carry A. Nation who was arrested thirty times for smashing saloons with her axe. By the early years of the 20th century the prohibition movement gained momentum as the Anti-saloon League, won supporters, operating not as a political party, but as a powerful lobby putting pressure on

Temperance. Carry A. Nation.

Prohibition. An illegal still.

members of both parties in Congress. Many states went "dry" and in 1913 Congress passed the Webb-Kenyon Act which prohibited the shipment of intoxicating liquors into states which had anti-liquor laws.

In 1913 the prohibitionists introduced a national prohibition amendment into Congress. The attempt failed, but wartime conditions in 1917 and the shortages of food grains in Europe gave prohibitionists the opportunity they needed. In December 1917 the Eighteenth Amendment was initiated in Congress. It was ratified by January 1919, and went into effect in January 1920, making illegal the possession, manufacture, or transportation of any beverage containing more than one-half of one percent of alcohol. The enforcement of the law was a farce, crime and vice flourished as crooks took over the enormously profitable production and selling of liquor, and what President Hoover was to call "a great social and economic experiment, noble in motive" became a national disgrace.

In 1932 the Democratic party called for the end to Prohibition, and in December 1933 the Twenty-First Amendment was ratified and immediately repealed the Eighteenth Amendment, the only amendment to repeal a previous amendment.

Review Questions

GREAT BRITAIN

Section 1
1. What were the conditions in early-19th century England that led to demand for parliamentary reform?
2. In what ways was the repeal of the Corn Laws unfavorable to farmers, but favorable to businessmen and to factory workers?
3. In what respects was the Chartist platform regarded by some people as "radical" at the time? Would it be so regarded today?

Section 2
4. How was the policy of laissez-faire expected to improve British industry and trade?
5. Why were some reformers strongly opposed to laissez-faire?
6. What Acts passed by Parliament were contrary to the doctrine of laissez-faire, and in what respects were they contrary?

Sections 3 and 4
7. Is it true to say that Great Britain was not an actual democracy until the 20th century?
8. Why did the Budget of 1909 raise the question of putting limits on the power of the House of Lords?
9. Was the Parliament Act of 1911 a gain or a loss for democratic government? How?
10. Explain how each of the Social Security measures tried to help people overcome the "accidentals" of life.

FRANCE

Section 5
11. How did the Second Republic become the Second Empire?
12. Was Napoleon III's foreign policy advantageous or disadvantageous to France?

Sections 6 and 7
13. What was the cause of the rise of the Paris Commune? What did the Commune hope to achieve?
14. Why did the Dreyfus Affair split the French nation?

UNITED STATES

Section 8
15. For what reasons did Utopian communities have little success?
16. In what respects did women have fewer rights than men?

Section 9
17. How did each of the following give people a closer control on government: Direct Primary; Initiative; Referendum; Recall?
18. What arguments did the United States Supreme Court use to invalidate state laws regulating working conditions? Do the arguments sound reasonable?

4

The British Empire and Commonwealth

Canada

Australia and New Zealand

Ireland

South Africa

The British Commonwealth and Empire

The American Revolution taught the British government the lesson that English people living in British possessions could not be denied the rights enjoyed by citizens in Great Britain. Consequently, when minor rebellions broke out in Canada in the 1830's the British government determined to find a political solution that would satisfy the people. Out of that experience Britain evolved dominion status, and later the politically mature concept of an association of equal partners.

Towards the end of the 19th century Great Britain began granting to white-settled areas of the empire the right to choose their own provincial prime ministers and cabinets. Later Britain gave them the right to run all their own domestic affairs without any obligation to be answerable to Britain, a condition known as dominion status. This was confirmed at the turn of the century by the recognition of Canada, Australia, New Zealand, and the Union of South Africa as independent nations associated together for common interests in the British Commonwealth. Colonial possessions had only limited rights, and were parts of the "Empire" but not members of the Commonwealth of sovereign nations.

Ireland presented a particularly difficult problem because British people living in Northern Ireland did not want to be absorbed into the rest of Ireland. This led to tension and physical violence throughout the 19th century and in the 20th century.

Terms

1. Quebec Act, 1774
2. United Empire Loyalists
3. Canada Act, 1791
4. Durham Report
5. British North America Act
6. Hudson's Bay Company
7. Dominion of Canada
8. Emancipists
9. Act of Union
10. Catholic Emancipation
11. Home Rule
12. Ulster Covenant
13. Easter Rebellion, 1916
14. Sinn Fein
15. Government of Ireland Act
16. Dail Eireann
17. Irish Free State
18. Eire
19. Republic of Ireland, 1949
20. Boer
21. Bantu
22. Great Trek
23. Uitlander
24. Union of South Africa
25. British Commonwealth
26. Imperial Conference
27. Statute of Westminster

People

28. Guy Carleton
29. Louis Papineau
30. William McKenzie
31. Lord Durham
32. Captain James Cook
33. Isaac Butt
34. Eamonn de Valera
35. Cecil Rhodes
36. Paul Kruger
37. Louis Botha
38. Joseph Chamberlain

Places

39. Quebec in 1774
40. Maritime Provinces
41. Upper Canada
42. Lower Canada
43. Toronto
44. British Columbia
45. Newfoundland
46. Australia
47. New Zealand
48. Botany Bay
49. Tasmania
50. New South Wales
51. Victoria
52. Queensland
53. Western Australia
54. South Australia
55. Ulster
56. Londonderry
57. Cape of Good Hope
58. Cape Colony
59. Transvaal (South African Republic)
60. Orange Free State
61. Natal
62. Rhodesia

Events

1763	Acquisition of Canada by Great Britain
1791	Canada Act: Upper and Lower Canada
1837	Rebellions in Upper and Lower Canada
1840	Upper and Lower Canada joined
1867	British North America Act: Dominion status inaugurated
1769–1771	Discovery of Australia by Captain Cook
1778	First convict settlement in Australia
1901	Commonwealth of Australia
1907	Dominion of New Zealand
1608	Ulster plantation
1696	Restrictive Acts on Irish Catholics
1800	Act of Union
1829	Catholic Emancipation Act
1916	Easter Rebellion
1920	Government of Ireland Act
1922	Irish Free State: member of British Commonwealth in 1931
1937	Eire: independent sovereign state
1949	Republic of Ireland
1814	Cape of Good Hope acquired by Britain
1833	Abolition of slavery in the British Empire
1835	Beginning of Great Trek by the Boers
1886	Discovery of gold in the Transvaal
1895	The Jameson Raid
1899–1902	The Boer War
1910	Union of South Africa
1926	Imperial Conference: British Commonwealth
1931	Statute of Westminster

1. Canada

When the British took Canada from the French in 1763 the population was only about 65,000, or 5 percent of the 1,300,000 population of the thirteen British colonies. The Quebec Act of 1774, passed by the British government, extended the area called Quebec southward to the Ohio River, and allowed the French to practice their own religion and to retain French civil law.

The years 1763 to 1867 were the formative years of Canada, because during this period many settlers came into the area, the Canadians repulsed attempts by some United States citizens to take Canada, and England gave Canadians important rights of self-government. The first substantial migration to Canada, which was still settled only along the St. Lawrence River and in parts of the Maritime Provinces of New Brunswick, Nova Scotia, and Prince Edward Island, occurred during and soon after the American Revolutionary War. As the British situation worsened in New York and New Jersey, the loyalists who supported George III became refugees, whose plight presented a serious problem to the British authorities. At least 30,000 were transported by sea to Nova Scotia, Cape Breton Island, and New Brunswick.

At the end of the war the British government spent over $15,000,000 to make "a liberal and handsome compensation" to loyalists. Sir Guy Carleton, the Governor-General of Canada, not only helped in the organizing of new settlements for the loyalists but persuaded George III to express his royal favor by permitting them and their descendants to use after their names the letters U.E.L., for United Empire Loyalists, to record their support for a United Empire.

One important settlement was along the northern shore of Lake Ontario, known originally as Upper Canada to distinguish it from Lower Canada, lower down the St. Lawrence River toward the mouth. At York, later renamed Toronto, several thousand loyalists were given about 100 acres of virgin land and a town lot each to encourage them to settle in groups.

The Canada Act, 1791

In Lower Canada the French settlers objected to the attempts of British emigrants to change the legal system and the religion. Sir Guy Carleton, now Lord Dorchester and Governor-General of all British colonies in Canada, sympathized with the French people. "This country," he wrote, "must to the end of Time be peopled by the [French] Canadian race who have already taken such firm root."

In 1791 the Westminster Parliament split the colony of Quebec into Lower, or French Canada, and Upper, or British Canada. Although the governor-general was supreme over both areas, each one was to have its own assembly, language, laws, and official religion, but to remain subject to the British Parliament. The Maritime colonies, inhabited mainly by English and Scottish emigrants, enjoyed a greater degree of self-government. By 1800 Canada was little more than Nova Scotia, Cape Breton Island, New Brunswick, and the relatively small settlements of Upper and Lower Canada along the St. Lawrence River.

Rebellions in Canada, 1837

Politics in Canada had not developed happily since the 1791 Canada Act. In French Lower Canada the French residents resented English influence, and brought government to a standstill when the Assembly refused to vote money to run the government during the years 1831 to 1835. The British government tried to resolve the issue by voting a special appropriation to pay the overdue costs of government in Lower Canada. Outraged by this attempt to reduce their power, the French under their leader Louis Papineau rebelled against the British government in 1837, but without success.

In Upper or British Canada a rebellion broke out almost simultaneously under William MacKenzie, who had been the first mayor of Toronto in 1834. New settlers were discontented because old settlers to a great extent monopolized political and economic life; both new and old settlers wanted more rights of self-government. The rebellion in Upper Canada soon collapsed after MacKenzie and his followers fled to the United States.

Lord Durham's Investigations

The British government, alarmed at such discontent and fearful that another American Revolution was looming, sent out Lord Durham in 1837 to investigate the situation and to make recommendations to Parliament. Significant was Durham's realization that what was happening in Canada was "a struggle, not of principles, but of races." He was convinced that Lower Canada faced the essential conflict that the English settlers would never agree to a French-dominated House of Assembly, and that the French would never submit to the British government.

The problem in Upper Canada was relatively easy to resolve by giving all the settlers a share in the English-type government. In the colonies of Prince Edward Island, New Brunswick, Nova Scotia, and Newfoundland the issue was simply a collision between executive and legislature, with the executive attempting to retain too much authority. There were other lesser grievances, and Durham strongly recommended that they be solved. For example, Prince Edward Island had only 100,000 acres under cultivation out of over 1,400,000 acres of arable land. The main reason was that too few people owned land, and many of these were "absentee" landlords who lived in England and made little attempt to use the land or permit others to buy it. Emigration had dwindled from 50,000 in 1831 to a trickle of 5,000 in 1838, because of political disturbances, the appalling accommodations on emigrant ships, and the failure of the British government to arrange proper land grants.

The Durham Report, 1839

Durham's first recommendation was that the French-speaking colony of Lower Canada must be absorbed into the English-speaking majority, just as the French of Louisiana had been absorbed into the English-speaking majority of the United States. The two colonies should be united. The second recommendation was based on the sound principle that the wishes of the majority of the people should be listened to and respected by the Westminster government. The governor of each colony in Canada should recognize the leader of the majority party as the man to run local affairs. He, and not some arbitrary appointee of the governor, should be the prime minister. This was "responsible" government, with the premier being responsible or answerable for his actions to the Canadian Assembly and not to an official in London.

The third recommendation was that the three areas; (1) a new colonial constitution, (2) foreign affairs and external trade, and (3) the disposal of public lands, all be left to the British government to decide. The fourth recommendation, one that was almost completely unexpected, was that one central government agency should help to develop the country's vast natural resources of mines and forests, and construct railroads to tie various parts of the country together and build its future.

In 1840 Upper and Lower Canada were joined, and in 1848 Lord Elgin, the Governor-General, introduced responsible government in

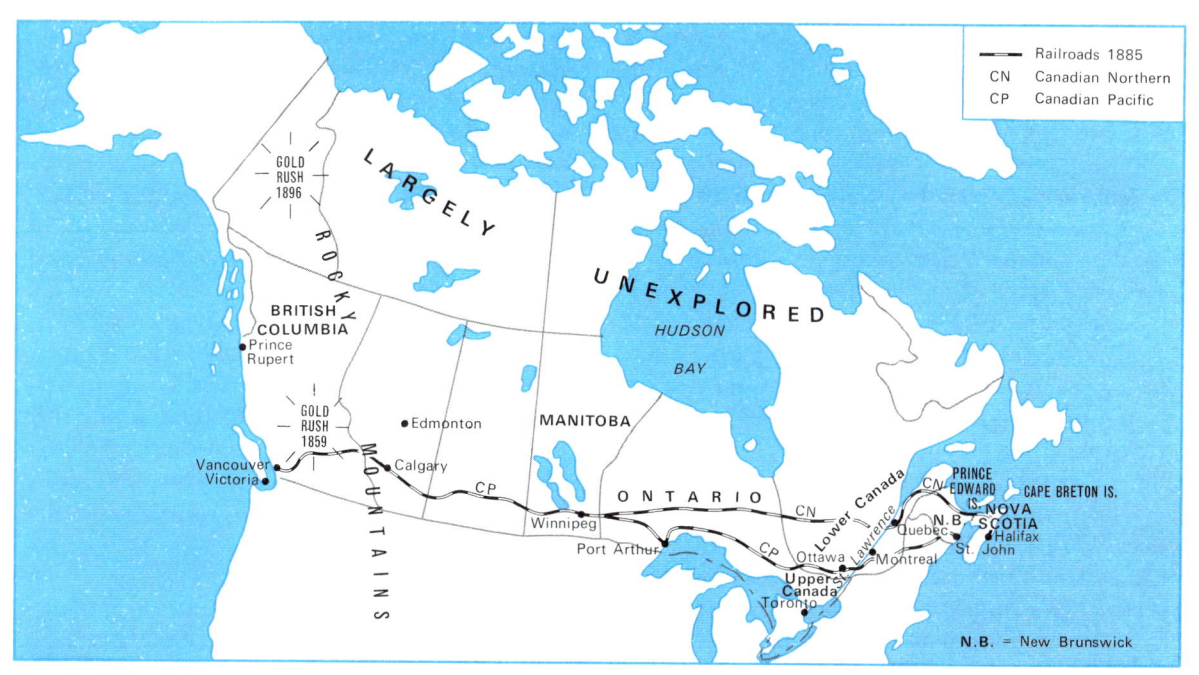

Canada, 1791–1912

Canada by always appointing as prime minister the leader of the majority party. This meant that the prime minister and his cabinet were answerable to the colonial assembly and not to the governor-general or England.

The British North America Act, 1867: Dominion Status

The basic problem in Canada was the diversity of the several colonies, which fell into five groups. The senior British colony was Newfoundland, which looked eastward and traded with Europe. They regarded men from the St. Lawrence region as poachers in their own fishing-grounds. They had no intention of joining any federation of any type. The Maritime Provinces of Nova Scotia, New Brunswick, and Prince Edward Island formed their own group, traded with Europe, and would probably only be persuaded to join a federation if there was the guarantee of a railroad across the country.

The third colony was that officially called Canada, the two colonies which had been joined in 1841. Durham's forecast had proved wrong, and the Union was turning out to be a failure. The French and English had pulled even farther apart, with the French preserving their own language and nationality, although the people had no loyalty to France as a home. While the French population had increased by 1,000,000, the population of Upper Canada increased by at least 1,500,000 and would probably increase faster as more settlers moved in.

The fourth "colony" was the vast area of the Hudson's Bay Company, founded in 1670 as the Gentlemen Adventurers of England Trading into Hudson's Bay. The company administered the expanse of Canada from the settlement in

Upper Canada to the west coast, and operated efficient trading-posts across the continent. But unless a railroad was built across Canada to link east and west and to aid in settling the vast plains between, then the Americans who were by this time pouring across the Great Plains in their thousands might simply push north across the border, and under the cry of "Manifest Destiny" claim the whole of the northwest.

Beyond the Rockies lay the fifth group, British Columbia and Vancouver Island, both originally trading-posts of the Hudson's Bay Company. When gold was discovered in British Columbia in 1855 more than 20,000 miners from the United States went northward.

During the American Civil War some patriots decided that the British should be driven out of Canada, and although attempts to do so were unsuccessful, the Canadians saw that there were several good reasons why some sort of federation was necessary.

In 1867 the British North America Act established Canada as a dominion or self-governing part of the British Empire; the event was celebrated one hundred years later in Expo '67 in Montreal. By this Act, (1) the colonies of Ontario and Quebec were separated, and were joined by New Brunswick and Nova Scotia to establish a federal form of government, the Dominion of Canada. The colony of Newfoundland preferred to remain a separate entity until 1949. The other terms of the Act were (2) a royal-appointed governor would represent Great Britain and would be responsible to the Crown for foreign affairs and defense, (3) the four provinces, as they were now called, would each have its own legislature modeled after the British parliament, but with delegated or specific powers, (4) the Federal government at Ottawa would consist of a Senate appointed for life, and a democratically-elected House of Commons based on universal suffrage; the federal government would have reserved powers, that is those not specifically delegated to the provincial legislatures, (5) other provinces were to be admitted as they became settled, and admitted on an equality with the original members. Manitoba joined the federation in 1870, British Columbia in 1871, Prince Edward Island in 1873, Alberta and Saskatchewan in 1905, and Newfoundland in 1949.

In 1869 the Dominion of Canada purchased the vast territories of the Hudson's Bay Company, and in 1885 completed a railroad across the continent to join British Columbia with the east. The opening up of the interior by rail attracted emigrants, so that between 1897 and 1912 the population increased by more than 2,000,000 to over 7,000,000.

2. Australia and New Zealand

The Voyages of Captain James Cook

Early in the 17th century the Dutch first sighted Australia along its harborless, dry west coast; they named it New Holland, and made Shark Bay a regular sailing mark. For more than another hundred years very little more was found out about Australia. Then in 1769 a rare astronomical event led to a fateful expedition and the real discovery of Australia. A transit of Venus across the sun which was about to occur would give geographers the opportunity to make useful navigational corrections. The British Admiralty organized a scientific expedition, provided a ship, a crew, and Lieutenant James Cook as commander; a wealthy civilian, Sir Joseph Banks, advanced the money for the expedition to the Pacific, and went along with a team of scientific assistants.

Cook made his observations and then for six months charted the waters of what proved to be the long narrow islands later called New

Voyage of James Cook. Taking possession of New South Wales, 1770.

Zealand. Cook then headed northwest for the eastern coast of New Holland. He sailed southward along a line of cliffs which had some resemblance to the Welsh coast, and named it New South Wales. In 1779, during his third voyage, Cook was killed in a beach brawl in Hawaii. His accomplishments were greater than those of any earlier navigator, and he was able to place on the map lands and seas that equaled one-quarter of the earth's surface. He sailed three times around the world, into the Arctic and Antarctic, charted the coasts of New Zealand, New South Wales, Hawaii and dozens of other islands, and he disproved the widely-held belief that there was a navigable Northwest Passage and a habitable Southern Continent.

Convict Settlement in New South Wales

With the end of the American Revolutionary War the British government had to find new lands for the loyalists, and a new place of exile for convicted criminals who could no longer be sent to Virginia under contract, as had previously been done. The housing of convicts in rotting ship hulks in the Thames River became such a national scandal that other arrangements had to be made. In 1786 Parliament authorized a convict settlement in Botany Bay, on the east coast of Australia. In those days the term "convict" was not limited to hardened criminals but included political prisoners, men who dared to try to organize trade unions, or people guilty of any one of two hundred crimes punishable by death, such "crimes" as stealing small sums of money, or poaching, which was unlawfully catching a bird or an animal on private estates.

In January 1788 Captain Arthur Phillip of the Royal Navy landed in Australia as Governor of New South Wales, with 529 male and 188 female convicts, and a guard of 200 marines, and founded the town of Sydney. Australia was "settled," but for another thirty years the settlement in New South Wales was little more than a petty kingdom run by a series of petty dictators of retired army and navy officers, one of whom was Captain Bligh of *Mutiny on the Bounty* fame.

Once the convicts had served their sentence they were turned loose as "emancipists," and since the British government made no provision for their return to England, they worked as servants for free immigrants coming into the country, or went out beyond the settlement to stake their own claims in the country.

Some of the settlers realized that the land was favorable for sheep-raising, and sent back to England for merino sheep, whose wool soon became a very profitable business. The increasing number of immigrants and officials who had served their tour of duty soon outnumbered the convicts, particularly after England ceased the practice of sending them out to Australia.

The first settlement at Sydney became the capital of New South Wales and of other settlements which spread out from there. So vast was the continent, and so separated were the settlements that they could not be administered from Sydney. In time, three areas split off into separate colonies: Van Diemen's Land, which was the island later named Tasmania; Victoria to the south of New South Wales, with its capital at Melbourne; and Queensland with Brisbane its capital, to the north.

In 1829 some wealthy Englishmen settled in Western Australia, established Perth as its capital, and carved out vast estates for themselves. This colony had a difficult time because labor was scarce, and the settlers attempted to remedy the situation by requesting that convicts be sent out from England. The colony flourished until other Australian settlements forced England to cease this practice.

The last settlement was South Australia, which was opened by the efforts of Edward Wakefield, a staunch advocate of colonization.

Not until 1851 did Australia enjoy boom days, and these were the result of the discovery of gold in several parts of the country. Before the gold rush there were only 250,000 colonists on the entire continent. In ten years the population tripled and enjoyed some quite liberal rights of self-government. The principle of limited self-government proposed for Canada in 1840 was extended to each of the five Australian colonies of New South Wales, Victoria, Queensland, Tasmania, and South Australia. Not until 1871 did the sparsely-settled colony of Western Australia receive a partially representative government.

The large area of the Northern Territory, over 520,000 square miles, is under the jurisdiction of the Commonwealth Government. The estimated population in June 1965 was nearly 20,000 Aboriginals and about 55,000 Europeans. Much of the area is desert, although there are extensive pastoral areas which support the important beef industry. By 1972 the aluminium and bauxite industries had developed substantially.

The Commonwealth of Australia, 1901

During the years 1895 to 1900 the six colonies gradually agreed to form a federation together, partly because of the activities of Germany in the Pacific and partly because of the need for improved communications and of co-operation for common interests. In 1901 there were only 2,000,000 people in a continent that was 2,400 miles from east to west, and with a land area of a little under 3,000,000 square miles.

Unlike the British North America Act, which was the result of rivalry between races, the Constitution of the Commonwealth of Australia was founded upon a democratic social principle. The Constitution set up a central Federal government, with a Senate of six senators from each of the six states, chosen by the voters of

Opening of the First Federal Parliament

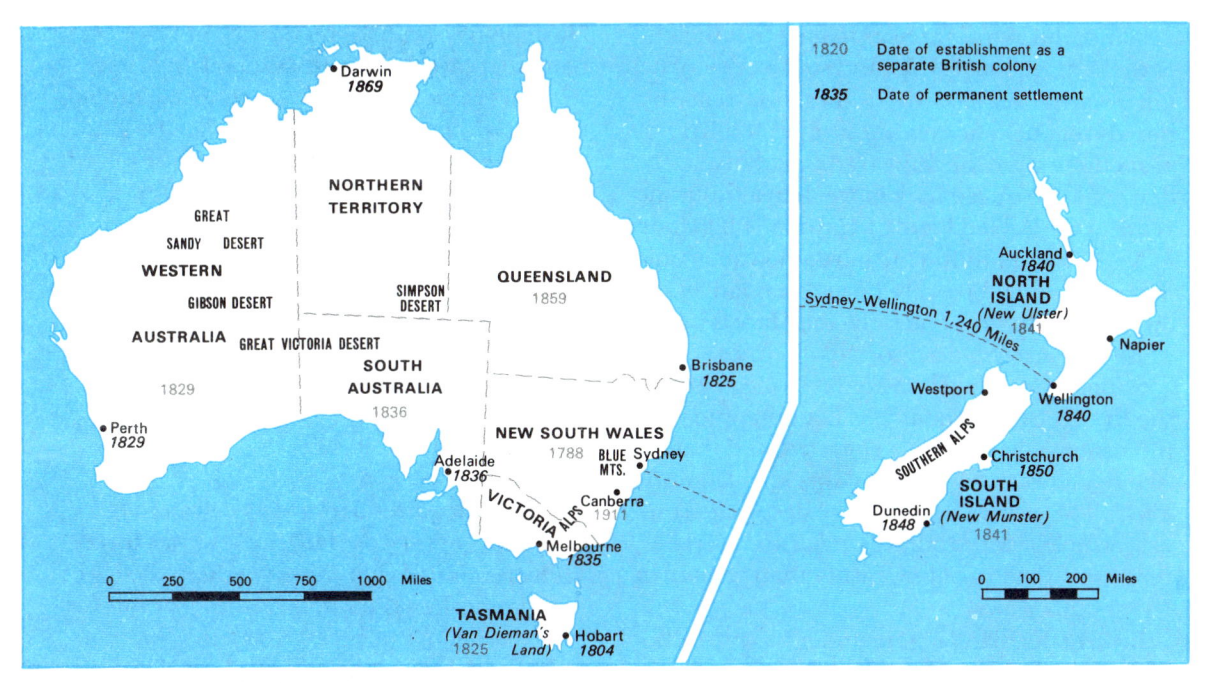

Australia and New Zealand

each state as a single voting district. Representation in the federal House of Representatives was based upon the proportion of population in each state, with women having the right to vote for both Houses. The powers of the federal Parliament, like those of the United States Congress, were specifically enumerated, and included the important ones of trade, taxation, commerce, finances and money, defense, and federal railroads. All other powers were retained by the states, which had the same English-type government as the Commonwealth Parliament, with the Premier chosen by the majority party.

In 1911 the Commonwealth government obtained from the state of New South Wales a site of land on which to build the Commonwealth capital of Canberra, where construction was begun in 1923 and completed by 1927 when Canberra was officially opened by the Duke of York, later to be George VI.

New Zealand

Twelve hundred miles southeast of Australia lie the two large islands of New Zealand, charted by Captain Cook in 1769. Inhabitants of the islands were Polynesians, a gay, sophisticated people who lived in the Central Pacific area that included Easter Island, Hawaii, Fiji, and New Zealand. One group of them, the Maoris, occupied New Zealand about 1350 A.D., where life became far more difficult than in the more lush islands of the Pacific. The Maoris lived simply, had no form of writing, but knew from epic poems handed down from one generation to another that they had once been a great people. Relics of their monotheistic religion remain on Easter Island. Once they migrated to New

Zealand, the Maoris appear to have lost their earlier navigational skills, and so never returned northward. Comparative studies show that on islands that held no communication for 400 years there were the same traditional histories that could be traced back more than a thousand years to the 'fabled land' of Hawiiki. The Maoris in New Zealand found life hard; the yam would not grow, and there were no edible quadrupeds on the islands. Consequently, the Maoris became man-eaters and ferocious enemies.

Captain Cook had annexed New Zealand for the British Government, but London ignored the annexation, and in 1817 even stated that the islands were "not within His Majesty's Dominions." The earliest settlers were desperate convicts who escaped from Australia, and were ready to risk cannibalism rather than remain in New South Wales.

In 1840 the islands came under the protection of Great Britain by a treaty signed in novel fashion by over 500 chiefs, each of whom copied on the treaty the design tattooed on his face. Settlers came in increasing numbers, and missionaries helped to convert the Maoris, and in 1853 the islands were given a measure of self-government and became the most British of all colonies.

In 1907 New Zealand received the same rights of self-government that the Commonwealth of Australia had received in 1901, under the title of the Dominion of New Zealand.

3. Ireland

England acquired Ireland by conquest in the 12th century. In 1494 Ireland was forcefully reminded that she was a dependency of England when the English administrator Sir

European and Maori Students. Integration is not an issue in New Zealand.

Ireland

Edward Poynings "persuaded" the Irish Parliament sitting in Dublin to become subordinate to the English Parliament. The area controlled by England around Dublin was the Pale, from *palus*, a stake, and was the area originally protected by a fence or wooden wall. To be "outside the pale" was to be on one's own, outside the protected region.

According to the detested Poynings' Laws, Ireland's parliament could meet only when England approved, could consider only that legislation that England permitted, and must accept all laws passed for Ireland by the English Parliament.

From the days of Elizabeth in the 16th century English sovereigns organized "plantations" of English and Scottish settlers. When the Spanish Armada threatened England with invasion, Catholic Ireland was a possible base from which Catholic Spain might attack England. Serious revolts broke out in Ireland and Spain promised support. England answered the threat by sending in enough troops to do what it had never attempted before, completely take over the whole of the island. It did so with ferocity, even destroying grain to starve rebel peasants into submission.

The Ulster Plantation

English policy of settling Protestants in the northern counties of Ireland, collectively called Ulster, is still today a source of grievance to the Republic of Ireland which wants to unite the official Republic with the northern part which England has held since 1608. In that year Irish estates were forfeited for treason against England. Some London settlers received the grant of Derry and called it Londonderry, into which thousands of Scottish Presbyterians poured.

The Irish Parliament was "packed" with a majority of Protestants, and remained for two hundred years little more than a pawn of England. During the English Civil War of 1642–1649 Irishmen supported Charles I and brought down upon their heads the wrath of Cromwell and his veterans of the Model Army, fanatics who crushed the rebellion without mercy, killed all the priests they could get their hands on, and set out to drive the Catholic population of Ireland into Connaught, the westernmost section of central Ireland.

Restrictions on Irish Catholics

When James II was forced off the English throne in 1688, he fled to France, and then landed in Ireland with French troops to use it as a base for an invasion of England. William of Holland, invited to replace James II on the English throne, took an army to Ireland, and once again that country was crushed. This time the consequences of rebellion were even harsher than before, for England was determined that never again would rebellion raise its head in Ireland.

Roman Catholics, who comprised three quarters of the population, (1) had their property confiscated, (2) lost all civil rights, (3) could own no land, (4) were denied an education, (5) could not own a gun or a horse, (6) were not allowed to have priests to conduct their religion, and (7) could not export their products to any country but England, which had already prohibited them. The Protestant-filled Parliament of Ireland was manipulated by the Lord Lieutenant of Ireland, who represented the English king and carried out his orders.

The Act of Union, 1800

Britain gradually released its control over Irish affairs, and in 1782 repealed the spirit of Poynings' Laws of 1494 and renounced the right of the British Parliament to legislate for Ireland.

But the opportunity for rebellion again was

too much for the Irish to resist, and in 1798, while Great Britain was fighting the French, a revolution broke out in Ireland, with only meager, ineffectual assistance from France. So outraged were the Protestants in Ireland that even the English Parliament dared not leave Catholics to the mercies of the Irish Protestant Parliament. Finally, after lengthy negotiations with Great Britain, the Protestant members of the Irish Parliament agreed to vote itself out of existence for $7,000,000 to be spent in buying up "pocket boroughs," paying pensions, getting titles, and other rewards.

The Act of Union which passed both Parliaments in 1800 eliminated the Irish Parliament, and added 100 members from Ireland to the British Parliament and 32 Irish lords to the House of Lords.

Catholic Emancipation, 1829

For over two centuries Catholics had been denied the right to hold any public position because they refused to take the Test Act of 1673, which demanded the rejection of the Catholic doctrine of transubstantiation. Daniel O'Connell, a Catholic from County Clare, was elected to the Parliament at Westminster in 1828 but could not take his seat because he would not take the Test Act. After agitation in England the Test Act was repealed in 1828, and a year later a Catholic Emancipation Act freed Catholics from previous restrictions, and permitted them to sit in the Westminster Parliament if they would simply take an oath denying the Pope's right to interfere in British domestic affairs.

Home Rule for Ireland

In 1870 Isaac Butt, a Protestant lawyer, organized the Home Rule Association which favored the repeal of the 1800 Act of Union, and requested the establishment of a separate Irish Parliament in Dublin, in which Catholics, now relieved of various restrictions, would be allowed to sit. Charles Parnell succeeded to the leadership of the Association, and instituted a policy of obstructionism in the British parliament. Rules of debate permitted the debate to continue as long as members wished to speak to the subject under discussion. The Irish organized their members to speak in relays and at length. They actually obliged the House to change its debating rules. Gladstone unsuccessfully tried to get a Home Rule Bill through Parliament in 1886 and again in 1893, when the Commons passed it but the Lords rejected it.

The Irish Nationalist delegation of some 80 members at Westminster was politically powerful enough to convince the Liberal Prime Minister Asquith to introduce another Home Rule Bill in 1912. This Bill provided a parliament for the whole of Ireland, including the minority Protestants of the north. These men bitterly equated Home Rule with "Rome Rule," and maintained that they would never allow themselves to be ruled by Catholics. Another reason for opposition was that Ulster, or Northern Ireland, was industrial and the rich part of the country, and it feared crushing taxation from Catholic Ireland. Because the Lords were opposed to Home Rule, the Bill would take over two years to be passed, under the terms of the Parliament Act.

Protestant Ulsterites rallied under Sir Edward Carson, who advocated force against acceptance of Home Rule for United Ireland. "Ulster will fight and Ulster will be right," became the slogan. They organized their own Ulster Volunteers and an Ulster Covenant pledging those who signed to fight against Home Rule. As a consequence Southern Ireland organized its own army, ready to fight Ulster. The only compromise that Ulster would make was the permanent exclusion from a "Home Rule Parliament" for the six Protestant counties, which must be represented at Westminster.

Prime Minister Asquith believed he had no choice but to go ahead with Home Rule, and so in late May 1914 the House of Commons passed the Bill for the third time. It was officially law. But before it could be put into operation World War I broke out. Rather than face an almost inevitable rebellion in Ireland, the British government decided to postpone its operation until after the war ended.

The Easter Rebellion, 1916

Unfortunately the British government was tactless in handling the Irish during the war. Many Irishmen were ready to fight against Germany, but the formation of an Irish army division was delayed, and only a few Irish Catholics were commissioned officers. As a result, a revolutionary group known as Sinn Fein (We Ourselves) was organized to bring pressure on Irish members of Parliament to withdraw from Westminster and to reject Home Rule but demand complete self-government for the whole of Ireland. This minority group sought assistance from England's enemies, in the old tradition of Irish appeals during the days of Louis XVI of France and the French Revolution. They planned for an insurrection throughout Ireland and the seizure of Dublin.

On Easter Monday, 1916, the Sinn Feiners seized the Dublin post office, railway stations, and a large part of the city, and proclaimed an Irish Republic. The British army captured several ringleaders, tried them in secret and executed fifteen, thus giving added prestige to Sinn Fein. With the end of World War I Sinn Fein carried on its tactics by refusing to permit its members to go to Westminster, allow taxes to be paid to England, or use British law courts in Ireland. The British increased the size of the constabulary force in Ireland by enrolling auxiliaries dressed in the black hats of the Royal Irish Constabulary and army khaki, the hated "Black and Tans."

The Easter Rebellion 1916. The General Post Office in Dublin during the rebellion.

Government of Ireland Act, 1920

In 1920 Britain enacted the Government of Ireland Act which gave Southern Ireland and Northern Ireland each its own parliament for domestic affairs, and with representatives at Westminster for defense and foreign matters. In May 1921 elections were held, but in Southern Ireland Sinn Fein won 124 out of the 128 seats and refused to send its members to Southern Ireland's parliament.

The British held two conferences with representatives from both parts of Ireland, but Eamonn de Valera, leader of Sinn Fein, refused to accept Home Rule for Ireland, and when other Sinn Fein representatives later accepted dominion status for Ireland, as the Irish Free State, allowing to Northern Ireland the choice of being represented in Westminster, de Valera again denounced the agreement. Finally, in December 1922, Dail Eireann, the Irish Parliament, accepted the settlement. Unfortunately for Ireland, a bitter civil war was then waged between the Irishmen who accepted the Irish Free State agreement and de Valera and his "Irreconcilables" who refused to do so. The Irish Free State was in 1922 a dominion in the British Commonwealth, with a British governor-general representing the British sovereign.

In 1932 the moderate Cosgrave was replaced as prime minister of the Irish Free State by de Valera, who ignored the governor-general, changed the title to Seneschal and appointed an obscure Irish workman to the position.

Eire, and the Republic of Ireland

In 1937 de Valera prepared a new constitution that changed the Irish Free State to Eire "an independent and sovereign state," owing no allegiance to the British monarch, and severing its ties with the British Commonwealth. The extremists still wanted the whole of Ireland to be united, and organized the illegal Irish Republican Army, which continued to bomb buildings in Northern Ireland and England. Northern Ireland, with a majority of non-Catholics, refused to consider joining with Eire for fear that they and their industrial area would be taken over by the Catholic, agricultural Eire.

When war broke out between Great Britain and Germany in 1939, the government in Dublin declared its neutrality and refused to permit Britain to use any bases or airfields in Eire, despite their potential strategic value in anti-submarine warfare. De Valera refused the British and American requests that he close down the German and Japanese ministries in Dublin, and on May 3, 1945 expressed official condolences to the German minister in Dublin upon the death of Hitler. Between 1948 and 1951 de Valera was out of office, but the more moderate Prime Minister, James Costello, was no more successful than de Valera in persuading Northern Ireland to join Eire as a united Irish nation.

On April 18, 1949, the anniversary of the Easter Rebellion of 1916, the title of Eire was officially changed to the Republic of Ireland, but down to recent times the problem of Irish unity remains to be solved. Northern Ireland's Catholic minority believes that it is discriminated against politically and economically by the non-Catholics, who control the politics of Northern Ireland (*see* Vol. IV, 7).

4. South Africa

Acquisition of Cape of Good Hope by Britain

When the French Revolution endangered the Netherlands, the British decided to keep the strategic Dutch-owned Cape of Good Hope on the southern tip of Africa out of French hands. If the French should get control of it they could seriously interfere with Britain's commercially valuable sea-route to India. The Dutch East India Company had early in the 17th century established a small settlement there to provide its ships with fresh food for the long sea voyage between Europe and India. Despite the company's attempt to control the settlers, they insisted on expanding farther inland and eastward. The 18th century mixture of Dutch farmers and French Huguenot refugees became one people known as Boers, the Dutch word for farmers. They drove off marauding Bushmen, seized the land and cattle of the Hottentots, and gradually reduced the blacks to a form of slavery. The Boers were a self-reliant, independent people who, believing that they had been badly treated by the Dutch East India Company, revolted and set up the first independent republics in South Africa, the two little republics of Graaff Reinet and Swellendam.

In 1795 the British were authorized by the exiled ruler of the Netherlands to take and hold the Cape settlement for his nation until the end of the war. Britain did so and gave it back to the Netherlands, now called the Batavian Republic, under the terms of the Treaty of Amiens between France and Britain in 1802. Britain took it back when war broke out with France once more, and this time intended to stay there. At the peace conference of 1814 the Netherlands showed little interest in the Cape, and readily accepted the British offer of $10,000,000 for it. Economically, the Cape settlement benefited greatly from British ownership. The garrison of several thousand troops and Britain's world-wide markets brought prosperity. But one serious problem arose between the British authorities and their new subjects.

The Boers favored slavery, but the British did not, and the appearance of missionaries from the London Mission Society greatly excited the Boers, who realized that their own slave-holding society would be turned upside down. Missionaries wrote home to explain their great efforts against slavery, and in justifying their own efforts they greatly exaggerated the situation. Nevertheless, the British government found itself under growing pressure to take action against slavery throughout the British Empire, and even to lend their weight against it on the international scene.

In the spring of 1807 Britain abolished slave trading, some eight months before it became illegal in the United States under the Constitution. However, the promoters of this measure had no intention of abolishing slavery itself. It was assumed that in time slavery would die out.

Once Napoleon was exiled to Elba after his surrender in 1814, a widespread revival of the international slave trade seemed probable. During the summer of 1814 the British government received over 700 petitions with 1,000,000 signatures demanding the universal abolition of slavery. Finally, after twenty years of agitation slavery was abolished in 1833 in the British lands, and some 750,000 blacks were liberated.

Friction between the Boers and Britain

In South Africa the problem was a peculiar type of slavery that was economic dependence rather than actual slavery. The Hottentots were pastoral nomads who had been deprived of grazing lands and their herds. They had almost no means of subsistence, they worked for almost no wages, and they cost nothing to get because

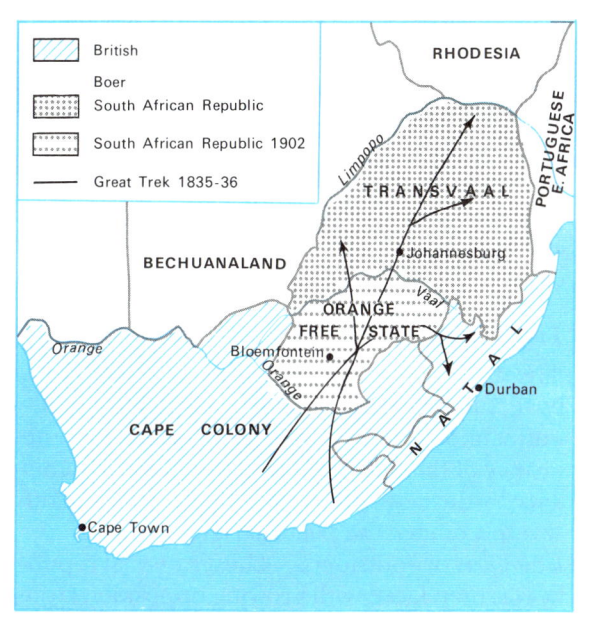

South Africa.

there were always more Hottentots than there were jobs. The Bantu tribes were a threat to settlers who were attempting to push farther northward because there was not enough land for the Boers in their old settlements. The Bantus could not support themselves and were being squeezed between the advancing settlers in front of them and more native tribes behind them. Because British policy seemed to sympathize with the natives, the Boers grew restive under British control. As British subjects they were under British jurisdiction, so they decided to leave Cape Colony and start life anew and use the blacks as slaves, as God had intended, they claimed, and where they could get more land to satisfy their growing numbers.

In 1835 they began their Great Trek, and during the next few years more than 12,000 Boers moved northward, taking with them their household possessions, their cattle, and even seedling trees. They crossed the Orange River and established the republic of the Orange Free State, while others moved on across the Vaal River to found the Transvaal republic. Great Britain formally recognized in 1852 the independence of the South African Republic, previously the Transvaal, and in 1854 the Orange Free State. South Africa then consisted of four white settlements, the two Boer republics ringed around with natives, and the two British colonies of Cape Colony and Natal.

The Boer War, 1899–1902

The discovery of gold in 1886 near Johannesburg, the capital of the Transvaal, led to a great influx into the area of gold seekers, much to the dismay of the Boers, who feared political dominance by the newcomers. The Boers consequently severely limited the political rights of these *Uitlanders* or "outsiders." The Transvaal republic was then faced with growing opposition from the Uitlanders, who claimed that they were a majority of the population, that they paid the greater part of the taxes, but were unjustly denied their political rights. The situation was worsened by the ambitions of Cecil Rhodes, who wanted to establish a line of English states, not London-ruled colonies, bound together in the common interests of a white empire stretching from Cape Town to Cairo. Rhodes had gone out to Africa as a young man seeking his health, made a fortune in diamonds, and became first a member of the legislature of Cape Colony and then its Prime Minister. He set out to get control of Bechuanaland, then south-central Africa, organized the British South Africa Company and established what was then known as Rhodesia. Rhodes, who was at this time Prime Minister of Cape Colony and the actual ruler of Rhodesia, saw the grievances of the Transvaal Uitlanders as an opportunity to further his ambitions. He planned a joint operation for 1895 which would overthrow the Transvaal government, arranging with the Uitlanders in Johannesburg to organize a revolt at the same time that he sent in an armed expeditionary force of 660 men under a colleague, Dr. Jameson.

At a given signal from Johannesburg, Jameson was to ride across the Transvaal frontier and bring the revolt to a successful conclusion by overthrowing the Transvaal government. However, the group in Johannesburg decided to postpone their revolt, but Dr. Jameson, despite a warning from Rhodes not to proceed, set out on what came to be known as the Jameson Raid and was attacked by the Boers who captured him and turned him over for trial in England at the request of the British government.

Rhodes was obliged to resign as Prime Minister of Cape Colony, and was officially censured by the British government. The German Kaiser undiplomatically but deliberately sent a telegram to Paul Kruger, president of the Transvaal, congratulating him on the failure of the conspiracy.

In 1899 the Uitlanders, now worse off than before in the hostile atmosphere of the Transvaal, appealed to London for help. Paul Kruger issued an ultimatum to the British government, offering to give political rights to the Uitlanders provided Britain would recognize the complete independence of the Transvaal. Britain rejected this offer, and tension grew because Kruger was convinced that the British intended to take over the Transvaal, and the British were convinced that Kruger intended to drive the British out of South Africa and set up a confederation of Boer republics.

Kruger decided that further negotiations were useless and that by issuing an ultimatum he could take advantage of the small British force. On October 12, 1899 the Orange Free State joined the Transvaal in war against Great Britain.

For three years the Boers fought a guerrilla war as commando groups struck sudden blows at the British, then dispersed to strike elsewhere. At no time did the Boers muster more than 50,000 men and lads against the British army of 250,000. Finally, General Kitchener surrounded the Boer territory, drove the Boers into an ever-closing circle, burned and destroyed farms and crops, and herded Boer women and children into refugee camps.

The Boers were finally obliged to give in and recognize the sovereignty of the British Crown. In return they were not to be deprived of their personal liberty or property, were to retain their language and use it on a parity with English in schools and courts of law, and were to receive the sum of $15,000,000 from Britain to assist in their rehabilitation. Actually, more than ten times that amount was spent by Britain for livestock and to irrigate and cultivate land. A few years later a Liberal government in England gave responsible government to the Transvaal and the Orange River Colony, in which the local prime minister and his cabinet were chosen by the people, and were not appointed by the British government.

In 1910 the four British colonies of the Transvaal, Orange River Colony, Natal, and Cape Colony were formed into the Union of South Africa, with Louis Botha, the former commander-in-chief of the Boer army, as its Prime Minister. South Africa had now joined Canada, Australia, and New Zealand as dominions with the right of home rule for domestic affairs.

5. The British Commonwealth and Empire

Imperial Conferences

To Joseph Chamberlain, the British Colonial Secretary, the year 1897, Queen Victoria's Diamond Jubilee as reigning monarch, was an excellent occasion to bring the self-governing colonies into closer partnership with the mother country. The 1897 Imperial Conference consisted of twelve men, with Chamberlain presiding and the prime ministers of eleven self-governing parts of the British empire discussing common problems.* The conference did not accomplish any major change but it did go on record as favoring future such conferences.

During World War I the self-governing colonies and India contributed 3,000,000 men to the common cause, and after the war Canada, Australia, New Zealand, and the Union of South Africa were admitted as charter members to the League of Nations. Now that the populations of these dominions were growing far more rapidly

---

*Canada, Newfoundland, New Zealand, Cape Colony, Natal, and the six Australian colonies of New South Wales, Queensland, Victoria, Tasmania, South Australia, and Western Australia.

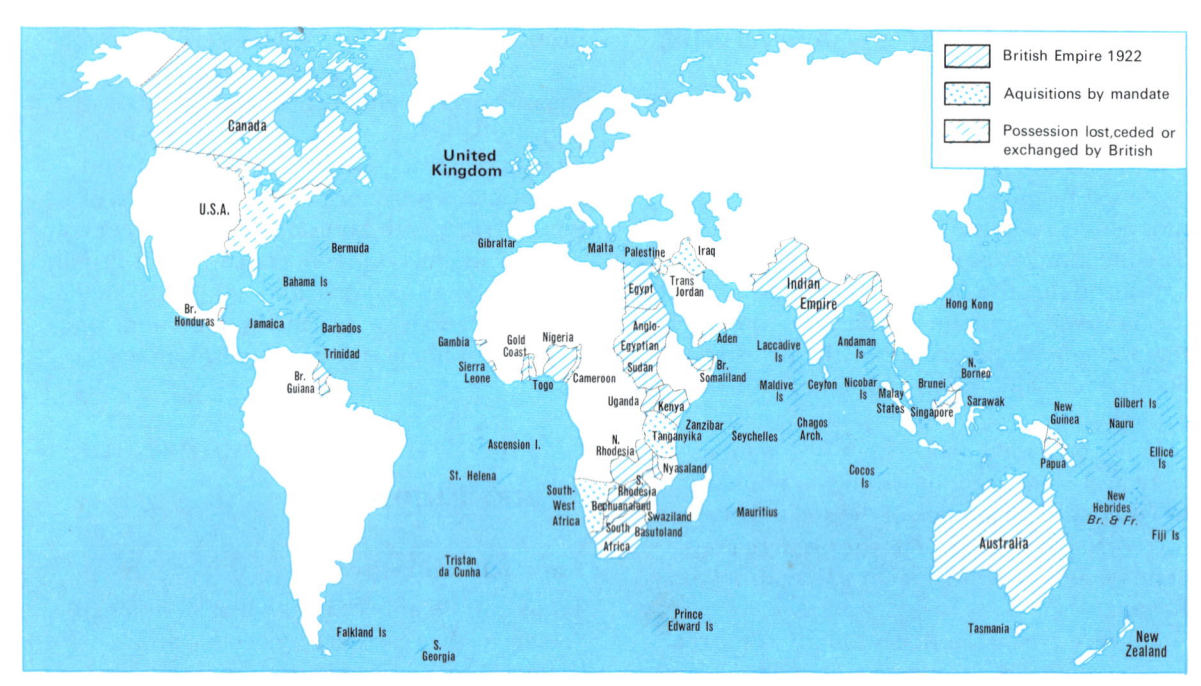

British Empire and Commonwealth, 1922.

than the population of Great Britain, some more suitable relationship with Parliament was necessary.

The Imperial Conference of 1926 used the term British Commonwealth to distinguish the self-governing communities from such colonies as India, the British West Indies, Gibraltar which were directly under the control of Great Britain. The self-governing dominions were defined by the conference members as "autonomous Communities within the British Empire, equal in status, in no way subordinate to one another . . . and freely associated as members of the British Commonwealth of Nations."

The Statute of Westminster, 1931

The intention of the Imperial Conference of 1926 that the dominions be regarded as autonomous, or self-governing, was enacted into law in 1931 by the Statute of Westminster. By its terms (1) Parliament may pass a law which operates in the dominions only upon their request, (2) Parliament may not invalidate any law passed by any dominion, and (3) no change in the succession to the British throne may be made without the consent of the dominions.

By this Act of Parliament the term "dominion" refers to those former British colonies which are now completely self-governing and which may, if they wish, recognize a common sovereign. Together with Great Britain they constitute the British Commonwealth of Nations, which has no constitution, no Parliament, no central defense force, no physical ties whatever. Its members are freely associated together through historical ties, sentiment and common interests, and by broadly similar political ideals.

The "Empire" territories of Great Britain included nearly forty colonial possessions that were not self-governing, and ranged from tiny St. Helena, the naval base of Gibraltar, to the subcontinent of India with its hundreds of millions of people. Many of these were to become members of the Commonwealth, such as Ghana, Nigeria, and Ceylon.

India

India was first governed by the English East India Company from 1600, and then directly by the British government from 1858. Because it did not receive any rights of self-government until well into the 20th century, the history of India as a British possession and then as an independent nation is discussed in Volume V.

Review Questions

Section 1
1. What were the causes of the 1837 rebellions in Upper and Lower Canada?
2. In what ways did the British North America Act of 1867 show a great change from Britain's colonial policy of the 18th century?

Section 2
3. What was unusual about the early settlement of Australia?
4. How did the settlement of New Zealand differ from that of Australia?

Section 3
5. Explain how Ireland was, from its earliest acquisition by England until 1800, little more than a possession of England.
6. What political and social rights were denied to Catholic Irishmen before the passing of the Catholic Emancipation Act?
7. What was meant by Home Rule in Ireland? Why were the people of Ulster so opposed to it?
8. What did the Sinn Fein party object to in the Government of Ireland Act of 1920?
9. How did the Irish Free State, Eire, and the Republic of Ireland differ from each other, even though each referred to Southern Ireland?

Sections 4 and 5
10. How did the Boers of South Africa come under British rule, and why did they object to it?
11. How were the ambitions of Cecil Rhodes and the actions of the British government both partly responsible for the Boer War of 1899–1902?
12. How did the Statute of Westminster of 1931 change the term British Empire to British Commonwealth and Empire?

5

Nineteenth Century Imperialism

Motives for Imperialism
The Opening of China
Japan Westernizes and Expands
Reaction to the Partitioning of China
Imperialism in Southeast Asia
Imperialism in Africa

One of the dynamic results of the Industrial Revolution was the revival of colonization in the later 19th century. During the period 1870–1914 almost the entire continent of Africa and large parts of Asia became possessions of European powers. This sudden interest in overseas expansion was the more surprising because the large colonial empires of the early modern age had already broken up. France, Spain, Portugal, and Great Britain had lost large parts of their overseas empires in the New World, where former colonies had become independent nations.

During the early 19th century nations which still possessed colonies believed that they cost more to administer than they were worth. This point of view changed radically about 1870, and the new form of colonialism called imperialism developed with remarkable speed. China and Africa were the main victims of this new drive for overseas possessions.

In China the new technique of spheres of influence and concessions was used. The sphere of influence gave a foreign nation important economic rights; concessions were land leased to foreign powers which exercised their own laws and took charge of the protection of their own nationals.

The African continent had been virtually unexplored except for its coastal fringes. In the 1870's the "scramble for Africa" began, and by the beginning of World War I in 1914 most of Africa was partitioned among various European powers.

Terms

1. Imperialism
2. "White Man's Burden"
3. *Origin of Species*
4. Survival of the Fittest
5. Social Darwinism
6. Natural Selection
7. "Middle Kingdom"
8. Confucianism
9. Opium War
10. Treaty of Nanking
11. Extraterritoriality
12. Concession
13. Treaty of Wang-hsia
14. Taiping Rebellion
15. Sovereign nation
16. Treaty of Tientsin
17. Shogun
18. Samurai
19. Boxer Rebellion
20. Open Door Policy
21. Sphere of Influence

People

22. Charles Darwin
23. Confucius
24. Caleb Cushing
25. Commodore Perry
26. John Hay
27. David Livingstone
28. Henry Stanley
29. Cecil Rhodes

Places

30. Yellow River
31. Yangtze River
32. Canton
33. Hong Kong
34. Amoy
35. Foochow
36. Shanghai
37. Ningpo
38. Tokyo
39. Nagasaki
40. Korea
41. Vladivostock
42. Seoul
43. Liaotung Peninsula
44. Dairen
45. Port Arthur
46. Formosa
47. Pescadores Islands
48. Trans-Siberian Railway
49. Chinese Eastern Railway
50. Kiaochow Bay
51. Kwangchow Bay
52. Kowloon
53. Wei-Hai-Wei
54. Tsushima Straits
55. Java
56. Malaya
57. Hawaii
58. Samoa
59. Marshall Islands
60. Caroline Islands
61. Sudan
62. Abyssinia
63. Kenya
64. Nigeria
65. German West Africa
66. German East Africa
67. Togoland
68. Kamerun
69. Belgian Congo
70. French Equatorial Africa
71. Angola
72. Mozambique
73. Mauritius
74. Italian Eritrea
75. Italian Somaliland
76. Liberia

Events

1839–1842	Opium War
1842	Treaty of Nanking
1844	Treaty of Wang-hsia
1858	Treaty of Tientsin
1854	Treaty of Kanagawa
1894–1895	Sino-Japanese War
1895	Treaty of Shimonoseki
1904–1905	Russo-Japanese War
1905	Treaty of Portsmouth

Art in Color

Left. Rain, Steam, and Speed painted in 1839 by *Joseph Turner (1775–1851).*

Above. View of the Tivoli Gardens from the Villa d'Este, painted 1843 by *Jean Baptiste Corot (1796–1875).*

Below left. The Balcony by *Eduard Manet (1832–1883)*, painted in 1868.

Below. The Washerwoman painted c1848 by *Honoré Daumier (1808–1879).*

III-1

Above. Impression, Sunrise painted 1872 by *Claude Monet (1840–1926)*. He and his friends were the leading spirits of the Impressionist School.

Right. Her First Evening Out painted c1880 by *Pierre Auguste Renoir (1841–1919)*. He focused his art on the human figure, painting the joy of living.

Below. Paul Cézanne *(1839–1906)* painted the Card Players c1885.

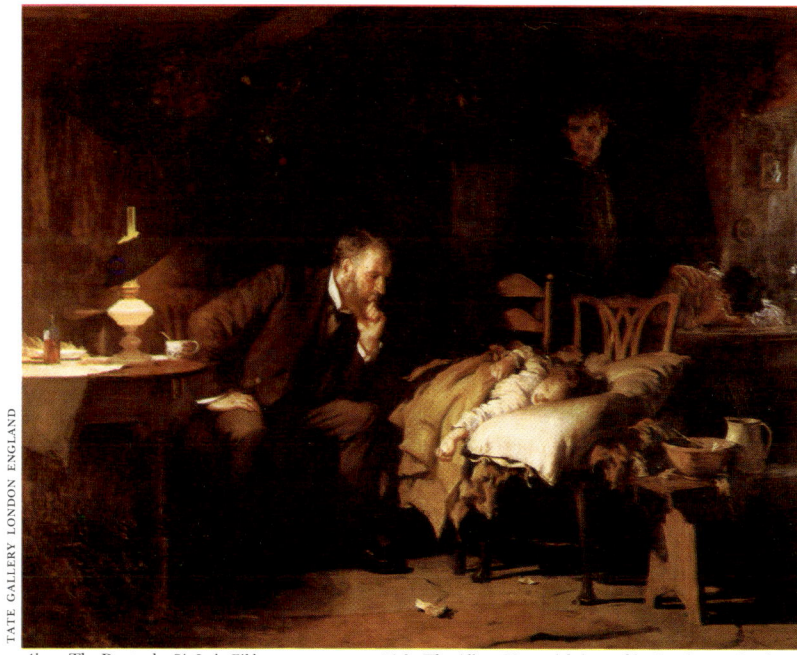

Above. The Doctor by *Sir Luke Fildes (1843–1927)*. Painted in 1891.

Below. Poster designed 1892 by *Henri de Toulouse-Lautrec (1864–1901)* of Aristide Bruant.

Right. The Albert Memorial situated in Kensington Gardens, London, was built for Queen Victoria in memory of her beloved husband Prince Albert. Completed in 1872, it was not unveiled until 1876.

Below right. The Mango Eater painted c1895 by *Paul Gauguin (1848–1903)*.

Right. La Porte St. Martin painted c1911 by *Maurice Utrillo (1883–1955)*, who painted many of his pictures from postcards.

Below right. The Breakfast Table painted in 1932 by *Pierre Bonnard (1867–1947)*.

Below left. Kissing the Moon. Painted in 1904 by *Winslow Homer (1836–1910)*.

1. Motives for Imperialism

Economic

Until the 1870's British manufacturers could find adequate markets at home and in other European countries for their textiles, their machinery, and other products. Belgium and Germany, and to a lesser degree France, were industrializing rapidly and were not only able to satisfy the needs of their own people but were determined to protect their own manufactures against foreign competition. The increasing saturation of European markets obliged industrial nations to look overseas for markets, for sources of raw materials, and for opportunities for the investment of surplus capital.

Strategic Reasons

While economic needs were a significant reason for the new imperialism of the 19th century, they should not be regarded as the only ones. And it would be incorrect to assume that the war which broke out in 1914 was caused essentially by rivalry for overseas possessions.

Political tensions and rivalries in Europe by the end of the 19th century were leading to the formation of rival groupings and alliances among nations and seriously threatening the peace (*see* p. 136). Since there was the threat of war, each nation wanted to protect its interests by getting strategic naval bases, coaling stations, and ports of call wherever they could, and deny them to other nations. In the atmosphere of the later 19th century even prestige was a significant factor, and overseas possessions were sometimes acquired to prevent other nations from getting them. The force of nationalism, the support for one's own country and the desire to see it "get ahead" strongly motivated the acquisition of parts of Africa that could actually offer very little more than simply being marked on the map as the possession of a particular nation.

Humanitarian and Administrative Motives

Undoubtedly there were humanitarian reasons which motivated sincere people to become missionaries and attempt to take to the natives of Africa the benefits of civilization. Often referred to as the "white man's burden," this announced intention to improve the lot of backward people could sometimes cover up the injustices and even the brutality of imperial rule. So important did the role of missionaries become that one of the most famous of all African missionaries, David Livingstone, was taken back to England after his death and buried as a national hero in Westminster Abbey.

Another motivating factor was the great opportunity for administrative and other positions for the white masters. The African and the Indian civil services provided well-paid jobs for several generations of younger sons who became the "empire-builders" for the mother country.

The Influence of Social Darwinism

Scientists had long speculated about the evolution of man, perhaps influenced by the thesis of Karl Marx that history was based on continuing economic change. Earlier hypotheses had suggested that man was descended from some primitive, non-human form, and that acquired characteristics could be inherited, but the evolutionary concept could not progress far until three essentials existed: a large body of carefully-observed facts, an acceptable explanation of how and why species should change, and a public sufficiently educated to accept so historically revolutionary a doctrine.

Charles Darwin (1809–1882) spent several years on scientific expeditions to South America and the Pacific islands, made careful observations of fossil remains, compared them with living organisms, and also recorded the variations of species under differing environments.

Charles Darwin. A contemporary cartoon.

He gradually decided that species were subject to changes, and concluded that the changes were caused by need and circumstances. Darwin was influenced in his thinking by Malthus who was concerned with the pressure of increasing population upon food supply. If man was obliged to change his habits under adverse circumstances, was not this true of all nature?

For many years Darwin investigated and thought about this theory, and in 1859 published his findings in the *Origin of Species*. Its full title, *On the Origin of Species by Means of Natural Selection, or the Preservation of Favored Races in the Struggle for Life*, indicates more clearly what he was investigating.

Darwin's conclusion that the "fittest" survived did not necessarily mean that the physically fittest survived. He meant that the organisms which possessed "advantageous" characteristics survived. Advantageous characteristics were those such as the ability to obtain food, particular skills in combat, elusive speed, camouflage such as the polar bear's, and other assets. Species with these advantages would survive longer and would tend to reproduce more of their kind. By such natural selection the "weaker," possessing no advantage, would gradually become extinct. In his *Descent of Man*, published in 1871, Darwin traced man's descent from animal species through the process of "natural selection."

Darwin's theory of life as a "struggle for existence," in which the *adaptable* survived, was highly disconcerting to theologians because it indicated a natural rather than a theological origin of man, but for later 19th century imperialism this thesis of natural selection provided a very useful excuse for the subjection of weaker nations and colonial people by strong nations. Since any "fit" people could survive, then nations should arm themselves and be able to survive wars. This was used as an argument in favor of Bismarck's policy of "blood and iron," and it came at a time when competition between nations indicated a very probable European war.

Racists who believed in the superiority of one race over another strongly supported Darwin's thesis, and twisted it into what is called Social Darwinism, or the application of Darwin's laws of nature into laws of nations. These people ignored the basic difference between nature and man. Animals attempt to survive in a natural situation of competition, whereas man lives in a protective society and must necessarily cooperate in order to survive.

2. The Opening of China

Geography and Historical Background

China of the 19th century was a vast land that stretched from the Amur River in the north to Indo-China, Siam, and Burma in the south, from the Pacific Ocean westward to India and the Himalayas. Although it was once believed that the Chinese were migratory groups from the Middle East, the discovery in 1929 of the skull of Peking Man in a north China cave indicates that man lived there at least 360,000 years ago, and the assumption now is that these were ancestors of modern Chinese.

Early Chinese civilization developed around the Hwang Ho (Yellow) River and the Yangtze River. People lived there much as any early peasant people did, simply wresting a livelihood from the soil. Isolated by geography from most of the outside world, protected in the north from barbarian invasions by the Great Wall of China, built more than 2,000 years ago and stretching 1,500 miles across the countryside, the Chinese called themselves the "Middle Kingdom," the center of the world.

China's long history followed a pattern for nearly 2,000 years of the same social, political, economic existence, based upon a feudal system of agriculture. The vast majority of peasants supported a small ruling class of landowners and government officials. Historically, this nation with the longest continuous existence of any nation on Earth has been ruled by a series of ten families or dynasties since 1700 B.C. down to 1911 A.D., when China became a republic.

Changes in ruling families occurred whenever a dynasty became too oppressive or corrupt. The Chinese would then simply "withdraw their support" and the ruling family would be replaced with another. If the ruling dynasty resisted, the people had the right of revolution, and exercised it whenever necessary. Even Chiang Kai-shek suffered this same fate in 1949.

Confucianism

The tradition of Chinese society was that life should remain unchanged. Much of that tradition was based upon the teachings of Confucius (probably 550–480 B.C.) and his successors for the next 2,500 years. Even Mao Tse-tung, the leader of modern Communist China, in his early years respected the teachings of Confucius and visited his birthplace in Shantung province.

Confucianism was not a religion in the usual sense, but a system of ethics or behavior and a political philosophy or belief designed to keep society unchanged and stable. Confucius made no attempt to deal with man's relationship to the universe or with a Supreme Being. His main concern was the rule of reason. If men were reasonable in their relationships with each other, in government, in family life and everyday experiences, then the state could keep the country secure and maintain a stable society. Poor government would result in dissatisfied people, an unstable society, and anarchy. The essence of Confucian teaching was in the maxim, "Whatever you would not have done to you, do not do unto others." The main driving force in life, and the highest purpose in life, was the happiness of men. This aspect of Confucianism made Confucius one of the great prophets of history, for it is still a universal aim of mankind.

But Confucianism had a negative effect in Chinese history because its basic beliefs were increasingly used to prevent change, sometimes to support tyranny and even to give an air of "divine right" to rulers who punished those who dared to question authority. Besides, Confucianism favored only the scholars who could afford the time to learn the Confucian classics.

The first great change for China came when contacts were made with the west in the 19th century. Aliens had come into China much earlier, with the Mongols who ruled for nearly a hundred years between 1280 and 1370, and the Manchus who came in from the north in 1644 and ruled until 1911. But these alien people were generally absorbed into China and adopted her customs. Westerners were never absorbed.

The Opium (Anglo-Chinese) War, 1839–1842
A modest trade between China and the outside world had been limited to a few officially-appointed Chinese merchants at Canton, and on terms laid down by the Emperor. Chinese goods were in greater demand in the West than were Western goods in China, and European merchants were obliged to pay in silver, the currency of China. By the early years of the 19th century foreign merchants, particularly British, were selling large amounts of opium to China from India. The Chinese found themselves paying out so much silver that the Emperor, alarmed at the loss of money and the bad effects of opium on the Chinese people, attempted to put a stop to the opium trade. Chinese authorities at Canton tried to carry out the Emperor's wishes, but were opposed both by foreign importers and the Chinese merchants who were making enormous profits from the trade. An official named Lin Tse-hsu, appointed by the Emperor to stamp out the trade, was himself adamantly opposed to the use of opium and was strongly anti-foreign. He insisted that all stocks of opium owned by foreigners and by Chinese merchants be surrendered to him to be destroyed without payment. Until the order was

The Chinese Opium War, 1839–1842

carried out all foreign merchants were forbidden to leave Canton. The British superintendent of trade turned over opium worth $6,000,000 but refused to agree that foreign merchants pay a bond as pledge that they would not allow their ships to bring in more opium in the future. Lin Tse-hsu, not content with immediate success, decided to attack British ships. This led to the first China-West war, and began a completely new and different period of China's history.

The British then captured Canton, sailed up the Yangtze River, and anchored offshore ready to bombard Nanking, the most important city in central China. In 1842 the Chinese capitulated and accepted terms they had formerly refused, terms that were the entering wedge which forced open China to Western influence and interference for the next hundred years.

The Treaty of Nanking of 1842, and an additional treaty of 1843, provided the following terms: (1) China would pay an indemnity of $21,000,000, including $6,000,000 for the destroyed opium, (2) the island of Hong Kong was ceded outright to Britain, (3) the five "treaty" ports of Canton, Amoy, Foochow, Shanghai, and Ningpo were opened to foreign trade, (4) China agreed to charge no more than a 5 percent duty on foreign goods, (5) an "extra-territoriality" clause exempted foreigners from Chinese law. The customs restriction meant that China no longer could raise tariffs to protect their own industries or to use as government income. The extraterritoriality clause in course of time permitted foreign nations to get "concessions" or actual settlements inside China.

Chinese tradition and way of life prevented any real opposition to threats from outside her borders. The government was largely decentralized, family loyalty could not bind the people together in united efforts against the foreigner, and the government failed to do the one thing that might save her from further interference, that is to adopt Western methods of industrialization and defense. Japan benefited from China's experience, for she quickly modernized along Western lines as the one way to protect herself. Perhaps all that prevented China from being completely "colonized" was the rivalry between European powers to get on the bandwagon of imperialism. Russia and Germany wanted Manchuria; Germany and Great Britain were rivals for northern China; and France and Britain were competing for southern China.

Another factor which saved China from conquest was that European Powers were not willing to go to war with each other over China, and the United States and Britain believed that their economic interests would best be served if China were not divided up completely among other nations.

The United States in China

Ever since 1784 when the first American ship, the *Empress of China*, sailed direct to Canton with a load of furs, Americans had been conducting a substantial trade with China. In 1844 President Tyler sent Caleb Cushing, a member of the Committee on Foreign Affairs, to China as Resident Commissioner. His directions were to obtain the right for American ships to enter Chinese ports and conduct trade on the same favorable terms that China had granted to Great Britain. The mission obtained the liberal Treaty of Wang-hsia in 1844, which opened official relations between China and the United States.

In some respects the terms were more liberal than those of the British treaty: (1) America had the right to trade in the original five treaty ports, (2) full rights of extraterritoriality were granted to United States citizens, (3) Americans were allowed to live in separate districts and could employ Chinese teachers and learn the language, a right which had previously been strictly forbidden to all foreigners. Cushing's treaty, as it was at first called, became the model for later treaties between China and other Powers.

The Chinese knew that they had a problem, and set up a Barbarian Affairs Bureau to keep records of foreigners. They probably hoped that the situation was only temporary, and attempted to play one nation off against another.

The Taiping Rebellion, 1850–1864

According to the Confucian philosophy, when a ruling dynasty failed to govern properly Heaven withdrew its mandate or command from that dynasty, and the people had the right to replace it. The evidence of Heaven's displeasure was a natural catastrophe, such as famine or a flood, or other disorder.

Even before the Opium War and the humiliating treaties with foreigners there had been increasing discontent throughout the country. The basic reason was that the old social and economic system, with its antiquated tax system and an increasing number of paupers, could no longer meet the needs of a rising population and the changing conditions of the 19th century.

The rebellion began in the province of Kwangsi as an outbreak of the local population

94 *Industrialism, Imperialism, and War*

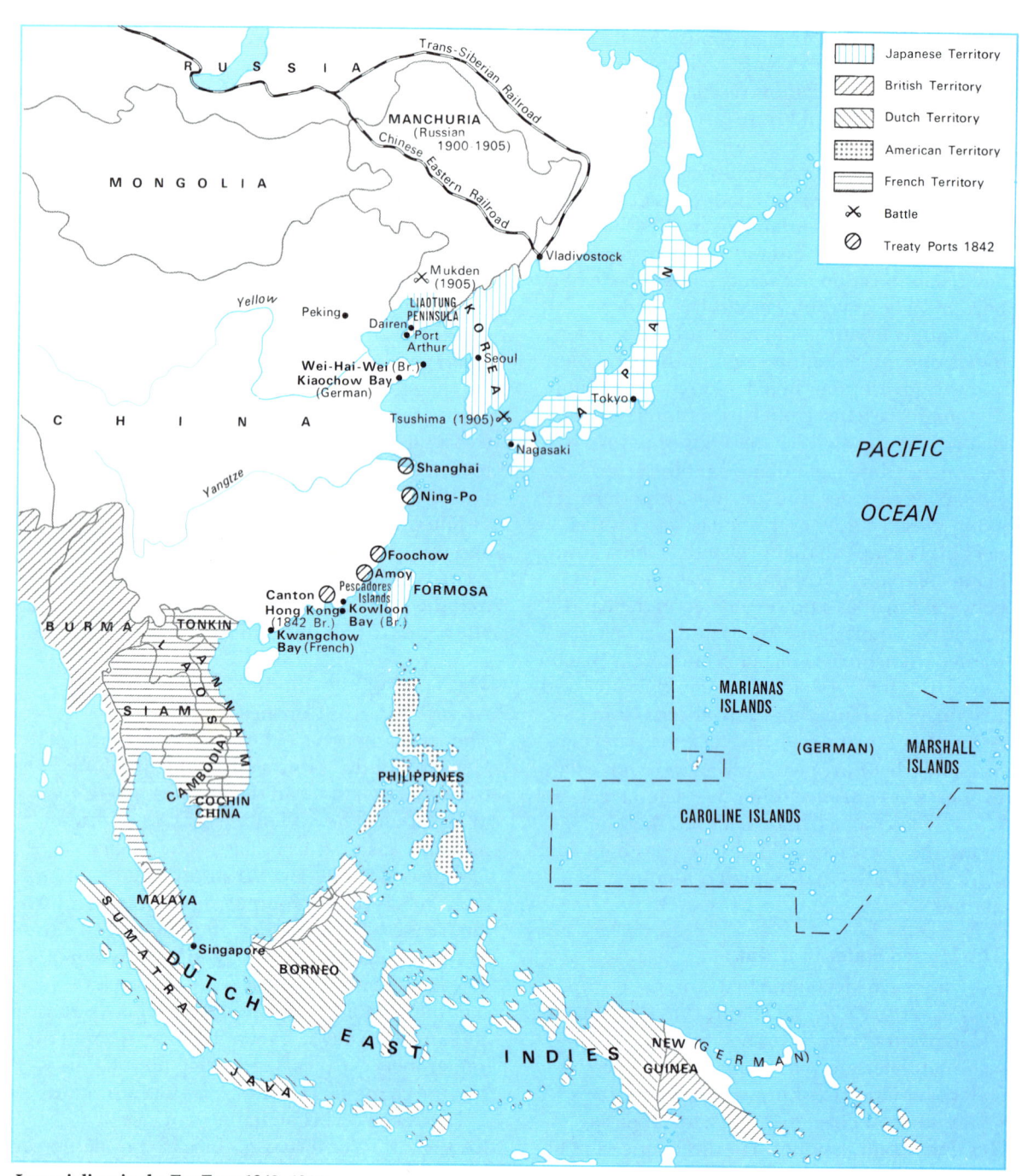

Imperialism in the Far East: 1842–1914

against tribal groups and Chinese immigrants from the north. Discontented people joined a man named Hung who claimed to be a younger brother of Jesus ordered to set up a Heavenly Kingdom on earth. By 1850 he had 30,000 followers who moved north, secured control of the Yangtze valley, captured Nanking and made it their capital. Forerunners of later communists, the Taiping forces seized land from its owners and redistributed it to peasants according to need—in theory. In actual practice the leaders lived in great luxury, divided the area under their control into kingdoms, and instituted a dictatorship of local warlords. By 1862 the Manchu government was able to commence decisive attacks upon the Taiping forces, and by 1865 the rebellion was ended, at a cost of some 20,000,000 lives.

The Taiping Rebellion was profoundly significant because it was the beginning of a vast upheaval in China which is still in progress today. Foreign nations took advantage of the breakdown of the weak central Chinese government to win for themselves further advantages in China.

The Treaty of Tientsin, 1858
This treaty was an enlargement of the treaties of 1842 and 1844 and extended privileges to France and Russia, as well as to Great Britain and the United States. The treaty was the result of another "incident" between the Chinese authorities and Britain. Chinese ships flying the British flag were safe from Chinese interference. This mis-use of the British flag led to Chinese seizure of a Chinese smuggler flying the British flag. The British retaliated by the bombardment of Canton, and this outrageous attack resulted in a widespread demand by the Chinese people to exterminate the British. The second war, if so one-sided an engagement can be called a war, involved the French, who had their own grievance, and ended with negotiations for a new treaty. This time Russia and the United States sent representatives, and although the Chinese attempted for two years to resist new demands, they finally had to agree to the terms presented in 1858. By the Treaty of Tientsin the status of China was completely changed, because she lost her position as a "sovereign" nation able to determine its own affairs. The terms of the treaty clearly show China's position: (1) the Four Powers—Great Britain, United States, France, and Russia—had the right to send diplomatic representatives to Peking, much against the wishes of China, (2) their citizens could travel anywhere in China and enjoy their rights of extraterritoriality wherever they went, that is, they were not subject to Chinese law, (3) eleven more treaty ports were opened up, including one on the island of Formosa, (4) foreign ships had the right to navigate the Yangtze River, which was navigable to small vessels for a thousand miles, (5) the importation of opium was legalized, and (6) Christian missionaries had the right to go anywhere in China and to own property there.

These last two rights are startling in their contrast, for Christianity and legalized opium trade were jointly a curious paradox of white man's claim to be civilizing China.

3. Japan Westernizes and Expands

The Opening of Japan
Just as agricultural nations in Europe were changing into industrial ones, so the age-long simple feudal society of Japan was also changing into an urban way of life. A small middle class was developing there and would have changed Japan even had the American Commodore

Perry not visited in 1853. Japan had remained completely closed to European foreigners, except for a very limited trade permitted to the Dutch on the island of Deshima in Nagasaki harbor, and Japan enforced this seclusion between the years 1638 and 1854. Nevertheless there were serious incidents involving Japan and foreign sailors, because as the Pacific trade increased there were occasions when sailors were shipwrecked on Japanese coasts. They were treated as criminals, exhibited around Japan in cages, and deliberately allowed to die from exposure. Furthermore, Japanese ports were needed by foreign nations as coaling and supply stations. In 1852 President Fillmore of the United States appointed Commodore Perry to command a naval expedition to open Japan to trade with the United States.

Perry's visit in 1853 to Yedo Bay, later Tokyo, was a critical incident in Japan's history. His steamships were the first seen in Japan's waters and their power impressed Japanese officials. When Perry demanded the right to present President Fillmore's letter to the Emperor, he was allowed to deliver it to two high-ranking officials, and was then ordered to leave with his ships. He refused to do so under compulsion, and later left in his own good time, and after sending word that he would return the following year to receive an answer from the Emperor, indicating quite clearly that he expected the answer to be favorable.

The Treaty of Kanagawa, 1854

In February 1854 Perry returned and was able to negotiate the Treaty of Kanagawa. Its terms were far more significant than they appeared to be. The two rather inferior ports of Hakodate in the north and Shimoda near Yedo Bay were opened to foreign ships, and an American consul was allowed to reside in Shimoda to protect American interests. Although the treaty was little more than one of friendship, it established a principle which was in great contrast to Japan's previous total exclusion of foreigners.

Probably Japan was influenced not only by Perry's steamships but also by the example of China's treatment in 1842, and by the recent frequent appearances of Russian vessels off the Japanese coast.

The Westernizing of Japan

Once one nation secured rights in Japan, other nations soon benefited. The British in 1854, the Russians in 1855, and the Dutch in 1856 all established the right to trade and to get supplies in Shimoda, Hakodate, and Nagasaki, to appoint consuls to the latter two ports, and to have their traders live in Nagasaki. Later treaties, negotiated initially by the American consul Townsend Harris, and including the other Powers, changed Japan's destiny. She now decided to westernize and meet the western Powers on an equal footing. The treaties themselves led in part to violence in Japan and an upheaval of its traditional organization. For the previous 250 years the emperor had been a figurehead in Japan, with the real power in the hands of a *Shogun* or generalissimo who,

Perry's Visit to Japan

although he received his title from the emperor, was a member of a powerful ruling family whose daughters traditionally married the young emperors. He commanded the military forces, which were really an association of Knights of the *Samurai* class, a graduated system of landowners from the Daimyo or great landholders, down to the small landowners, all of the privileged class. The Tokugawa family of shoguns was criticized for its treaties with foreign powers, and a great anti-shogun, anti-foreigner, pro-emperor movement spread throughout Japan.

Anti-foreign incidents led to reprisals by warships of foreign powers, and in 1867 the Shogun surrendered all his power to the new young emperor, who was to reign under the name of Meiji, the Enlightened, for 45 years; during this period Japan rose with incredible speed to the position of a first-rate power. The government built railroads, promoted textile mills and shipping lines, encouraged banking, and helped to finance strategic industries which would later serve for the defense and expansion of Japan.

The Sino-Japanese War, 1894–1895: Beginning of Japanese Expansion

Japan's decision to westernize brought her into the modern world of industrialization, the search for raw materials and markets, and rivalries in international politics. Russia's policy of advancing into eastern Asia alarmed Japan, particularly since China was too weak to resist any future Russian threat southward.

Korea was one of the strategic parts of southeast Asia, and despite its moderate size of 600 miles long and 150 miles wide it had suffered the fate of any area which is strategically located. Its history goes back to Christian times, and over the centuries Korea has been the road for invasion and conquest, and has suffered severely. It leads from the Pacific into China, Central Asia, and Russian Siberia. In the hands of a powerful nation it could threaten China, Russia, or Japan. In the 1890's Japan was particularly concerned, because Korea was a peninsula pointed straight at Japan and could be exceedingly dangerous to Japan's safety if it were in the hands of an expansionist nation. China claimed that Korea was subordinate to her as a protectorate of China, and that foreign nations must negotiate through China for trade and other purposes. By 1894 almost 90 percent of Korea's foreign trade was with Japan; but Russia was building the Trans-Siberian Railway across eastern Asia to Vladivostock, and was indicating that she had "rights" in Korea. Japan believed that her own security would be seriously threatened unless Korea became independent or she herself took control of it. If Korea remained under Chinese control, it could be taken over by Russia, who could then deny to Japan the potential markets and sources of raw materials on the mainland.

In early 1894 an anti-Japanese, anti-foreign, and anti-missionary rebellion broke out in Korea. Korean government troops were defeated, so China sent troops into her "tributary" state, notifying Japan of her action, in accordance with a previous agreement. Japan sent in her own troops, the Korean government managed to quell the rebellion, and then Chinese and Japanese troops faced each other in Seoul. Japan suggested joint Chinese-Japanese reforms in Korea, but China insisted, with incredible inconsistency, that she herself had no right to interfere in the internal affairs of Korea. Japan decided to act for herself.

Japanese forces seized the Korean king and replaced him with a puppet government which immediately requested Japan to expel Chinese troops. War was declared between the two nations, and Russia gave China verbal encouragement because Russian interests would better be served with Korea in the hands of a weak

China than a strong Japan. The short Sino-Japanese War proved that China was literally a paper dragon and that Japan had become unexpectedly powerful. In April 1895 the Treaty of Shimonoseki stated that (1) China had to recognize the independence of Korea, (2) China was required to cede to Japan the strategic Liaotung Peninsula in southern Manchuria, and Formosa and the Pescadores Islands, (3) China had to pay an indemnity of $165,000,000, and (4) China was required to grant Japan most-favored nation treatment, that is, she must be granted the best trading rights that any nation received.

This war not only showed how weak China was, but it then made her the target for European expansion, and initiated Japan's expansionist ambitions and policy on the mainland that were to continue until her World War II defeat in 1945.

The Partitioning of China

Within a week after the signing of the Treaty of Shimonoseki in April 1895 the three powers—Russia, Germany, and France—"advised" Japan to "retrocede" or give back to China the strategic Liaotung Peninsula. The European Powers had been caught off balance by Japan's quick success against China, and they were not disposed to allow Japan to become too great a power on the Chinese mainland. Russia did not want Japan in the Liaotung Peninsula because it was too close to Manchuria and the Trans-Siberian Railway which she had commenced building in 1891. Manchuria in the weak hands of China was no threat, but in the hands of Japan it could present a danger to Russia's Pacific provinces. Germany was anxious to develop a commercial empire in China and at the same time lessen the threat of conflict in the Balkans by turning Russia's attention toward a possible empire in the Far East. France simply supported Russia as its ally.

Two months later a treaty between Russia and China granted Russia the right to build the Chinese Eastern Railway across northern Manchuria to connect the Trans-Siberian Railway with Vladivostock and give Russia an advantageous economic position in Manchuria. In quick succession other Powers decided to obtain more concessions for themselves. Germany acquired a 99-year lease of Kiaochow Bay; Russia leased from China the Liaotung Peninsula with its strategic ports of Dairen and Port Arthur, the very territory which Japan had been "advised" to return to China; France leased Kwangchow Bay; and Britain leased Kowloon opposite Hong Kong, and Wei-Hai-Wei.

4. Reaction to the Partitioning of China

China: The Boxer Rebellion

Defeat at the hands of Japan was deeply humiliating to China. Voices which had vainly

THE OPEN MOUTH; OR, THE INTEGRITY OF CHINA.
British Lion. "It's all right, Johnny Chinaman, we've come to a perfectly Friendly Arrangement."
Russian Bear (pleasantly). "We're going to Divide you."

The Partitioning of China

warned of the dangers of Japan's westernization were now listened to, and influential Chinese advised that China must defend herself against extinction by industrializing, by educating her people, and by completely reorganizing the government.

Already Western ideas and techniques were penetrating into China through the foreign concessions in Shanghai, Foochow, Hankow, Canton, and other coastal ports. Plans were drawn up on paper by the young Manchu Emperor to build railroads, open mines and factories, educate the young, and reform the system of land ownership. But long tradition and habits opposed him, and he was forced to desist.

Another force, however, was already gathering momentum as an anti-foreign and an anti-Manchu movement. If the government could not prevent further losses of Chinese land and authority, then it should be replaced. In 1898 a secret group was organized into a gymnastic society popularly named the Boxers by foreigners. Its anti-Manchu objectives were cleverly manipulated by the Emperor and his supporters into anti-foreign activities. Demonstrators and rioters attacked foreign property and then people. In Shansi province over 200 missionaries were killed, and further excesses were carried out around Peking where the foreign colony of diplomats and families was isolated from outside contact. After the murder of the German minister, all foreign residents were brought into the legations, which were soon besieged and attacked. Chinese troops joined the demonstrators, and the government declared war on the foreign powers and offered a bounty on the heads of all foreigners. One of the announced reasons for the declaration of war was the series of aggressions by foreigners since the Opium War.

Seven nations, including the United States,

The Boxer Rebellion. The fighting at Tientsin.

hastily sent troops that totaled 16,000 men to relieve the desperate foreigners in Peking. Once they were rescued, foreigners of all types, diplomats, soldiers, businessmen, and even missionaries, looted public buildings and private homes, and carried off whatever pleased their fancy.

The tone had perhaps been set by Kaiser William of Germany, who had instructed his departing contingent of troops to give no quarter, take no prisoners. "Just as the Huns a thousand years ago under the leadership of Attila gained reputation ... so may the name of Germany become known in such a manner in China." That reputation followed the Germans back to Europe, where in World War I the name Hun was used to describe German troops.

The immediate punishment for China was severe. A prince of the royal family had to journey personally to Germany to apologize for the death of the German minister; four high officials were ordered to be executed; two royal princes were condemned to death but had their sentences commuted to life exile; many officials were removed from government service for life; and an indemnity and interest of $738,800,000 was exacted. Foreign nations were not only to be allowed to station guards in their legations, but all forts between the coast and Peking were to be pulled down, and foreign troops were to be stationed all along the route.

The consequences of this treatment of the Chinese, who had been goaded into action by the humiliating events of the 19th century, were to continue down to present times as bitterness and enmity toward all foreigners.

United States: The Open Door Policy

At this point in Chinese history, the United States adopted a policy which, in the long run, led inevitably to the clash between Japan and the United States in December 1941.

The Spanish-American War of 1898 resulted in American acquisition of the Philippines, and made the United States, whether she wanted to be or not, a Pacific power. The United States had long been trading with China and had benefited commercially from Western concessions and economic rights there. Toward the end of the 19th century the United States feared that if the Western European nations continued to wrest economic rights and territorial possessions from China, the United States might become increasingly excluded. The Secretary of State, John Hay, addressed similar Notes in 1899 to Western European Powers asking them to agree not to discriminate between each other, but to let every nation enjoy the same economic rights in any foreign concession and treaty port, and not to charge higher harbor dues or higher railroad freight rates for the goods of other countries than its own. This was the basic idea of the Open Door Policy, that no foreign concession should be closed to any nation. Actually the United States had no power to enforce these proposals, and the Western Powers had no need even to consider them, except for one reason. No one nation trusted any of the others, but no one nation dared to get special rights for itself for fear that all the others would gang up on her. It just happened that the idea of the Open Door suited the interests of the nations, and they agreed to it.

The Boxer Rebellion changed the Open Door Policy from one of equal opportunities for all powers—without much concern about what happened to China—to one which really meant that China be protected from further loss of territory and sovereign rights. Just as the relief columns were on their way to relieve the besieged foreigners in Peking, Secretary of State Hay sent another set of similar Notes to the several nations in July 1900. The United States, he said, wished to find a "solution which may bring about permanent safety and peace to China, and *preserve Chinese territorial and administrative integrity.*" The United States had thereby committed herself to the policy that China must remain an independent country.

Because Japan had already started on its expansionist policy by making Korea technically independent from China, but in reality subject to Japan's influence, and because Japan was soon to drive Russia out of Manchuria, there were two contradictory policies about the future of China. Japan apparently intended to secure influence there, perhaps acquiring parts of it, while the United States had recently committed itself to guaranteeing China's physical and political independence.

Japan: The Russo-Japanese War, 1904–1905

Japan did not forget the humiliation of being deprived of the Liaotung Peninsula, only to see it being taken over by Russia within weeks. An added grievance was the danger that Russia's increasing influence in Korea and Manchuria would cut right across Japan's intention to exercise control herself over those regions. The Boxer Rebellion had given Russia the excuse to move troops into Manchuria in order to protect the Chinese Eastern Railway, and there the troops remained until the end of hostilities. When Russia made it clear that she intended to control, if not take, the whole of Manchuria, Japan had to decide whether to watch Russia do so or whether to stop her by force.

She attempted to negotiate with Russia, but each time an agreement seemed about to be reached, Russia would make further demands. History has shown that the tactics of Soviet Russia have differed very little from those of Czarist Russia in this regard. Japan decided that the Russians were not negotiating in good faith, lost patience, on February 6, 1904 broke off diplomatic relations with Russia, and on February 8, without an ultimatum or a declaration of war, ordered her ships to bombard Russian-leased Port Arthur. Japan's diplomatic tactics apparently did not change over the next 35 years.

If Japan's action could possibly be defended it must be on the grounds that Russia clearly

The Russo-Japanese War. The battle of Tsushima.

meant to dominate Manchuria, Korea, and apparently north China. Japan regarded her attack on Russia in Manchuria as self-defense, and other nations tended to agree.

To the great surprise of Western nations, and perhaps Japan herself, Japanese troops won victory after victory, at great expense in lives, but with decisive results. The Russian armies were driven back across Manchuria, and the Russian Baltic fleet sailed halfway around the world via the Cape of Good Hope, only to be sunk in the Tsushima Straits off Japan, before it could reach Vladivostock.

The United States Again: Balance of Power

Both sides were ready for peace after a year and a half. Russia was fighting thousands of miles from its headquarters in Moscow, and at the end of the single-track Trans-Siberian Railway which could not possibly keep the Russian armies in Manchuria supplied. And Japan was almost at the end of her resources. Both sides were ready for negotiations, and President Theodore Roosevelt of the United States was very willing to offer his services. The interests of the United States would best be served if neither Japan nor Russia became too powerful and threatened to upset the balance of power in the Far East.

Representatives of the two belligerents met at Portsmouth, New Hampshire, in August 1905, and a month later agreed to terms: (1) Russia recognized Japan's paramount, or dominant, military, economic, and political interests in Korea. This was a death warrant for Korea, and in 1910 Japan simply annexed it, (2) Russia transferred to Japan all her rights in South Manchuria and the Liaotung Peninsula, without China being consulted, (3) Russia ceded to Japan the southern half of Sakhalin Island, which pointed directly at Japan, (4) Japan acquired the rights to the southern half of the Chinese Eastern Railway, which now became the South Manchuria Railway, (5) both sides agreed to withdraw their troops from Manchuria.

The great significance of the Russo-Japanese War was not only that Japan had become a World Power, but that an Asiatic nation was able to defeat a Western Power, one that had apparently been feared by other Western nations. The ability of an Asiatic nation to be so successful was read as a sign by other Asiatic peoples that the day would come when they too could be free from white domination. This was to become one of the great issues of the 20th century.

5. Imperialism in Southeast Asia

The Dutch East Indies

By 1600 the Dutch had a large merchant marine and owned the greater proportion of shipping in northern Europe. Wishing to extend their trade to the Far East the Dutch government organized their own East India Company, which gradually took over Portuguese trade in the Far East. In 1619 they founded the city of Batavia, now called Jakarta, on the island of Java, and in 1641 were permitted to establish the only European trading station with the Japanese, on an island near Nagasaki.

By 1815 the Dutch occupied the island of Java, and over the next several decades established a Dutch empire throughout the 3,000-mile archipelago which became known as the Dutch East Indies. With their great natural resources of rubber and other products not possessed by European nations, these islands became typical examples of 19th-century imperialism. For some time the Dutch exploited cheap native labor, much as Leopold of Belgium was to do in the Congo Free State, by requiring from each village a stated amount of crops. The Dutch encouraged education in native languages, but discouraged the teaching of Dutch in order to keep out of the Dutch East Indies any Western ideas of nationalism and democracy. The natives were not trained in self-rule, and when they secured their independence after World War II they suffered from this lack of training.

British India

When the English East India Company was first established in 1600 the company sold shares to investors for each voyage out and back. After each successful voyage the company divided up profits and capital proportionately among the shareholders, and then organized another expedition.

Within a few years the company set up a permanent organization with a permanent capital, much like any modern business concern, and paid out periodic dividends to its shareholders. Its charter gave it sole rights to trade between England and the East Indies and to act as a local government in administering the lands it controlled. The British East India Company governed large parts of India, trained its agents and employees in its own college in England, and built and maintained its own fleet and its own troops.

Before the middle of the 19th century the British government and British people were increasingly critical of the Company's trading monopoly and of its administration of India. The critical situation which finally ended the Company's rule in India was the Sepoy Mutiny of 1857, British interference with native customs such as widow-burning, and with religious beliefs aroused strong resentment. In 1857 there were 250,000 native troops and only 40,000 British troops in the employ of the Company. Rumor had it that native troops were being issued cartridges greased with pork and beef fat. Since it was profane for a Moslem to touch

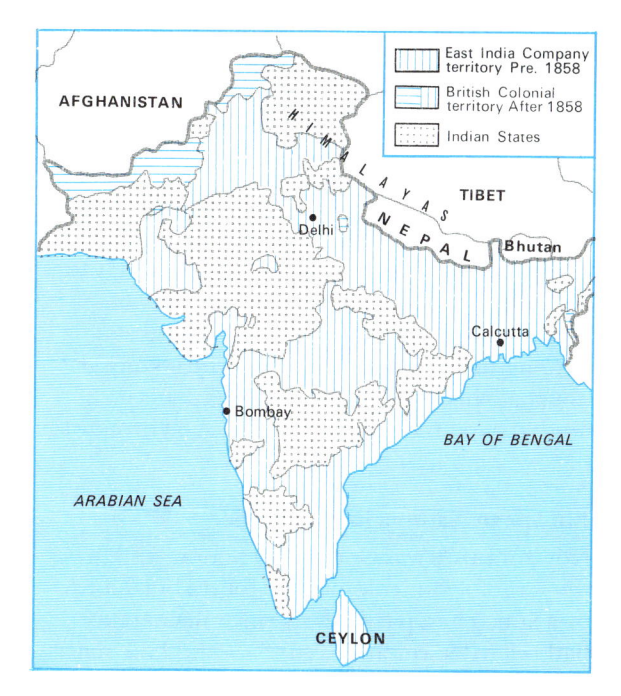

British India

pork fat, and because the cow was sacred to Hindus, native Hindu and Moslem troops, called Sepoys, mutinied. Not until 1859 was the mutiny completely crushed, after thousands of mutineers had been executed in retaliation for the deaths of European residents and British troops.

In 1858 the East India Company lost its administrative control of India, which now became a British colony ruled from London by an official Secretary of State for India, chosen by the British cabinet, and assisted by a council for India. From this time on the British government gradually gave native Indians some say in the government of their country, but at too slow a pace to suit many Indian leaders.

British Malaya

The British were in Malaya by the end of the 18th century, and by mid-19th century several provinces had been brought under British rule. Singapore was developed as one of the great seaports of the world, and with the invention of the automobile Malaya became increasingly valuable to Britain. Its great supplies of rubber and tin made it one of the most valuable colonies of the 20th century. Its great wealth spurred other nations to search for colonies in order to get similar advantages. Britain's possession of Malaya was in general recognized by most nations, and Britain's control of the colony was not challenged until 1941, when Japan's intended expansion into Southeast Asia brought the two nations into conflict.

European Nations in the Pacific

Not until 1870 was Germany a nation, and in the scramble for colonies she found herself to be a latecomer, particularly since Bismarck had regarded colonies as useless and had made no attempt to acquire any. Kaiser William II thought quite the opposite, and participated in the successful attempts by European powers to stake out for themselves the most strategic and useful of literally thousands of islands throughout the Pacific. In 1886 Great Britain, the Netherlands, and Germany shared in the acquisition of New Guinea or Papua. Germany then took possession of the Marshall Islands, and in 1899 purchased from Spain for about $4,000,000 the Caroline, Peleu, and Mariana Islands.

In 1875 the United States and Hawaii ratified a treaty which placed the Hawaiian Islands within an American sphere of influence. But Americans in general opposed annexation, so the Grant administration compromised to the extent that none of the privileges enjoyed by the United States should be extended to any other power, and no other nation should lease or control any Hawaiian territory. By 1890 Hawaii was dominated by white planters and traders, particularly by Americans, who were the principal advisors to the native rulers of Hawaii, and who in general controlled the government.

In 1891 Queen Liliuokalani denounced the leasing of Pearl Harbor to the United States and decided to reduce American influence on her government. In 1893 the "foreigners" forestalled her by staging a revolt, connived at by the United States government, and carried out in part by the American Minister. Marines were landed from an American warship to protect the local committee, the American flag was run up, and the Queen obliged to surrender under protest. A committee of Hawaiian businessmen formed a provisional government, and in February 1893 signed a treaty of annexation. Congress took no action until 1898, when Japanese activities suggested threats from that quarter. By 1895 there were 25,000 Japanese in the islands, at least equal to all Americans and Europeans. Japan had just defeated China in Korea, and now believed herself to be a Power with world interests. On August 12, 1898, the islands were officially annexed to the United States.

The Samoan Islands were to Britain and her colonies of Australia and New Zealand what Hawaii came to be for the United States and the Philippines. The Samoan Islands control the sea approaches from the north and east Pacific to Australasia. The harbor of Pago Pago on the island of Tutuila was only less strategic than Pearl Harbor. German settlers on the islands were of increasing concern to New Zealand which repeatedly asked Britain to annex them. The Samoans themselves became alarmed at German activities and asked the Americans and the British, but never the Germans, to annex them. The final solution was a tripartite agreement among the three powers to maintain the independence and neutrality of the islands.

During the later decades of the 19th century the United States acquired several overseas possessions in the Pacific. The Aleutian Islands, 1,500 miles westward from the mainland, were included in the purchase of Alaska in 1867. That same year the United States annexed the uninhabited Midway Islands. American Samoa was annexed by executive agreement in 1880, and Hawaii by joint resolution of Congress in 1898. After the Spanish-American War the United States extended itself deep into the Western Pacific with its annexation of Wake, Guam, and the Philippine Islands.

6. Imperialism in Africa

Long before the Christian era a vigorous and widespread commerce was carried on throughout the Mediterranean Sea and along the north coast of Africa, and colonies were established there by the Phoenicians and Romans.

Not until the 15th century, however, did explorers begin to sail down the west coast of Africa and around into the Indian Ocean. During the 17th and 18th centuries a very profitable slave trade along the west African coast assumed enormous proportions in order to satisfy the demands of the hungry labor markets of the New World continents. But even so, very little was known of Africa beyond the narrow tidewater coastal region, and the great part of that vast land mass remained the "Dark Continent," not because of the color of its people but because of European ignorance about it.

A primary cause for this lack of knowledge was the geography of Africa. The Sahara Desert stretched forbiddingly for 3,000 miles from the Atlantic eastward to the Red Sea, in a band nearly 1,000 miles wide. The Sahara and the vast area of Africa southward is a vast plateau with a narrow coastal plain, and rivers which are navigable only a short distance inland before rapids interfere with navigation. From the 16th century down to the middle of the 19th century the New World and the Far East offered so many opportunities for colonies and trading companies that the continent of Africa was largely ignored.

European Interests in North Africa

In 1815 the lands along the Mediterranean coast of African were, with the exception of Morocco, all technically subject lands of the Sultan of Turkey. Tripoli, Libya, and Egypt were actually parts of the Turkish Empire, but Algeria and Tunisia were in practice free from Turkish control.

For hundreds of years these territories harbored pirates who preyed upon shipping and exacted tribute from European maritime nations which used the Mediterranean. United States ships suffered from the Barbary pirates, particularly during the War of 1812. In 1812 Congress authorized Stephen Decatur to lead an expedition against the Dey of Algiers, who had dismissed the United States consul, declared war on the United States, and enslaved American crews because he had not received sufficient tribute. Decatur successfully led his 10-vessel fleet against Algiers, Tunis, and Tripoli, and obliged these states to release United States citizens and pay compensation for captured American vessels. Great Britain and France later followed this up with vigorous action of their own, and in 1830 France began the occupation of Algeria as the final step in eliminating piracy in the Mediterranean. Almost by accident France became a colonizing nation in North Africa, but did little to extend its possessions there until in 1881 at the suggestion of Bismarck it added Tunisia to its African territory.

Great Britain became a colonial power in North Africa because the ruler of Egypt failed to repay substantial loans advanced by Great

Britain and France. The Khedive of Egypt, Ishmail Pasha, was a semi-independent ruler under the Sultan of Turkey and wanted to Europeanize Egypt and make it a modern nation. He arranged for large loans from British and French bankers, commenced ambitious projects of road-building, railroads, and harbors, and spent over $80 million on the construction of the Suez Canal. For more than ten years the Khedive's indebtedness increased until finally he requested Britain and France to appoint experts to advise him how to repay the loans. In 1875 the Khedive raised some money by selling his own Canal shares to Great Britain, but this sum was far from enough to solve his financial difficulties. In 1879 the French and British persuaded the Sultan of Turkey to replace Ishmail, and arranged for the Dual Control, of Britain and France, to manage Egypt's finances. The threat of revolt against the Dual Control endangered the lives and property of Europeans, who appealed for help to Britain and France. The two nations sent warships, and Britain decided to land troops in Egypt to defend the Suez Canal, her "lifeline" to India and the East. The French withdrew but Britain carried out her plans, and from 1882 Egypt became in fact a protectorate of Great Britain. During the following years the British extended their occupation up the Nile as far south into the Egyptian Sudan as Khartoum, where General Kitchener raised the British flag in 1898.

Meanwhile the French were extending their possessions in the Congo, and ordered Captain Marchand to head an expedition to the Upper Nile. In July 1898 Marchand and his small force reached Fashoda, 500 miles south of Khartoum, and there raised the French flag. A short time later General Kitchener arrived at Fashoda with gunboats and artillery to inform Marchand that the French occupation was in violation of Anglo-Egyptian rights in the Sudan. Marchand insisted upon his right of occupation, Kitchener upon his right to raise the British and Egyptian flags, and Marchand persisted in his refusal to lower the French tricolor. Both men had satisfied their honor as commanders, they parted on friendly terms, and left the solution of the problem to London and Paris.

At first neither nation would back down, and it looked as though the Fashoda Incident could lead to war. France called upon her ally Russia for support, but was quickly told not to count upon Russia in the event of war. France, appreciating that Britain had the military advantage, extricated herself from the dilemma by recalling Marchand, who had been sent as an "emissary of civilization" and presumably not as a representative of the French government. The French later gave up all claims to the Sudan. In 1922, after Egypt became an independent nation, France and Britain jointly exercised rights as a condominium in the administration and development of Anglo-Egyptian Sudan.

The Opening of the Suez Canal

The Scramble for Colonies in Sub-Sahara Africa

Earlier predictions that colonial empires would disappear proved completely inaccurate. The "Little Englanders" who wanted no colonies for the mother country were now overshadowed in many European countries by those who formed colonial societies and wrote books and pamphlets advocating the desirability of colonies. Between 1875 and 1900 almost the entire continent of Africa was divided up among the European nations.

Great Britain had in 1814 acquired from the Netherlands the former Dutch settlement of the Cape of Good Hope at the southern tip of Africa, but it had remained only a modest settlement over the years. European interest in Africa was first aroused through the Scots missionary David Livingstone, who had for years worked with the natives of East Africa in the Lake Tanganyika region, and had won their respect because apparently he had no desire for gain for himself or for others. He explored the Zambesi River valley and because he was so completely at home and happy with the natives, he made little attempt to keep in touch with the outside world. For three years no word came from him, so the *New York Herald* took the opportunity to get the paper some publicity by sending the reporter Henry M. Stanley to find him. The famous meeting took place in 1871 when the two met, with the famous remark from Stanley, "Dr. Livingstone, I presume."

Stanley's expedition attracted wide attention to Equatorial Africa. Stanley himself was so impressed by the country's natural resources that he went to Europe to try to find backers to develop the resources. In 1878 he was introduced to King Leopold II of Belgium who had already called an international conference at Brussels "for the Exploration and Civilization of Central Africa." Leopold quickly appreciated Stanley's business acumen and engaged him to establish trading posts, build bridges and roads, and make treaties with the natives in the Congo area. Leopold then persuaded businessmen friends to join him in a private business venture under the high-sounding name of the International Congo Association. In 1885 the 900,000 square miles which Leopold acquired was called the Congo Free State, of which Leopold was the sovereign and the owner of all ivory and rubber, which the natives were forbidden to sell to anyone else.

Africa now was of such interest to other European nations, and had become such a potential source of international friction, that in 1884 Bismarck called a Berlin Conference of fourteen nations, including the United States, to discuss the issue of African colonization. Africa was regarded much as America had been regarded in the 17th century, as a land without government and therefore open to settlement by any nation which chose to colonize there. The conference concerned itself with defining spheres of influence and agreed that any Power that occupied any African territory would merely have to notify the others, who would recognize the action.

The keenest rivalry existed between Great Britain and France, and to a lesser degree Germany which came late upon the European scene and had no African colony as a base of operations.

Great Britain, Germany, and France

British power in Africa had already been established in the north and in the south, in Egypt and at the Cape of Good Hope, and by 1870 its authority extended into Cape Colony and Natal. In 1867 diamonds had been found in an area between British Cape Colony and the Boer Orange Free State Republic; later this area proved to have the richest diamond deposit

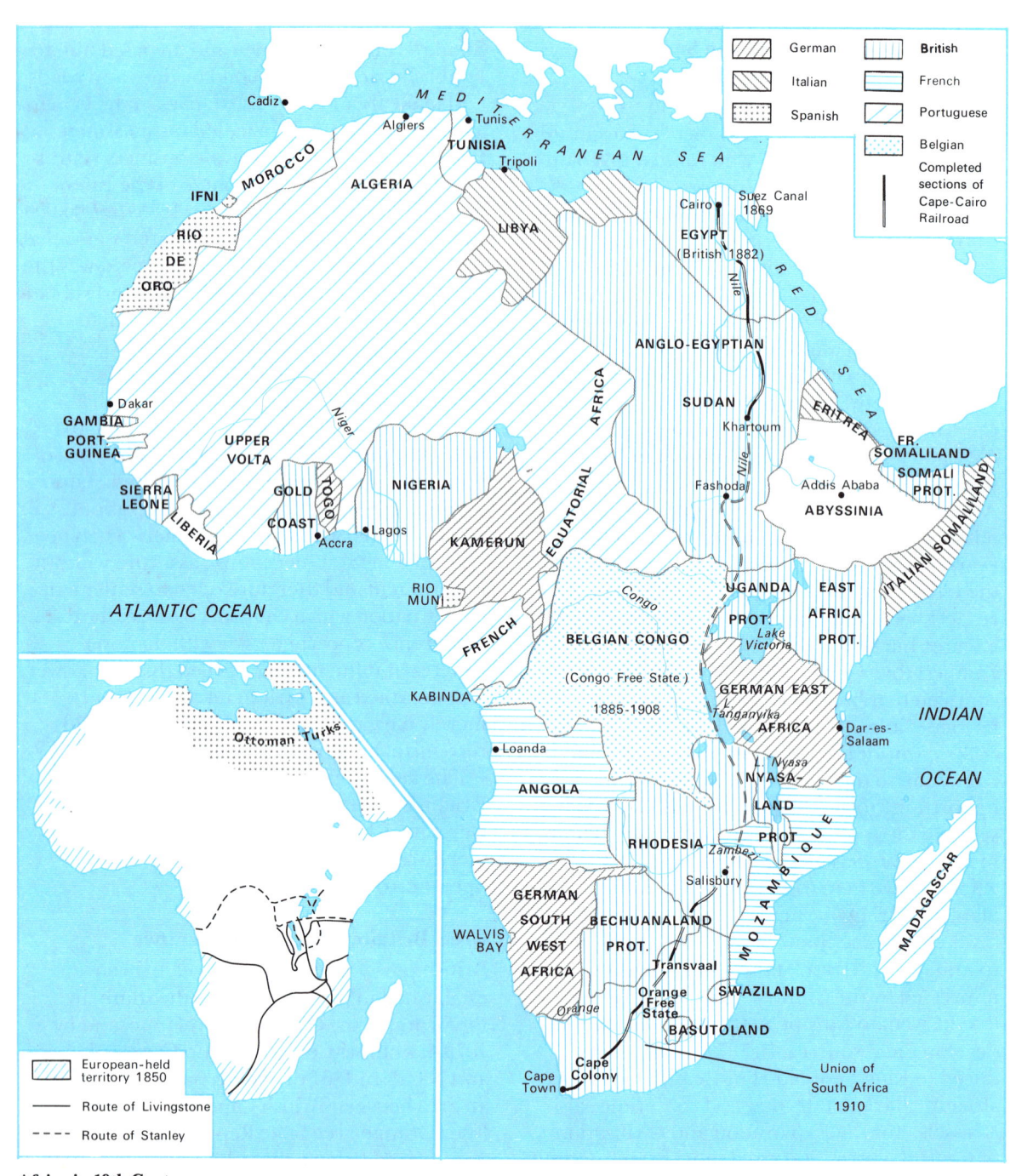

Africa in 19th Century

in the world. Cecil Rhodes, an English lad who came out to Africa for his health at the age of seventeen, bought up diamond claims from prospectors who came from the four quarters of the globe, and by 1890 had formed the De Beers Consolidated Mines, which had a monopoly of 90 percent of diamonds in Africa, and also the Consolidated Gold Fields of South Africa, which was to monopolize gold production in that area.

Now enormously wealthy, Rhodes decided that Africa should become part of the British Empire, and as Prime Minister of Cape Colony he planned a Cape to Cairo railroad through territory which would become British. Through his efforts Great Britain got control of Bechuanaland, between the Boer Transvaal and German West Africa, and then the territory known as Rhodesia, a vast fertile area rich in natural resources and owned by the British South Africa Company organized by Rhodes.

Britain then took Kenya in East Africa as part of the Cape to Cairo plan, but Germany interrupted further expansion by herself taking Tanganyika, then known as German East Africa. The railroad never was completed, although it did run northward from Capetown to the Zambesi River, and southward from Cairo up the Nile into Anglo-Egyptian Sudan. Just as German-controlled Tanganyika prevented Britain from owning territory all the way from the Cape to Cairo, so Britain's acquisition of Nigeria in the west and other territory prevented Germany from establishing possessions that could have given her control of the middle region from east to west. In a few years Germany added the colonies of Kamerun and Togoland on Africa's west coast, but she was to lose all her African colonies at the end of World War I.

France founded Dakar on the west coast in 1857, acquired territory along the Niger and Congo Rivers, and took possession of the valuable island of Madagascar off the southeastern coast of Africa.

Belgium, Portugal, Italy, and Spain

Leopold of Belgium expected that his personal Congo Free State would bring in vast riches in rubber and ivory, but the natives saw no reason to go to work for Leopold, even for pay. So the managers of the Congo Free State simply levied on every village a tax in the form of a prescribed amount of rubber and ivory. Native armies were organized to enforce the edict, native women were frequently held as hostages until the required amounts were collected, and native protests were savagely handled. Atrocities such as torture, the severing of hands, and personal servitude became such a scandal that an international investigation caused even the Belgian government to intervene. Leopold gave up his claim to the Congo Free State, which in 1908 became the Belgian Congo as a colony of Belgium.

Portugal had as early as the 16th century commenced settlements in Mozambique on the east coast, and in Angola on the west coast. In the 19th century it extended its claims in these two areas, and in recent years it has claimed them to be an integral part of Portugal, not simply colonies of the mother country; thus Portugal considers these areas to be of no concern to any other nation.

Spain had held the small possession of Rio de Oro on the upper west coast since 1478, and in 1906 added Spanish Morocco.

Italy, whose ambitions to acquire Tunisia had been thwarted by France in 1881, seized Eritrea on the Red Sea, and the southern part of Somaliland on the Indian Ocean. These two areas were of little use to Italy unless she could also occupy Abyssinia, or Ethiopia, which separated the two colonies. In 1896 the Italians attacked the Abyssinians but were soundly defeated at Adowa. The Italians did not forget that humiliation, and in 1935 Mussolini revenged the defeat by taking over Ethiopia, one of the oldest nations in history.

Many African natives served in various colonial armies during World War I. Their experiences in the service at home and abroad sparked the beginning of the desire for independence.

Native demands for rights were regarded as dangerous to colonial rule, and native leaders were not infrequently jailed for their activities. World War II greatly accelerated the demands for independence, and resulted in the granting of independence by Britain to Ghana in 1957, to be followed by the creation of some 30 independent African nations in the following decade.

Review Questions

Section 1
1. Explain the important economic motives for 19th-century imperialism.
2. Explain how the Social Darwinians justified the acquisition of colonies. Were their arguments reasonable or simply an excuse for colonizing?

Section 2
3. In what ways was Confucius a prophet of history?
4. Explain in what ways treaty ports and concessions were an interference with the independence of China.
5. In what ways was the Treaty of Tientsin, 1858, an even greater interference with Chinese sovereignty?

Section 3
6. What were the immediate and the long-range results of Commodore Perry's visit to Japan?
7. The Sino-Japanese War of 1894–1895 was a deliberate action of Japan to serve her own interests. Explain what those interests were.
8. Explain in what ways the actions of the Great Powers in China in the 1890's led almost inevitably to the Russo-Japanese War of 1904–1905.

Section 4
9. What were the causes and results of the Boxer Rebellion?
10. Why did the United States initiate the Open Door Policy, and why did other nations agree to it?
11. Why did Japan decide that she had to go to war with Russia?
12. Why did President Roosevelt participate in the Treaty of Portsmouth? Was it because Russia and Japan could not come to terms by themselves?

Section 5
13. Why were the Dutch East Indies and Malaysia such valuable colonies?
14. Why were Hawaii, Samoa, and other Pacific Islands apparently so important to nations in the later 19th century?

Section 6
15. Explain how France and Great Britain became involved in North Africa.
16. List the colonies in Africa of each of the following nations: France; Great Britain; Germany; Belgium; Portugal.

6

The United States: Industrial Nation and World Power

The Growth of Corporations and Railroads

Regulation of Railroads and Corporations

Attempts of Labor to Organize

The Agrarian Revolt

The Progressive Movement

The Emergence of the United States as a World Power

The last quarter of the century was a period of unprecedented material growth in the United States. The nation changed from an agrarian and small-business economy to one dominated by great corporations that controlled nationwide industries. Great natural resources were used to build the United States into one of the wealthiest and most powerful of nations. The minerals, timber, grain, and cattle of the West, the petroleum, sulphur, and cotton of the South, and the industrial skills and money of the East were all combined to bring the Age of Industrialism to the United States.

The old frontier of the West disappeared under the advance of industrialism and the transcontinental railroads. Farmers found themselves the victims of overproduction and falling prices and became increasingly burdened with mortgages on their farms. They revolted against conditions, blamed railroads and bankers for their plight, and demanded reforms. Labor attempted to organize in order to enforce demands for better conditions and wages, but had an uphill fight before gaining recognition and the rights of collective bargaining. Small businessmen, who believed in free enterprise, found themselves unable to compete with impersonal and frequently ruthless railroads and corporations. Public sentiment became so aroused that reformers were able to oblige them to recognize their responsibility to public interests.

Terms
1. *Wabash, St. Louis and Pacific Railway v. Illinois*
2. Interstate Commerce Act
3. Sherman Anti-Trust Act
4. *United States v. E. C. Knight Company*
5. Pullman Strike
6. Greenbackers
7. Free Silver
8. Populists
9. Progressives
10. Bull Moose
11. Clayton Anti-Trust Act
12. Federal Reserve System
13. Roosevelt Corollary

People
14. John D. Rockefeller
15. Andrew Carnegie
16. J. Pierpont Morgan
17. William Jennings Bryan
18. Theodore Roosevelt
19. William Howard Taft

Places
20. Cuba
21. Philippine Islands

Events
1887 Interstate Commerce Act
1890 Sherman Anti-Trust Act
1894 Pullman strike
     Populist Party
1898 Acquistion of Philippine Islands, Guam, Puerto Rico
1899 Open Door Policy initiated
1901 Assassination of President McKinley
     Theodore Roosevelt becomes President
1902 Anthracite strike
1904 Election of Theodore Roosevelt to presidency
1905 Roosevelt Corollary
1908 Election to the presidency of William Howard Taft
1912 Election to the presidency of Woodrow Wilson
1912 Federal Reserve Act
1914 Clayton Act
1917 Declaration of war on Germany

1. The Growth of Corporations and Railroads

Inventors and Entrepreneurs

The factor most responsible for the great change in American society was the expansion of industry, whose total value increased at least six times between 1875 and 1914. In the same period the number of workers in industry increased from 6,000,000 to 26,000,000. Before 1870 such inventions as the McCormick reaper, the Colt revolver, and the sewing-machine were in mass production. The Civil War stimulated the demand for steel, textile, and other products, and the post-war years brought a flood of new discoveries and inventions—the air-brake, the typewriter, the Kelly-Bessemer process for producing steel, the use of the gasoline engine, and the development of the electrical industry which revolutionized industrial techniques, transportation, and communications.

There had been inventors and industrialists before the Civil War, but after 1870 conditions were such that the demand for large resources of capital for machines and for nation-wide marketing methods led to the growth of the large corporation. A large population to supply labor, a transportation system to move raw materials and manufactured products, enormous resources of raw materials, and government tariffs to protect young American industries from foreign competition were all favorable conditions for industrial expansion.

Outstanding among the entrepreneurs, men who took risks of business investment and management, were men like John D. Rockefeller, Andrew Carnegie, Cornelius Vanderbilt, and many others. It took not only vast sums of money to drill for, refine, and distribute oil, to build the great furnaces and rolling mills for steel, and to build the great railroad systems, but it took great management ability also. Rockefeller's very efficient management and financial skill organized the Standard Oil Company, bought up refineries, controlled railroads and pipelines for the distribution of oil, and within a decade had a virtual monopoly on the refining and distribution of oil. Hundreds of small competitors were knocked out, but Rockefeller greatly helped to bring order out of a chaotic business, to increase oil production, and in the long run benefit the consumer with a cheaper product.

Andrew Carnegie, son of an immigrant Scottish weaver, worked his way up the Pennsylvania Railroad Company from telegraphist to divisional superintendent, then left to work on the building of iron bridges, and then steel rails. He used his company's enormous profits to acquire raw materials, buy up competitors, and build an "integrated" industry of iron ore from the Mesabi Range; iron ore ships carried the raw material to his own docks, and then his own railroad carried it to his own blast furnaces and rolling mills. He crushed competitors and labor unions, increased his annual production of 320,000 tons to 3,000,000 tons in ten years, and multiplied the company's annual profits from $5,000,000 to $40,000,000 in the same period.

Meanwhile J. Pierpont Morgan, the banker, organized steel mergers until the Federal Steel Company was second only to Carnegie Steel in size. He then set out to consolidate the steel industry into one large corporation, and when Carnegie Steel blocked the project he bought it out from Carnegie in 1901 for Carnegie's own price of $450,000,000.

Railroads

On the eve of the Civil War railroads which had reached the Mississippi River, were beginning to push lines into Iowa and Missouri. In 1862 Congress enacted the Pacific Railroad Act

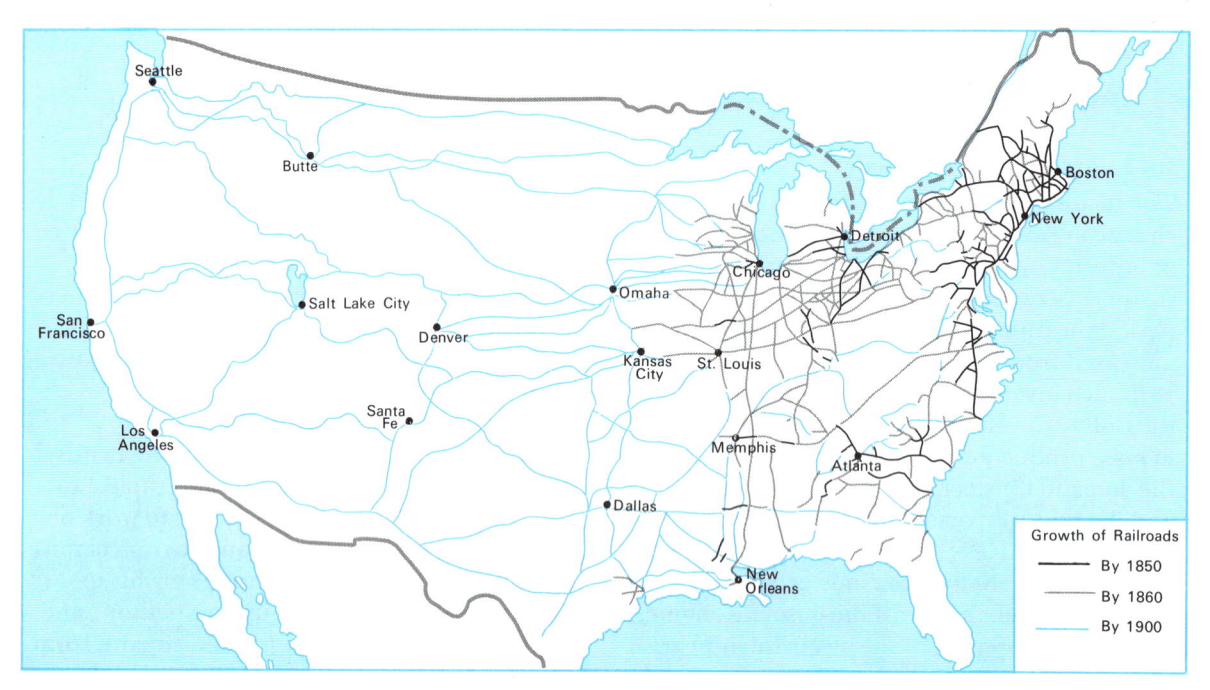

United States. Growth of Railroads.

which authorized the construction of a railroad to the Pacific coast, and subsidized it with large grants of public land, and with substantial loans up to $48,000 per mile of construction. Altogether the government gave away to transcontinental railroads a total of 131,000,000 acres, or more than 204,500 square miles of land, supplemented by additional grants from states, to a grand total of 183,000,000 acres, or 286,000 square miles, an area larger than New York, Pennsylvania, and the six New England states.

The railroads, the largest landholders in the West, sold land at $4 or $5 an acre, and brought in at their own expense many settlers to start farms and raise food and make other products for railroad business. Within twenty years the great transcontinentals spanned the continent, the Union and Central Pacific, the Northern Pacific, the Santa Fe, and the Southern Pacific. The only one which was not financed by any government aid was James J. Hill's Great Northern Railroad.

2. Regulation of Railroads and Corporations

Railroad Abuses

The transcontinental railroads received such large free grants of public land from the government that farmers regarded them as public utilities obliged to serve the interests and needs of the public. Instead, the farmers found that railroads were out to make as high a profit as they could by various means which farmers considered to be highly unfair. Where competition existed, railroads gave rebates or kick-backs

Early Railroads. Crossing the continent by rail remained an adventure in itself.

to big shippers to get their business, and where there was no competition railroads charged outrageously high rates, which frequently fell upon the small farmers who blamed railroads for their low incomes. In several western states where farmers controlled the legislatures they passed "granger" laws, named after farmers' associations with local granges or meeting-places, which set maximum rates that railroads could charge. The railroads fought back by claiming that since they were interstate lines that crossed more than one state they could be regulated only by the federal government, which had been given by the Constitution the power to "regulate commerce among the several states."

The Interstate Commerce Act

The decision by the United States Supreme Court in the case of *The Wabash, St. Louis and Pacific Railway v. Illinois* ruled that states could not regulate interstate commerce. The federal government then enacted the Interstate Commerce Act in 1887 which regulated freight and other rates charged by railroads, and set up the Interstate Commerce Commission, the ICC, to enforce the rates. Although at first the ICC was hampered by Supreme Court decisions, it finally did secure the power to oversee all railroad relationships with the public.

The Sherman Anti-Trust Act

The spirit of the last decades of the 19th century was one of laissez-faire, or non-interference with business by the government, a theory of non-interference that included wages, hours of labor, conditions of labor, and controls of any kind in business operations. Public opinion generally supported laissez-faire because many people believed that men had the right to form large corporations, even though they formed trusts or monopolies that could secure the complete control of the sale of goods.

But the small businessmen realized that they could not compete with giant corporations, and they demanded that monopolies be prohibited. In 1890 Congress enacted the Sherman Anti-Trust Act which prohibited any "contract, combination in the form of trust or otherwise, or conspiracy in restraint of trade or commerce among the several states." The first case brought before the Supreme Court as an alleged violation of the anti-trust act was unsuccessful.

The Knight Company had bought up several sugar refineries in Pennsylvania, and controlled about 90 percent of refined sugar production in the country. The government brought suit in *United States v. E.C. Knight Co.* on the argument that the company was a "conspiracy in restraint of interstate trade." However, the Court ruled that E. C. Knight only *manufactured* sugar, and had nothing to do with its distribution throughout the nation. The Court could have argued that obviously the company refined 90 percent of the nation's sugar for nationwide consumption, but it chose to argue that manufacturing preceded commerce but was not part of commerce. Therefore, said the Court, the company was not a monopoly restraining interstate commerce, and it could not be ordered by the government to be broken up into several competing companies. Not until the Progressive period of Theodore Roosevelt and Woodrow Wilson was the anti-trust act enforced against monopolies.

3. Attempts of Labor to Organize

Over a period of time industrialization provides more jobs for labor and raises the standard of living for the workers, but the immediate results of the factory system and of unrestrained competition are usually severe on the working class. In the late 19th century the worker in the United States found himself to be no longer a skilled workman in a small enterprise in which the relations between employer and worker were personal. More often than not he was simply a machine tender who fed the machine and did little more than look after it.

His job could always be threatened by the constant flood of immigrants who would work for lower wages. The factory owner and the manager, hard pressed by competition and by the increasing costs of expensive machinery, tried to reduce costs by lowering wages and working conditions. Attempts by labor to organize were fought by employers by any means they could use, including the technique of the company town where living quarters, stores, and all town services belonged to the company and could be denied to workers who complained. This meant that the workers would be out of a job, which they could hold only while they lived in the company town.

Early unions were idealistic organizations that did not believe in strikes, and were more concerned about getting an 8-hour day than the more pressing needs of higher wages and better working conditions. The first large labor organization was the Noble and Holy Order of the Knights of Labor, which admitted to its ranks all "toilers" regardless of race, sex, skills, or lack of skills. It denounced strikes and hoped for remedies through Congressional legislation. Although at its peak membership was more than 750,000 it declined rapidly because it produced no real benefits for labor.

Meanwhile an organization called the American Federation of Labor, organized in 1881, approached the problems of labor's injustices from a completely different viewpoint. The AFL set as its goal an economic rather than a political program; it wanted to improve labor conditions by organizing skilled workers to bargain collectively for the union as one group, and the right to strike. These proposals confronted employers with a completely unacceptable concept. Employers had long claimed that they, and they alone, had the right to determine wages and conditions of work, based upon the law of supply and demand of labor, and not upon the idea of a minimum wage. The demand of the workers to have any say whatever about wages was flatly turned down by employers.

The Pullman Strike

In 1887 wage cuts on major railroads resulted in unsuccessful but violent strikes in which millions of dollars of property were destroyed, federal troops were used to break strikes, and scores of people were killed. In Idaho miners fought against company guards with dynamite and rifles, and at Carnegie's Homestead Steel plant in Pennsylvania, three hundred armed Pinkerton detectives were brought in by Henry Frick, the plant manager, to break a strike and destroy unionism in steel plants.

The most significant strike of the period was the 1894 railroad strike that began in the Pullman Palace Car Company plant in the model town of Pullman, near Chicago. The year 1894 was a bad one for labor, with unemployment rising steadily. Pullman cut wages five times in one year but refused to reduce rents that were higher than those for comparable quarters in other parts of Chicago. The Pullman workers had recently joined the American Railway Union, under the leadership of Eugene V. Debs, and as the strike continued the ARU refused to handle any trains to which Pullman cars were attached. Pullman refused to negotiate, and all major railroad lines fired switchmen who refused to handle Pullman trains. By the middle of June nearly all men working on railroads west of Chicago were on strike.

President Cleveland was persuaded to have a federal court injunction issued against the strikers, ordering them to cease boycotting trains. They were obstructing the delivery of

Trusts. This contemporary cartoon sums up the problem as seen by the ordinary citizen.

the United States mails illegally. To enforce the injunction and to keep order, Cleveland ordered 2,000 federal troops into Chicago, despite the strong protest of Governor Altgeld of Illinois who said that local militia had not been called out because there was no need of troops. As soon as the federal troops appeared, the union lost control of its men, violence broke out, and the strike was suppressed. Eugene Debs and other union officials were found guilty in a federal court of violating the Sherman Anti-Trust Act because the strike was defined as a conspiracy by the union to interfere with interstate commerce. For the immediate present labor unions were seriously restrained by this interpretation of a strike and the Sherman Act, and not until the Clayton Act of 1914 could unions avoid the threat of strike injunctions.

4. The Agrarian Revolt

After the Civil War farmers suffered from falling prices for farm products, from surpluses created by new farm machinery, from high freight rates charged by railroads, and from a steady drop in their incomes. Other targets were the "middlemen" who handled grain and other produce from the farm to the market, the dealers, the storage agents, the brokers, and others. National banks were blamed for not giving easy loans on real estate, and the government was criticized for putting protective tariffs on foreign goods and forcing the farmer to buy higher-priced American goods.

The Grange

To protect their own interests, farmers joined together in an organization called the Patrons of Husbandry, better known as the Grange. It declared itself to be "non-political," and attempted to eliminate the middleman in the purchase of goods needed by farmers by setting up co-operatives. Members contributed funds to buy fertilizer, seeds, farm equipment and other items in wholesale lots, and then sell to themselves at cost. But poor business management and competition from efficient businesses drove out most of the co-operatives. Membership was about 500,000 in 1874 but declined rapidly, until by 1880 it was only 4,000.

The Greenback Movement

Farmers were attracted to the Greenback Movement which wanted more "greenbacks" or paper money printed, in the belief that more money in circulation would mean larger incomes. The demand for more money was a fairly constant one for fifty years after the Civil War, appearing under the banner of Greenbackers, the Free Silver men, and the Populist Party. A recurring problem in the United States was that of determining how much money was "enough." As a population grows and more goods are produced, more money must be put into circulation by the government. Money is a means of exchange, and it represents buying power. As farmers' incomes dropped so the demand for more money grew, although a period of prosperity would lessen the clamor of demand.

Another "soft" money or "easy" money group was the Free Silver movement, which wanted all the silver that was mined to be bought up by the government and made into money when the commercial price of silver dropped, as it did when the flood of silver from the Comstock Lode and other mines knocked the market price down. The Free Silver group was absorbed by the Populist Party whose political platform appealed to Greenbackers, discontented farmers, idealists of all stripes, among whom were Mary Ellen Lease, the Kansas suffragette who advised farmers to "raise less corn and more hell," and the man from Nebraska, William Jennings Bryan, who eventually took over the Populist Party and merged it with the Democrats.

The Populist Party

The Populist Party demanded a broad range of reforms: government ownership of railroads and telegraph lines; a graduated income tax; an 8-hour working day; the end of injunctions in labor disputes, as in the Pullman strike; the direct election of senators; the secret ballot, the initiative and the referendum; and a minimum of $50 per person in circulation. The Populist presidential candidate in 1892 was James B. Weaver, who scored 1,000,000 votes, or 9 percent of the popular vote, a remarkable showing for the first run by a third party.

Conditions worsened across the country in 1893; businesses closed down, unemployment rose, but the Democratic administration of Cleveland followed a traditional laissez-faire policy and made no attempt to alleviate distress. In 1894 thousands of discontented workers and farmers voted for Populist candidates in the Congressional elections. In 1894 the Democratic Party appeared to be in danger of breaking up as the Populists gained strength. Then the situation was saved by the appearance of William Jennings Bryan, already a congressman, and now a spokesman for the "Free Silver" supporters of the Populist Party, but a staunch Democrat. Bryan became the choice of Populists and Democrats for the presidency in 1896 but his program appealed less to the town worker and middle class than to the farmer, and his Republican opponent, William McKinley, won by 51 percent of the popular vote to Bryan's 47 percent.

5. The Progressive Movement

The Northern Securities Case

In September 1901 a young anarchist who said he believed in the assassination of all rulers, shot President McKinley, recently elected for his second term. Eight days later McKinley was dead, and Vice-President Theodore Roosevelt became president at the age of forty-two, the youngest man to hold that office up to that time.

His occupancy of the White House was a turning-point in American history. The profound change was almost abruptly introduced by government use of the Sherman Anti-Trust Act against the Northern Securities Company controlled by the bankers J. P. Morgan and Company, Kuhn, Loeb and Company, James J. Hill of the Great Northern Railroad, and Edward Harriman of the Union Pacific Railroad. This was a huge railroad holding company that had bought up a controlling number of shares of the major transcontinental railroads. Morgan and Hill were stunned by Roosevelt's "ungentlemanly" conduct of interfering in business, but despite their efforts to halt proceedings, the case went to the Supreme Court, which in 1904 ordered the railroad monopoly to be dissolved.

During Roosevelt's administration the government proceeded against 44 more corporations including the Beef Trust, the American Tobacco Company, and the Standard Oil Company.

The Anthracite Strike

The second incident which shocked business and shook the foundations of the laissez-faire belief of no government interference in business was Roosevelt's handling of the Anthracite strike of 1902. The United Mine Workers went on strike in May in support of demands for an 8-hour day, an increase in wages, and recognition of the union. Eight railroads which dominated the mining industry refused to negotiate or recognize the union as the bargaining agent for the miners, and the strike continued into the fall. Labor's willingness to negotiate, and the operators' attitude that "God in His Infinite Wisdom has given control of the property interests" to the directors of large corporations, gained public sympathy for the miners.

Roosevelt called the contesting parties to a conference at the White House, to the resentment of the coal operators at this implied recognition of the union by the government. Refusing to make any concessions, they demanded that the government issue an injunction and if necessary call upon the army to break the strike. Roosevelt let it be known that he would order the government to take over direction of the mines in order to get coal produced before winter set in. The mine owners gave in and accepted a compromise settlement suggested by an arbitration board which awarded a 10 percent increase in wages, reduced working hours, but not recognition of the union.

Roosevelt's purpose in intervening was to give both sides a "square deal," an attitude which typified his administration. He was the first president to bring labor and management to the White House to attempt the settlement of a dispute, to coerce a large industry, and to persuade two sides to accept the findings of a commission appointed by the president.

The Nature of the Progressive Movement

The programs of the two Progressive presidents, Roosevelt and Wilson, between 1905 and 1916 were successful because they had the support of civic-minded citizens, of a solid group of 6,000,000 middle-class voters, who were vitally concerned with the problems of monopolies, slums, corruption in large cities, the waste of tax money, the discriminatory practices of railroads, and the fear that unless remedial measures were taken organized labor might become too powerful and radical. Intellectual leaders, editors, college presidents, clergymen, and sincere business leaders supported the need for "progressive" change.

Millions of Americans lived in poverty in a land of enormous resources and great wealth; workers toiled in factories for sixty hours a week; thousands of railroad workers were killed at work every year; and over 2,000,000 children worked in factories. Wages were fixed by supply and demand, there was no pension system for workers, no assistance for the unemployed, no compensation for injury or death on the job. Progressives did not quarrel with industrialism but did insist that the worst aspects of poverty could be remedied. Their attitude was in part molded by a group of journalists and writers to whom Roosevelt gave the name "muckrakers," who exposed inexcusable conditions in society. Ida Tarbell showed the ruthlessness of Rockefeller in his *History of the Standard Oil Company*; Upton Sinclair exposed the incredibly bad conditions in the meat-packing industry in *The Jungle*; and Lincoln Steffens exposed city corruption in *The Shame of the Cities*.

Roosevelt won the presidential election of 1904 on a platform which made the Republicans the party of reform. He secured Congressional support to enact remedial legislation in several areas of national affairs. By the Hepburn Act the Interstate Commerce Commission was given effective power to regulate railroads in the public interest. A Pure Food and Drugs Act protected the consumer against dangerous products. He used his authority to conserve valuable forest lands and natural resources for the public use, instead of allowing them to be exploited by private interests for their own use.

Roosevelt's contribution to government was his firm belief that he was the steward or agent of the public and that he had the duty and the power to determine the nation's interests, and that its future should be in the hands of the government, not of private interest groups. Government had the duty and the authority under the Constitution to exercise that power.

Progressive Legislation of Wilson's Administration

In 1908 Theodore Roosevelt had supported the nomination of William Howard Taft as the Republican presidential candidate, and had himself gone off to Europe and Africa as a private citizen. Upon his return to the United States he decided that Taft had not lived up to his campaign promises and to the spirit of the Roosevelt administration. As a result, he announced that his hat was in the ring, but lost out to the Taft forces which controlled the convention. His followers bolted the convention and named him as the candidate of the Progressive Party, and Roosevelt, announcing himself to be "as strong as a Bull Moose," accepted the nomination, and split the Republican vote. As a result Woodrow Wilson, the Democratic candidate, won with 42 percent of the popular vote, with 6,293,000 against Roosevelt's 4,119,000, and Taft's 3,485,000. The Democrats carried both Houses of Congress also.

As president, Theodore Roosevelt had taken the position that the federal executive had the authority to use the Anti-Trust Law against obvious misuse of their power by monopolies. He did not believe in breaking up large corporations simply because of their size, but only if they exercised their size and power against the public interest.

Wilson believed that trusts had been given too free a hand, and that competition must be preserved by ever closer regulation of corporations and trusts. His Congress enacted the Clayton Anti-Trust Act in 1914 to place close controls on businesses, and to stop unfair practices through "cease and desist" orders. The Clayton Act was also hailed as the Magna Carta of labor because it stipulated that labor unions were not conspiracies or combinations under the terms of the Sherman Act, and could not be prevented from striking by the courts, as had been the case in the Pullman strike.

The Tariff and the Federal Reserve System. Two areas which had remained almost untouched since the Civil War were tariffs and banking. Wilson had criticized protective tariffs for reducing United States trade abroad, because nations whose goods were taxed by the United States usually retaliated with their own taxes on American goods. He reduced tariffs down to an average 27 percent, the first real change in tariff policy for fifty years.

Wilson believed that banks had been serving the interests of too few people, and that the general public had too little say in a business which was of tremendous concern to the entire nation. There had been too many financial crises in the past, and the President intended to remedy the situation. In 1913 Congress enacted legislation that set up a completely new addition to the normal banking system, the Federal Reserve System. The government had a great deal of control over the system, which provided a more "elastic" money supply to the country.

The Federal Reserve bank is a "banker's bank" because it can make loans available only to banks, not to private individuals. If, for example, manufactured products are not being sold in sufficient quantities to keep factories producing more, the Federal Reserve bank can lend money at a low rate of interest to local banks, which then can lend more to their customers. If people can borrow money easily and cheaply, they will do so, and buy more goods, and help to keep factories producing goods that consumers demand. Later, the borrowers will repay the bank, which will in turn repay the Federal Reserve bank. Thus the money is "elastic" and can be regulated to meet the nation's needs in times of depression and inflation.

Other Progressive Legislation. In several other ways Woodrow Wilson carried out his determination to serve the people's needs. By workmen's compensation legislation federal employees were paid when injured on the job. Interest rates on farm loans were lowered, and a special farm banking system was set up so that farmers could store their non-perishable crops in warehouses and receive a loan on them. This enabled farmers to store crops when there was such abundance available that farm prices dropped. When farm prices rose, the farmer could take his crop out of storage, sell it, and pay off the loan.

Reform measures commenced by Roosevelt and continued by Wilson justify the use of the term Progressive Period for the years of their administration.

6. The Emergence of the United States as a World Power

The expansion of the United States from a nation east of the Mississippi River to one which incorporated the American continent was evidence that the nation was not isolationist. The acquisition of Louisiana, Florida, Texas, the western lands of New Mexico, Utah, California, Oregon, and Alaska demanded negotiations with foreign powers. After the Civil War the nation withdrew from foreign affairs, an attitude sometimes incorrectly labeled isolationism, instead of withdrawal or non-intervention. Domestic problems and industrialization and the settling of the land west of the Mississippi became of major concern. The situation changed toward the end of the 19th century when the nation suddenly found itself a world power, at first more by accident of circumstance than by deliberate intention.

Cuba and the Philippines

The acquisition of the Philippine Islands during the Spanish-American War of 1898 forced the United States into the role of a world power with overseas interests to protect.

For most of the 19th century Cuba had been of great interest and of some concern to the United States because of its strategic position in the Caribbean. Britain had wanted it as "compensation" when the United States acquired Florida in 1819, and British and French naval maneuvers in the Caribbean in the 1820's disturbed the United States. On several occasions the United States unsuccessfully attempted to purchase Cuba from Spain. Repeated insurrections of Cuban natives against Spanish rule led the United States to fear that the island could some day be transferred by Spain to another power, or become the object of foreign acquisition. In 1895 a serious revolt broke out again, and the repressive measures of the Spanish troops won wide sympathy in the United States for the Cubans.

In April 1898 the United States officially declared war on Spain, claiming no intention of acquiring Cuba for itself. When the war was over a few months later, the United States found itself owning Cuba and the Philippines. Cuba was made a United States protectorate under the Platt Amendment which prohibited the government of Cuba from incurring a foreign debt that it could not repay, and from making any foreign treaty that restricted its own power or transferred land to a foreign power.

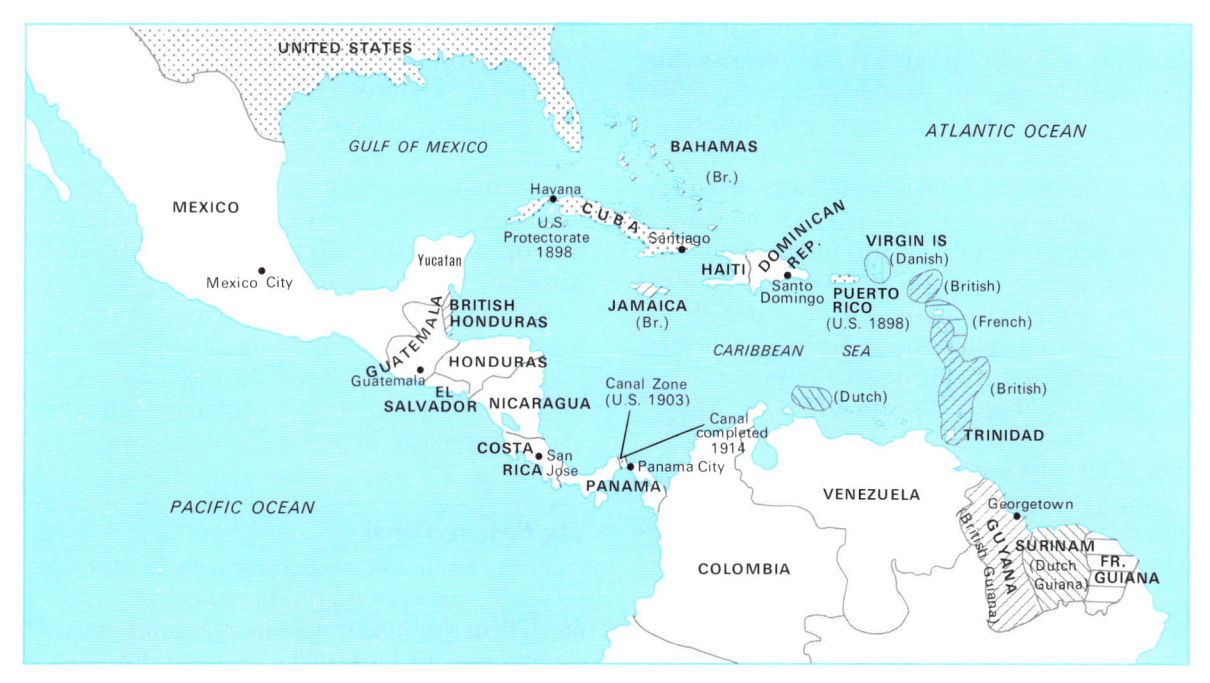

The United States and the Caribbean

The Open Door Policy

The Philippines presented the United States with a very different problem. Apart from the islands not being ready for self-government and being placed under United States control, they made the United States a world power, and a nation whose foreign policy could be affected by the actions of other nations.

The United States had for some time been aware of the increasing interference by foreign powers in China, because it had itself gained from China trade rights in several Chinese ports. Several nations had forced China to turn over to them "spheres of influence" and "concessions" over which China lost control. In 1895 Japan had forced China to give Korea its independence and to allow Japan to have special rights in the Liaotung Peninsula. When some European nations forced Japan to leave the Liaotung Peninsula, the Russians took it over for their own interests. Russia also had virtual control over Manchuria, and to the United States appeared to be a major threat in the Far East.

The United States sent official identical Notes to the Powers with concessions in China, suggesting that each one allow the others to trade freely in its sphere of influence, a policy that was later to be known as the Open Door Policy. A short time later the United States attempted to persuade those same nations to agree to respect China's territorial and political independence, and to take no more land from China.

When Japan declared war on Russia in 1904 and pushed that nation out of Manchuria, Japan began to appear as a serious threat, perhaps greater than Russia. President Theodore Roosevelt acted as mediator between the two nations, in order to maintain a balance of power in the Far East, and secured their consent to the Treaty of Portsmouth by which Japan secured rights in Manchuria, the Liaotung Peninsula, and the southern half of Russia's Sakhalin Island. Realistically, the United States recognized Japanese interests in the Far East by two agreements, the Taft-Katsura and the Root-Takahira, whereby Japan acknowledged the paramount interests of the United States in the Philippines and in the Pacific in return for recognition by the United States of Japan's paramount interests in Korea and Manchuria.

The Roosevelt Corollary

The attempt of several European nations to use force to collect debts from Venezuela in 1902 led President Theodore Roosevelt to add a corollary, or addition, to the Monroe Doctrine. Formerly, the Monroe Doctrine had warned European nations that the United States would not permit extension of their colonies in Latin America or interference in any independent nation in the western hemisphere. Roosevelt now warned Latin American nations that if they did anything that could cause European nations to intervene, such as failure to pay foreign debts, then the United States would herself intervene to correct the situation before foreign nations acted. Over the next decades the United States used this corollary to intervene in the Dominican Republic, Nicaragua, and Haiti.

The Panama Canal

Once the United States became a Far Eastern power it also became a two-ocean power and needed an isthmian canal through which fleets could move quickly into the Pacific and Atlantic Oceans. A French company had started to dig a canal some years earlier in Colombia but had gone bankrupt before completing it. The United States negotiated with the French to buy the incomplete canal, and with the government of Colombia to secure rights over a completed canal. When the Colombian government rejected the United States proposals, Roosevelt encouraged Colombia's province of Panama, where the canal diggings were located, to revolt and prevented Colombian forces from intervening.

    As a world power the United States was adopting a foreign policy that was based on her interests but conducting it realistically according to her ability to use pressure where she could, or make concessions where she had to.

Theodore Roosevelt and the Caribbean. This cartoon gives one view of U.S. foreign policy.

The First World War

When war broke out in Europe in 1914 President Woodrow Wilson declared United States

The Panama Canal. This view of the canal under construction gives an idea of the enormous size of the project.

neutrality and demanded that the belligerents recognize the rights of the United States as a neutral to trade in non-contraband goods anywhere it chose. This demand was technically correct but in practice unrealistic, because Britain had control of the seas and did not intend to allow Germany to get supplies, and Germany was equally determined to prevent supplies from reaching Britain. For the first time in history, entire nations were at war with each other, and therefore the term "contraband" would no longer distinguish between war goods and non-war goods. Food was needed for factory workers making munitions and other war supplies, and food was therefore included in contraband, as was anything which could help the war effort.

The United States protested to both nations at this interference with her traditional neutral rights, but nations that are fighting with their backs to the wall do not pay much attention to neutral claims. Britain and Germany took whatever steps they could to keep each other from getting supplies, but since Britain simply interfered with American trade, her injury to the United States was far less than that committed by Germany, whose submarines sank ships on sight and brought about the loss of American lives and ships.

Woodrow Wilson had been elected for his second term in 1916 on the slogan, "He kept us out of war," but by April 1917 German actions so threatened the interests and the security of the United States that Congress declared war on Germany. The United States had demonstrated that she was not an isolationist nation, and that when she considered that her interests and security were at stake she would intervene with force.

Review Questions

Sections 1 and 2
1. What factors changed the United States to a basically industrial nation after the Civil War?
2. What were the railroad abuses about which the farmers so bitterly complained? Were the farmers justified in their complaints?
3. In what ways was the Interstate Commerce Act intended to regulate railroads?
4. Why was the Sherman Anti-Trust Act passed by Congress? For what reasons were monopolies thought to be against the general public interests?
5. What argument did the United States Supreme Court use to claim that the E. C. Knight Company was not a monopoly, even though it actually was?

Section 3
6. Why was the American Federation of Labor more successful than the Knights of Labor at winning rights for labor?
7. How did the Pullman strike lead to a loss of rights for labor? Why was the injunction, as used in the strike, a serious threat to labor unions?

Section 4
8. What were the objectives of the Granger Movement? Why was it unsuccessful?
9. What were the demands of the "soft money" supporters? Were their demands reasonable?
10. Why did the Populist Party attract the "soft money" supporters?

Section 5
11. Why was the Northern Securities Case a turning point in American history?
12. How did Theodore Roosevelt handle the Anthracite strike differently from the method used by President Cleveland in the Pullman strike? Which was more statesmanlike? Why?
13. What were the Progressives attempting to accomplish? What reforms did Progressive President Theodore Roosevelt bring about?
14. What measures enacted during the Wilson administration were "progressive" in nature? In what way did each piece of legislation help the American people?

Section 6
15. Why did the Spanish-American War oblige the United States to become a world power?
16. What was the purpose of the Open Door Policy?
17. In what way did the Roosevelt Corollary change the original meaning of the Monroe Doctrine?

7

Background and Origins of World War I

The Rival Alliances

Tensions between the Alliances

Responsibility for the War?

No one nation in Europe brought about World War I, and no nation actually wanted a war. But by the end of the 19th century conditions in Europe were very different from the situation immediately after the Congress of Vienna. The Concert of Europe of Great Powers who could hope to keep the peace in Europe no longer existed. The Industrial Revolution had brought about competition among nations for raw materials and markets. Germany, a new nation which was unified only in 1870, was quickly becoming industrialized and beginning to threaten the interests of England, France, and Russia.

The desire for independence by ethnic groups in Europe, particularly in the Austro-Hungarian Empire, threatened Austria's safety and very existence, and encouraged Russia to continue her traditional policy of expanding westward into Europe and becoming influential in the Mediterranean.

Rivalry among nations for colonial possessions led to tensions among the Great Powers and to the creation of two alliances which became rivals. Nations believed that force could be used to gain their objectives, and no one nation could afford to stand idly by while its rival seemed ready to get an advantage.

And so Europe drifted closer to war, until an assassination in the little town of Sarajevo, in a remote corner of the Austro-Hungarian Empire, plunged European nations into a war which finally involved nations from every hemisphere.

Terms
1. Balance of Power
2. Dual Alliance
3. Triple Alliance
4. Dreikaiserbund
5. Re-Insurance Treaty
6. Dual Entente
7. Entente Cordiale
8. Triple Entente
9. Anglo-Russian Convention
10. Moroccan Crises
11. Bosnian Crisis
12. Balkan Crisis
13. Slavs
14. Balkan League
15. Haldane Mission
16. Sarajevo Incident
17. Trialism

People
18. Bismarck
19. Jean Marchand
20. Gavrilo Princep

Places
21. Nile River
22. Cairo
23. Khartoum
24. Fashoda
25. Congo River
26. Cape Colony
27. Natal
28. Transvaal
29. Orange Free State
30. Union of South Africa
31. Afghanistan – the Zones
32. Morocco
33. Fez
34. Agadir
35. Algeciras
36. Bosnia-Herzegovina
37. Sarajevo

Events

1873	Three Emperors' League
1882	The Triple Alliance
1887	Re-Insurance Treaty
1894	The Dual Entente
1898	The Fashoda Incident
1899–1902	The Boer War
1904	The Entente Cordiale
1907	The Triple Entente
1906, 1911	Moroccan Crises
1908	Annexation of Bosnia-Herzegovina by Austria
1914, June 28	Assassination of Archduke of Austria
July 28	Austria declares war on Serbia
July 31	Germany declares war on Russia
August 3	German declaration of war on France
August 4	Great Britain's declaration of war on Germany

1. The Rival Alliances

One of the basic causes of friction between European nations after 1871 was the growing hostility of France toward Germany. France had suffered a humiliating defeat in the Franco-Prussian War partly from her own weakness and partly because she was politically isolated and without powerful friends in Europe. Although she wanted to find allies as protection against continued isolation, she found herself thwarted by the clever maneuverings of Bismarck.

He intended to keep peace so that Germany could benefit from her recently-founded national unity, and become the leading industrial nation in Europe. He knew that France not only wanted revenge for the Franco-Prussian War but also that it feared Germany's growing power which was making her the greatest nation on the Continent. France could not count upon Great Britain as an ally because Britain was continuing her centuries-old policy of an island nation able to protect herself through the balance of power. She had long avoided any entangling alliance or positive commitment abroad, preferring to act only when one European power or group of powers threatened to become predominant on the Continent and so threaten her own safety.

The Dual Alliance, 1879; Germany and Austria-Hungary

Bismarck decided that a good countermeasure to any future threat from France would be an alliance with Austria-Hungary. And because Russian expansionist ambitions could very well threaten both Germany and Austria-Hungary, the two nations readily arranged the Dual Alliance in 1879, whereby (1) Germany assured Austria of her protection should Russia attack her, (2) each would assist the other in the event of a Russian attack, (3) if either were attacked by another power, the other would remain neutral. This was not an offensive alliance, and neither would be obliged to assist if the other was aggressive.

The Triple Alliance, 1882: Germany, Austria-Hungary, Italy

To push further his plans of isolating France, Bismarck cleverly played upon that nation's ambitions. He let her understand that Germany would not object if France annexed Tunisia and added it to her present Mediterranean colonial possession of Algeria. French annexation of Tunisia in 1881 so outraged Italy, who wanted to restore the former glory of Rome by acquiring it herself, that she asked to be allowed to join the Dual Alliance. Again, the terms were those of a defensive alliance: (1) Austria and Germany would support Italy if she were attacked without provocation by France, (2) Italy would support Austria or Germany only if either were attacked by two or more Great Powers, (3) Italy insisted that the Triple Alliance would in no instance operate against Great Britain.

One part of Bismarck's foreign policy had already failed. In 1873 he had arranged the Dreikaiserbund, or Three Emperors' League, between Germany, Austria, and Russia to protect their common interests. But this proved to be a distinctly uneasy partnership because Austria-Hungary and Russia had very opposing ambitions in the Balkans, where Russia hoped to gain increasing influence. By 1878 the Dreikaiserbund had fallen apart, and Bismarck then negotiated the Dual and Triple Alliances.

Although their terms were secret, France and Russia were aware that some kind of combination was being organized against them. Russia then approached Germany, and between them they arranged the three-year Re-Insurance Treaty of 1887, which in general terms provided that if either nation was involved in a war the other would remain neutral, unless Russia attacked Austria, or Germany attacked France. The unscrupulous clause was that Germany agreed to give diplomatic support to Russian ambitions in the Balkans, which was the very place where Austria feared Russian expansionist ambitions. Even the German Kaiser found this diplomacy extraordinary, and told Bismarck that he was like a juggler trying to keep five balls in the air.

The Dual Entente, 1894: France and Russia
In 1890 Bismarck was dismissed from his position as Chancellor by the young Emperor William II who objected to the major role that Bismarck had so long played in German politics. William wanted to be his own master, and in 1890 the "pilot" Bismarck was dropped. His successors may have been less astute than Bismarck, but times were rapidly changing, and Bismarck's policy of playing both ends against the middle — of supporting the contradictory policies of Austria and Russia — was becoming unworkable. The Re-Insurance Treaty lapsed in 1890, and France was ready to take advantage of the situation. In 1894 France and Russia signed a military convention in which (1) Russia agreed to go to war with Germany if France were attacked by Germany, or by Germany and Italy combined and (2) France agreed to support Russia if she were attacked by Germany or by Germany and Austria.

Since rival alliances were building up on the Continent, why did not England become involved? Germany was already her great trade rival, and if a war should break out between France and Germany, then England's interests would certainly be with France. The plain facts were that England and France were rivals in North Africa, and England and Russia were rivals in Afghanistan and Persia. Until their conflicting interests could be settled there could be no defensive alliance against their common rival, Germany.

Bismarck Dismissed. The famous *Punch* cartoon.

Africa: The Fashoda Incident, 1898
Unfortunately for France the search for colonies in Africa led to rivalry with England over a simple but potentially dangerous issue of whose flag should fly over a tiny fort in the Sudan, to the south of Egypt.

In 1882 England had occupied Egypt because its khedive or ruler could not repay a series of large loans advanced by British and French creditors. Opposition by Egypt to this intervention led to a British decision to land troops in order to protect British interests and the new Suez Canal, Britain's vital "life-line to India."

Britain then began to extend her influence up the Nile, whose water was so vital to the existence of Egypt, and in 1898 raised the British flag over Khartoum, more than a thousand miles south of Cairo. Meanwhile, the French had been building a large African empire from the Niger River eastward along the Congo River, and in 1896 ordered Captain Marchand to lead an expedition from the Congo to the upper Nile. In 1898, after hauling a disassembled steamship across hundreds of miles of Africa, he arrived at Fashoda, five hundred miles south of Khartoum, and raised the French flag. Within a few weeks Marchand was confronted with two thousand British troops and five gunboats under Lord Kitchener, who insisted on raising the Egyptian flag over the fort. Faced with overwhelming odds, Marchand consented to the flying of the Egyptian flag over an outlying part of the fort on the condition that the French flag continue to fly over the main fort.

Fortunately the popular British and French demands for war with each other were restrained by the foreign ministers. The French government was far more concerned over the growing power of Germany in Europe, and ordered the withdrawal of French troops from Fashoda, leaving the Nile-Congo watershed as the dividing line between British and French spheres of influence.

South Africa: The Boer War, 1899–1902

One of the first instances of tension between Germany and Great Britain was the proposal by Germany to England that the two nations should divide between them the large Portuguese colonies of Angola and Mozambique. But Britain preferred Portuguese ownership to German, because expanded German territories in Africa would interfere with British plans to control territory all the way from the Cape to Cairo. Germany did not forget the rebuff, and when

British Gunboats at Fashoda on the Nile

the British ran headlong into conflict with the Boer republics of the Transvaal and the Orange Free State, Germany seized upon the opportunity to twist the lion's tail by congratulating the Boer leader.

Germany's purpose in sending her telegram of congratulations was to warn Britain of the dangers of isolation, and to indicate the advantages of co-operating with the Triple Alliance. The incident only heightened Britain's suspicions of the Kaiser's intentions.

Germany's Naval Program
Germany had the best-equipped and the strongest army on the European continent, an army that was quite capable of defending her boundaries. Her naval-building program appeared to be, at least to Britain, a direct challenge to the British navy. A German navy that could defend Germany's coastline was understandable to Britain, and acceptable. But if that navy was planned to be second only to Britain's, the suspicion was growing that Germany was threatening the British navy, which had the task of defending the trade routes of a far-flung empire. Britain needed a multi-ocean navy, but Germany needed only a one-ocean navy for operations in the North Sea.

The German Naval Laws of 1897–1898 almost tripled German strength in battleships and cruisers, from a total of 16 to 45, a navy of the size to suggest operations beyond Europe. In 1900 further German naval expansion doubled the number of battleships planned in 1898. Britain, fearing a naval race, made repeated overtures for an agreement by both nations to limit naval construction. But the Kaiser brushed aside all proposals, and in 1904 Britain embarked upon her own naval-building program.

The Entente Cordiale, 1904: France and Great Britain
France was as concerned as Britain about Germany's naval-building program, and as a consequence those two nations decided that they would resolve whatever differences that still remained between them. They came to a cordial "understanding," the Entente Cordiale, by which France agreed to give up all claims to Egypt and recognize Britain's "historic rights" there, in return for Britain's recognition of French interests in Morocco. This was nothing more than a colonial settlement recognizing each other's rights in north Africa, and was certainly not a military alliance. It was not aimed at Germany, but it could pave the way for a possible alliance between the two nations if events proved the necessity.

The Triple Entente, 1907: France, Britain, Russia
Now that France and Britain, and France and Russia were on good terms, was it possible for the three to get together for reasons of common interests? The stumbling-block had been Anglo-Russian antagonism over China, Persia, and Afghanistan. Britain had feared Russian occupation of Manchuria, but the defeat of Russia in the Russo-Japanese War (*see* pages 101–2) had resolved that issue. In Central Asia, where Britain had gained a foot-hold in Afghanistan, Russia had expanded her Siberian frontiers to the border of Afghanistan, and threatened British interests — or so Britain thought. The businessmen of Britain and Russia had invested money in business ventures in Persia, and both nations wanted influence there.

They were able to come to an understanding in the Anglo-Russian Convention of 1907 by which (1) Russia agreed that Afghanistan was not within her sphere of influence, (2) Britain agreed to grant Russia trading rights in Afghanistan, (3) the two nations divided Persia into three zones, the northern exclusively Russian, the southern exclusively British, and the middle zone open to both nations. Russia and Britain agreed that no other nation should share in the exploitation of Persia. Once these sources of tension were removed, there was nothing to prevent France, Britain, and Russia from forming an "understanding" among the three, and that understanding became the Triple Entente.

So, by 1907 six nations were aligned in two groups of three each, the *military defensive* alliance of Germany, Austria, and Italy, and the *diplomatic understanding* of Great Britain, France, and Russia. Neither group could be regarded as designed for war.

2. Tensions between the Alliances

Once the Triple Entente was concluded, Germany professed to see danger to herself from encirclement deliberately organized to threaten her on both frontiers. But both alliances were defensive, and the causes of friction that precipitated World War I were much deeper. By 1907 two facts were certain. Germany was the greatest European Power, and the British Empire was the greatest World Power. Germany's political and military activities, coupled with her tremendous economic growth, were making her a rival to Great Britain.

Germany's Economic Power

Germany's industrial efficiency and development were also making her a great rival to Britain in shipping, insurance, banking, and in markets which had formerly been dominated by Britain. Her electrical industry became one of her valuable exports, she was the foremost producer of fertilizers, explosives, armaments, and dyes, and her magnificent network of railroads, planned fifty years earlier, opened up markets for her throughout most of Europe and into Turkey.

The Moroccan Crisis of 1906

Included in the settlement of the Fashoda Incident was Britain's recognition of France's interests in Morocco. Kaiser William objected to Germany's exclusion from economic opportunities there, and was persuaded by the German government to pay an unexpected visit. The situation in Morocco was that the Sultan had borrowed vast sums of money from the French but was unable to repay the loans. The French then requested that the Sultan agree to a French military force to keep order and a French-controlled bank to manage Morocco's finances.

The German Foreign Office decided that an official visit by the Kaiser to the Sultan might encourage the Sultan to regret French interference. The official visit had its amusing side as well as its serious one. The Kaiser's ship anchored off Tangier in a heavy sea with a stiff wind blowing. After a rough journey ashore in a small boat, the Kaiser was then presented by the Sultan's uncle with a high-spirited Arab horse for the ride to the palace. The streets were lined, as the Kaiser believed, with "Italian and South-French anarchists, swindlers, and adventurers," and the crowd added to the Kaiser's discomfiture and the general confusion by yelling loudly and shooting off guns in the air. A military band attempted to drown the noise of the crowd, but only succeeded in making the Kaiser's horse more excited. The official visit was brief, but the Kaiser's address to the Sultan's representative included these words to challenge the French position, "I am resolved to do all in my power

138 *Industrialism, Imperialism, and War*

The European Alliance System to 1914

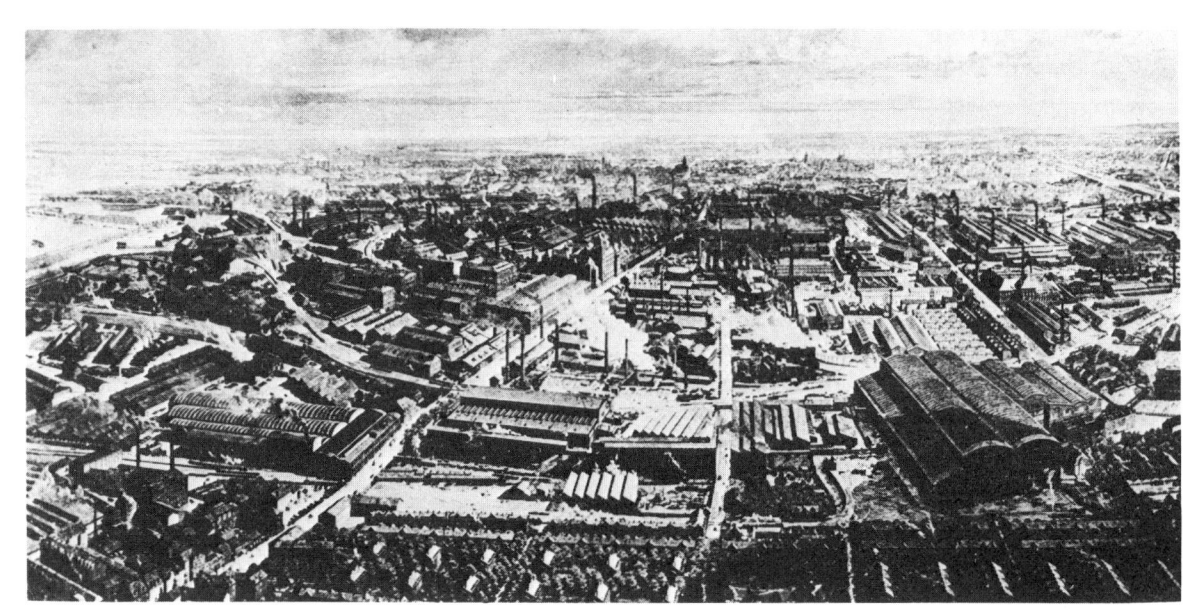

Krupp's Steel and Armament Works

properly to safeguard the interests of Germany, since I regard the Sultan as being an absolutely free sovereign."

As a consequence of the visit, the Sultan would not accept the French terms unless other European Powers agreed. Germany demanded an international conference and asked President Theodore Roosevelt to secure French participation. Roosevelt, fearing that the Moroccan crisis could precipitate a European war, was able to arrange a conference at Algeciras, Spain, and persuade Germany to accept the settlement which (1) stated that Morocco was independent, (2) guaranteed equal commercial opportunities for all nations, (3) set up an international bank to run Morocco's finances, (4) permitted France and Spain to train the Moroccan police force.

The Second Moroccan Crisis, 1911

The Algeciras settlement did not resolve the Moroccan problem because by 1911 the Sultan's debts were several times larger than they had been earlier. Disorder broke out and was put down by the French-controlled police force, and finally, on the grounds that foreign lives were in danger, the French sent in their own troops to occupy Fez, the capital city. Europe assumed that France intended to make a protectorate of Morocco. Germany protested and sent a gunboat to the Moroccan port of Agadir. War was almost certain unless either France or Germany backed down. Then Great Britain took an official and public stand, not only demanding that Germany withdraw her gunboat but announcing her intention to support France. Lloyd George, Chancellor of the Exchequer, speaking officially for the British government, said,

"I would make great sacrifices for peace.... But if ... peace could only be preserved by ... allowing Britain to be treated as if she were of no account in the council of nations, then I say emphatically that peace at that price would be a humiliation intolerable for a great country like ours to endure."

This diplomatic language meant quite clearly that Britain would support France if Germany should attack her. The incident intensified the dislike of French and Germans for each other.

The Bosnian Crisis of 1908 and Balkan Wars of 1912–1913

By 1878 Serbia, and to a limited degree Rumania and Bulgaria, had become independent nations after being for centuries a part of the Turkish Empire. Their example of freedom from foreign rule was of concern to the Austro-Hungarian Empire because half of its 50,000,000 people were Slavs, who were racially related to Serbia and to Russia, and who had very little share in the government. The Slavs consisted of Poles who wanted to join Russian and German Poland to form an independent nation; Czechs and Slovaks who wanted to form their own independent nation, which as Bohemia they had once been; Croats, Serbs, and Slovenes, who wanted to join independent Serbia and form a Greater Serbia nation.

The Austrian Emperor was naturally very much opposed to these ambitions because if satisfied they would mean the breakup of his empire. His particular concern was the independent nation of Serbia which wanted to annex the province of Bosnia-Herzegovina which the Congress of Berlin had in 1878 taken from Turkey and awarded to Austria to administer but not actually to annex. If Serbia could add this large province to herself she would double her size and acquire an outlet to the Adriatic Sea.

Serbia knew she could not do that alone, but she hoped that Russia would help her. And because Russia was now allied with France and Britain, Austria and her partners in the Triple Alliance believed that Serbia was being encouraged by the Triple Entente. So Austria decided to act before Serbia did. In 1908 she simply annexed Bosnia as part of the Austro-Hungarian Empire. Serbians reacted immediately by smashing the windows of the Austrian embassy in Belgrade, by publicly burning the Austrian flag, and by agitating for mobilization and war on Austria. Russia backed up Serbia; Germany announced that she would support Austria-Hungary, and although Great Britain and France protested the annexation, neither was willing to support Russia and Serbia.

Russia then tried other tactics. She helped to organize a Balkan League of Bulgaria, Serbia, Greece, and little Montenegro to attack Turkey and seize territory from her. In October 1912 the Balkan League attacked Turkey and took over almost all her European territory. When they attempted to divide the spoils Serbia quarreled with Bulgaria, which was then in turn attacked by her recent allies and Turkey. Fortunately, no Great Powers entered the fight, and the local Balkan crisis died down. But tensions were reaching the breaking-point elsewhere.

The Haldane Mission, 1912

As a consequence of the several European crises there was a general hope that relations between Germany and England could be improved. Britain wanted a slow-down in the expensive naval race, and after several overtures to Germany, sent a mission to Berlin under the leadership of Lord Haldane, who spoke fluent German and was minister of war. The Germans offered to drop a new naval-building program provided Britain would agree to remain neutral if war broke out. This Britain could not do without seeming to betray her commitments to her Triple Entente partners. The Kaiser missed an opportunity because had Germany been

German Militarism. A parade in 1913.

prepared to make an official agreement with Britain, then the Entente would almost certainly have collapsed, and Germany's fear of "encirclement" would have been groundless.

In answer to the German request for British neutrality, Haldane would only promise that England would "make no unprovoked attack upon Germany." This offer the Kaiser brushed aside as worthless. Who, he asked, would decide what "unprovoked attack" was?

The failure of the Haldane Mission led to what was in effect a military alliance between France and England. France was to concentrate her naval forces in the Mediterranean and look after British interests there, while Britain was to concentrate her navy in the North Sea and protect the northern and Atlantic coasts of France.

The Sarajevo Crisis, June 1914

Francis Ferdinand, Archduke of Austria-Hungary, was heir to the throne and a man of ability and intelligence who believed that the problem of the Slavs in the Empire could be solved by giving them the same kind of rights that the Hungarians enjoyed. He favored Trialism or a Triple Monarchy of three kingdoms of Austria, Hungary, and a Slav state. Independent Serbia bitterly opposed this because if the Slavs within the Austrian Empire were satisfied with their position they would see no reason to join an independent but poverty-stricken Serbia.

In June 1914 the Austrian Archduke and his wife journeyed to Bosnia to review two Austrian army corps stationed there. Part of the ceremonies included an official courtesy visit to Sarajevo, the capital city of the region. On Sunday morning, June 28, as the official cavalcade of cars drove down the main street to city hall a man stepped from the crowd and threw a bomb which landed on top of the Archduke's car, rolled off in front of the next car and exploded. Several wounded occupants of that car were

Assassination of Archduke Ferdinand. June 28, 1914.

rushed to hospital while the official party calmly went on with the scheduled program. After the ceremonies at the city hall the Archduke decided to visit the wounded in the hospital. His chauffeur began to follow the route originally planned, and had to stop and turn the car up a side street. At this precise corner another assassin, Gavrilo Princep, stepped forward, pulled out a revolver, and shot the Archduke and his wife.

3. Responsibility for the War?

The Austrian Ultimatum to Serbia

While definite proof was not available, there was a very strong suspicion that Serbian government officials and army officers belonging to the terrorist anti-Austrian organization called the Black Hand Society had planned and executed the assassination program. The murder provided Austria with the opportunity she wanted to eliminate Serbia as a political power, because Austria feared that Serbian propaganda and agitation were a threat to the existence of the Austro-Hungarian Empire. Austria had reason for her fears because Serbia was the center of a Pan-Slav movement demanding that all Slavs in the Austrian Empire be united and become independent. Serbia wanted to become a Greater Serbia of all these Slavs, and for the first expansion of her boundaries she wanted the Austrian province of Bosnia-Herzogovina, which Austria had incorporated into her Empire in 1908, and thus for the moment had blocked the Yugoslav, or Southern Slav, movement.

Believing that Austria would use the assassination as a pretext for war, Serbia maintained the officially correct position of condemning the outrage and sending her condolences to the Austrian government, but made no effort to restrain violent newspaper attacks on Austria. Without German support, Austria felt that she was unable to wage war against Serbia because she believed that Russia might very well come to Serbia's aid. The Kaiser allowed himself to be convinced that Germany's interests were vitally concerned, and virtually gave Austria a "blank check" to go ahead, and promised to stand by her. The Kaiser's basic error was in not realizing that there was a vast difference between permitting Austria to punish Serbia and encouraging her to make war on Serbia.

The Kaiser left for his annual Norwegian cruise aboard his yacht on July 6, and Austria started to draw up her ultimatum to Serbia. At 5 o'clock on the afternoon of Thursday 23rd July the Austrian ultimatum was delivered to the Serbian government, with the demand that a reply be returned by 5 p.m. on Saturday 25th July. The Serbians, who were busy with an election campaign, were astounded to receive the ultimatum. The long silence of nearly one month had apparently lulled them into a false sense of security. They had only 48 hours in which to reply to a document which Austria had taken nearly a month to work out and deliver.

That same day, July 25, Serbia sent her reply to the ultimatum. M. Pasic delivered it himself a few minutes before 6 o'clock at the Austrian legation. But the Austrian minister and his staff were on the train and on their way to the frontier by 6:30 p.m.

The basic terms of the Austrian ultimatum were (1) Serbia must condemn all anti-Austrian propaganda, and officially disavow annexation of any Yugoslav territories of the Dual Monarchy, (2) all anti-Austrian publications must be suppressed, and all anti-Austrian teachers and materials be removed from Serbian schools, (3) all military and civil officials designated by Austria as "guilty of propaganda against the

Monarchy" be removed, (4) Austrian officials must participate in suppressing any subversive Serbian movement and in investigating the assassination plot, and in trying persons involved in the plot.

The Serbian Reply

Serbia denied the government's responsibility for actions committed by private persons but did offer to hand over to Austria any Serbian whose complicity in the plot was proved, promised to censor anti-Austrian articles, and to remove anti-Austrian teachers and teaching materials. It refused, however, to permit Austrian officials to participate in the investigation, since this would be intervention in Serbia's independence. The government concluded its reply by announcing that if Austria was not satisfied with Serbia's answer then she was ready to refer the dispute either to the International Court at the Hague or to European powers.

This attitude was favorably received in Europe, and even the Kaiser changed his earlier charge that "Serbia is nothing but a band of robbers that must be seized for its crimes" to praise for Serbia, saying, "Every reason for war drops away." Firm pressure by Germany on Austria could probably have prevented hostilities, had it not been for a series of blunders that followed.

Blunders by the Powers

The first blunder was perhaps that of France. On July 20, three days before the Austrian ultimatum was delivered to Serbia, French President Poincaré and Prime Minister Viviani were in Russia on a three-day official visit. Poincaré publicly stated, "Russia has an Ally, France," a statement that looked very much like a blank check handed to Russia to write her own ticket.

A second blunder occurred on July 24, the day after the delivery of Austria's ultimatum, when the German government publicly announced its support of Austria-Hungary's charges. The situation to one British official looked as though the Great Powers were supposed to stand by while Austria slowly strangled Serbia. The blunder was that Germany seemed to assume that Russia would not intervene, despite the statement several days earlier by Sazonov, the Russian foreign minister, that Russia "would not be indifferent to any effort to humiliate Serbia." In diplomatic language "not to be indifferent" indicated intention to take action.

A third blunder was Russia's. On July 25 the Czar ordered partial mobilization of the Russian army, and announced that mobilization was not directed against Germany but was simply a means of exerting pressure on Austria.

That same day, July 25, the deadline for Serbia's reply to the ultimatum, the Austrian diplomatic corps left Belgrade in the evening less than two hours after a deadline which gave the Serbians 48 hours to answer a lengthy ultimatum that seriously endangered Serbia's independence. Such a hasty departure by the entire diplomatic corps was deliberate.

So, on July 25 the situation was that Austria-Hungary was determined to punish Serbia, Germany was ready to back her ally, and Russia was ready to back up Serbia. The British foreign minister, Sir Edward Grey, appeared not to wish to restrain Russia or France, and refused to state publicly that the Triple Entente would present a united front. Did Germany believe that Great Britain would remain neutral, whatever happened on the Continent?

A fourth blunder was the Austrian minister's refusal to consider peace proposals from other nations, and his declaration of war on Serbia on Tuesday, July 28, even though Serbia had accepted almost all of Austria's impossible demands. Other European Powers were sure that Germany was behind the plot. Their reasoning was simple. Austria's rejection of Serbia's conciliatory reply proved that she wanted to extend her influence in the Balkans. And she would not dare to act in this manner without the backing of Germany.

The next blunder was the Czar's agreement to general and full mobilization. He well understood the accepted belief of general staffs, "Mobilization means war." The nation which mobilized first had an advantage over nations which had not begun to do so, because it could then invade across a neighbor's frontier.

At 8 o'clock on the evening of July 30 the Czar gave the order for general mobilization, but then canceled it before midnight. The Russian foreign minister met next day with the Czar, who was now aware of the awful responsibility of bringing on a war, and finally persuaded the Czar to give the order for full mobilization.

Sazonov immediately telephoned the Chief of the General Staff, gave him the news and added, "Now you can smash the telephone. Give your orders, General, and then—disappear for the rest of the day." The Chief of the General Staff could then not be reached if the Czar again changed his mind.

On the afternoon of July 31 Germany sent Russia a telegram stating that unless Russia stopped mobilizing by 12 noon on August 1 Germany would declare war. When no reply had come from Russia by 5 o'clock Germany declared war on Russia.

The Alliance System Begins to Operate

Germany understood that France would help Russia, and had long ago planned that if ever she was engaged in a two-front war with France and Russia, she must attack France first because France could mobilize faster than Russia.

On July 31 Germany asked France what action she would take if war broke out between Germany and Russia. On August 1 France replied that she would consult her own interests, and immediately began to mobilize. On August 3 Germany declared war on France. What action would Great Britain take? On July 31 she had asked France and Germany whether they would respect Belgium's neutrality if they should go to war. France said she would, but Germany refused to answer. She had already decided that it would be much easier to advance through Belgium than to attack the forts on the French eastern frontier.

On August 2 Germany occupied Luxembourg and then demanded that German troops be allowed to go through Belgium. The Belgian king refused, so on August 4 German troops crossed the frontier into Belgium.

Great Britain was immediately greatly concerned because if Germany occupied Belgium this action would be directly opposed to her balance of power policy. She sent an ultimatum to Germany insisting upon respect for Belgium's neutrality. Germany replied that "necessity knew no laws," and accused Great Britain of making war "just for a scrap of paper"—the guarantee of neutrality that Great Britain and other powers had given Belgium in 1839.

That same day, August 4, Great Britain declared war on Germany.

None of the Great Powers wanted a European war because they all knew that it would be a dreadful struggle. None could foresee the final tragic consequences that led to the fall of four empires, the German, the Austro-Hungarian, the Russian, and the Turkish, but all realized the possible economic consequences to Europe.

And yet each nation thought that a war might give it what it wanted. Germany wanted economic advantages and the role of the greatest nation on the Continent. France wanted to recover Alsace-Lorraine and weaken the Triple Alliance. Great Britain wanted to destroy the menace of Germany's military and naval might. Russia hoped to get Constantinople and the Dardanelles. Austria-Hungary thought she could prevent the breakup of her Empire by crushing Serbia. And Serbia wanted to unite all Serbians within the Austro-Hungarian Empire into a Greater Serbia.

All the Great Powers were to a certain degree responsible because no one of them used all its capabilities to prevent the war, and the rival alliances believed that each was stronger than the other and could come out victorious.

Review Questions

Section 1
1. Explain the reasons for the Triple Alliance and state its terms. Was it a defensive or an offensive alliance? Why?
2. The Dual Entente was formed in 1894, but Great Britain did not join it until 1907. Explain the reasons for this delay by Britain.

Section 2
3. In what ways did Germany seem to threaten the interests of England and France during the first fourteen years of the 20th century?
4. Why should the Balkan Crises be of any concern of the Great Powers?
5. Was the death of the Archduke of Austria of any importance to Russia, or Germany, or France?

Section 3
6. Did any one nation, more than another, seem to be responsible for the war?
7. Why was each of the major powers finally willing to go to war? What was each afraid of? What did each hope to gain from the war?

8

World War I

German Preparations for War
The Germans Halted
Stalemate on the Western Front
The United States Enters the War
Peace Proposals and the Armistice

World War I was a watershed of European civilization, a "great divide," that separated the accepted traditions, 19th century diplomacy, and the relative peace of a hundred years from the vastly changed conditions after 1918. Three empires, the Austrian, Russian and German, collapsed as a result of the war; revolutionary Russia introduced the dynamic force of conspiratorial Communism into world politics; and nations believed that they must find some alternative to war as a solution to international rivalries.

In many countries, but particularly in France, the tragic loss of a generation of young men was reflected in later years in ineffectual governments that suffered from the absence of young, vigorous leadership. The success of revolutionary leadership in Russia brought to European politics a new diplomacy of deliberate disruption rather than the old diplomacy of negotiation and accommodation.

The avowed support by wartime allies of the principle of democracy inspired a growing feeling of nationalism among colonial and subject people that foreshadowed later demands for independence.

Terms
1. Schlieffen Plan
2. Salient
3. Zimmerman Note
4. Four Principles of Peace
5. Fourteen Points

People
6. General von Moltke
7. General Joffre
8. Paul von Hindenburg
9. Erich von Ludendorff
10. Winston Churchill
11. Aristide Briand
12. Woodrow Wilson

Places
13. Marne River
14. Antwerp
15. Calais
16. Boulogne
17. Tannenberg
18. The Dardanelles
19. Gallipoli
20. Verdun
21. Somme River
22. Jutland
23. Hindenburg Line
24. Caporetto

Events

1914 August	Declaration of war by Germany on Russia	
September	Battle of the Marne	
1915 April	Dardanelles campaign	
1916 February	Verdun offensive	
May	Battle of Jutland	
June	Somme offensive	
1917 February	German unrestricted submarine campaign starts	
March	Abdication of Czar Nicholas II	
April	United States declaration of war on Germany	
October	Bolshevik Revolution in Russia	
1918 January	The Fourteen Points proposed by Wilson	
March	Treaty of Brest-Litovsk: Russia and Germany	
November	The Armistice and end of World War I	

1. German Preparations for War

General Strategy

When hostilities broke out on August 1, 1914, with Germany's declaration of war on Russia, the advantages all seemed to lie with Germany. She had the best-trained and best-equipped army on the Continent; her general staff and officer corps were outstanding; her military supplies, particularly machine-guns and artillery, were without equal. Her navy was modern in ships, armor, and weaponry, and her small submarine fleet was a serious potential threat to Britain's overseas supply routes. Germany's geographical and industrial position gave her interior lines of communication based on a superb railway system that had been laid out under the supervision of the German general staff. In preparation for war Germany had stockpiled large supplies of raw materials.

The Allied nations had greater human and long-term industrial and financial resources, and had also the vital advantage of control of the seas to blockade the Central Powers of Germany, Austria-Hungary and their allies. Germany's advantages depended upon a short, swift war, while Allied advantages could only prove themselves over a longer period of time.

The Schlieffen Plan

Germany knew that once she attacked France she would have to attack France's ally, Russia, also, but she expected to be able to avoid a two-front war because Russia would be slow to mobilize. Germany had long planned her strategy of a rapid advance to take Paris and knock France out of the war, while she simply held off Russia.

The Schlieffen Plan had been developed by General Schlieffen in the late 19th century for

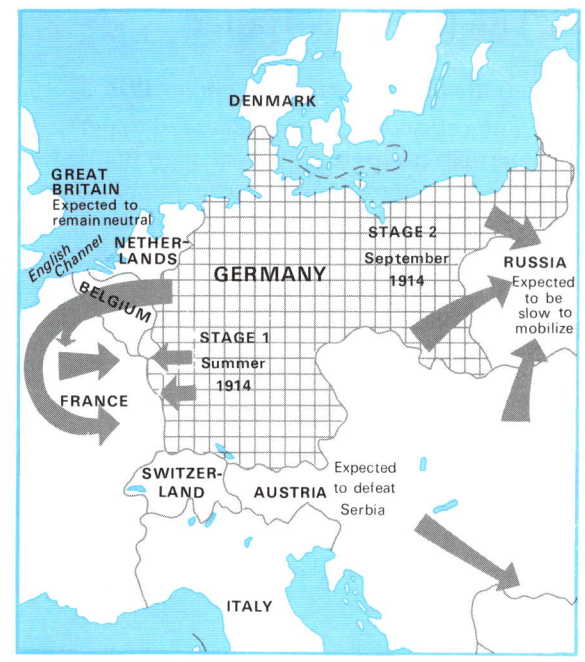

Schlieffen Plan

the conquest of France by the use of railroads to converge hundreds of thousands of troops on a small area or spread them over a large area.

A large German army would sweep through Belgium and northern France, swing around to the west of Paris, and then turn east and force the French army against the Alsace-Lorraine frontier where another German army would be waiting. The French, caught between two forces, would have no choice but to capitulate, and France would be out of the war before she could receive any help. Then the main German forces would be transported across Germany by rail to join the small force holding back the Russian army on Germany's eastern front. In a few weeks Russia would be defeated, and the war would be over.

2. The Germans Halted

The Battle of the Marne, September 1914

Belgium refused Germany's demand to permit German troops to march through her territory, and on August 4 Germany invaded across the Belgian frontier. The small Belgian army could do little more than delay German troops for a few days. The resistance of the Belgian forts at Liège and Namur gave French General Joffre time to shift his main forces northward and delay the Germans until British troops could be landed on the French north coast. The Belgians retreated to Antwerp where they were a threat to the German army's right flank and its supplies. This obliged the German General von Moltke to divert eleven divisions to take Antwerp and thus weaken the forward drive of the Schlieffen Plan.

World War I, 1914

On Germany's eastern front the Russians had mobilized faster than had been expected and obliged the German commander to ask for assistance. Four more divisions were diverted from the French front, further weakening von Moltke's army. Even so, the Germans advanced so rapidly toward Paris that they became exhausted and their supply lines broke down. The French and British troops fell back one hundred miles and took a stand on the Marne River, only fifteen miles from Paris. The fall of that capital appeared to be so imminent that on September 2 the French government fled to Bordeaux.

General Gallieni, charged with the defense of Paris, relieved the pressure by gathering together his army and rushing it in taxicabs to the Marne. For five days in early September the French, reinforced by troops from the Italian border, fought a series of engagements that forced the Germans to retreat to the Aisne River, where they "dug in" behind barbed wire and trench defenses that were to be typical of the next four years of fighting.

Six weeks after the war commenced the Germans had failed in their objective, and the war turned into a stalemate. The Battle of the Marne was one of the decisive battles of history because it forced the Germans into a two-front war and denied them their needed early decisive victory in the west.

Immediately, the English Channel ports became the target of both sides. The Allies wanted to take Antwerp as their northern base, while the Germans wanted to strike northwest to the mouth of the Somme River, then secure control of all the seaports between Antwerp and the Somme River. The Allies lost most of the Belgian coast but retained the vital ports of Dunkirk, Calais, and Boulogne. German successes gave her most of Belgium, and the important area of northern France that provided her with 40 percent of her iron ore, 70 percent of

The Machine Gun. This weapon was the main cause of the trench system.

her coal, and 80 percent of her iron and steel manufacturing. The war then took on two significant aspects. The opposing armies dug in for a long war on a 600-mile front from the North Sea to the Swiss border, and Britain was now obliged to import vast quantities of materials from overseas for her own use and for France.

The Russian Front

Russia had mobilized faster than Germany expected and planned first to crush Austria-Hungary and then concentrate her forces against Germany. But France's urgent plea for a second front against Germany to relieve the threat to Paris persuaded Russia to attack Germany. In mid-August the Russian armies invaded East Prussia and threatened its capital, Königsberg. This Russian advance caused the diversion of four divisions from von Moltke's forces in France, and brought out of retirement German General Paul von Hindenburg who had been a life-long student of problems of

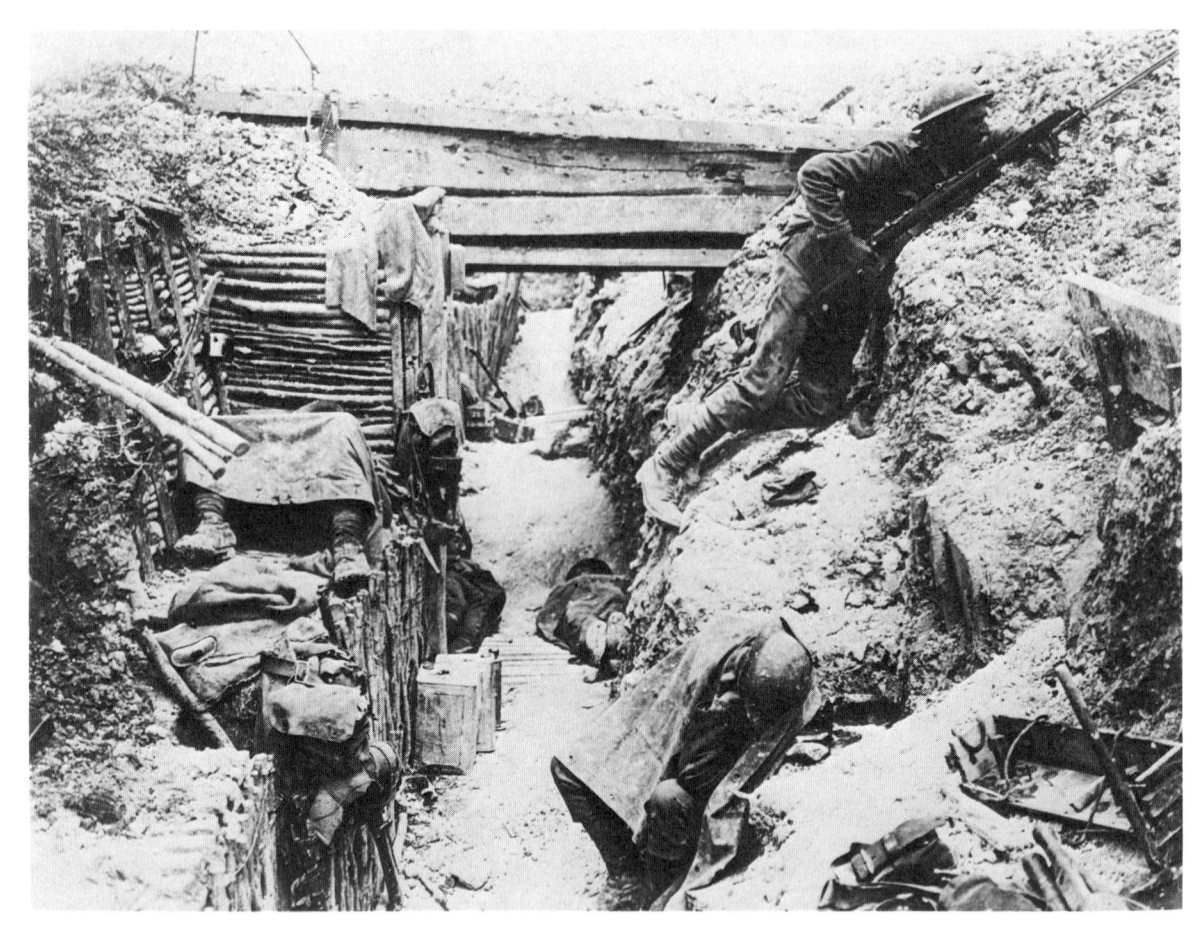

A Trench. During the winter and spring these were often filled waist-high in water.

campaigning in East Prussia. With him came Erich von Ludendorff, who had distinguished himself at the siege of Liège and was now appointed Hindenburg's Chief of Staff. These two men were soon to dominate German military campaigns and became from then on the virtual masters of Germany at war. In late August 1914, at the Battle of Tannenberg, the Russians were badly defeated in another decisive battle of the war. More than two-thirds of that Russian army was destroyed or captured, together with vast quantities of guns and munitions. Defeated though the Russians were, their attack on the Germans probably saved France from defeat in the fall of 1914.

The War at Sea

Britain's task of bringing supplies from overseas was threatened by German surface raiders and submarines. The immediate threat from

World War I   153

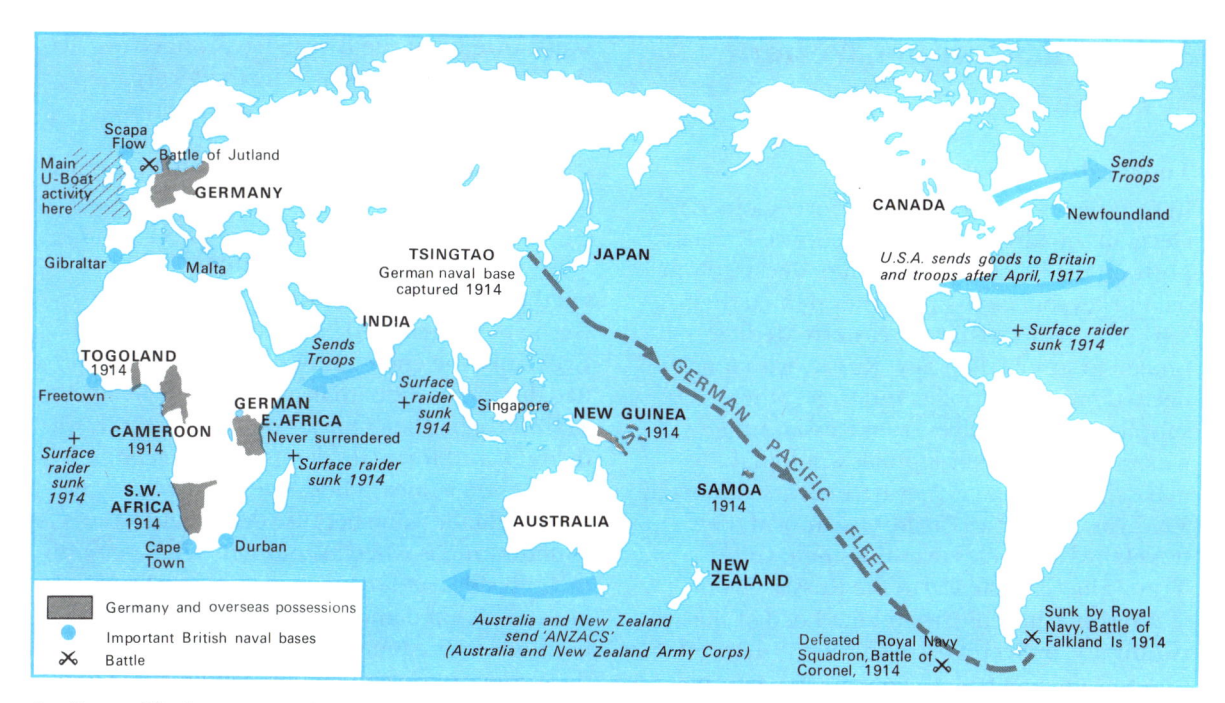

Sea Power. The importance of a navy to protect colonial interests is shown here.

The Russian Surrender at Tannenburg

the German navy was its Far East squadron, which had been forced out of its China base of Tsingtao when Japan declared war on Germany on August 23, 1914. Japan came into the war because she saw the opportunity to take numerous German merchant ships in Far East waters, and because she planned to demand as her share of the spoils at the end of the war all German concessions in China and German islands in the Pacific. The commander of the German squadron, Admiral von Spee, was joined by other German warships, and set out with his five cruisers to attack Allied shipping.

Off the Chilean coast he destroyed a small British squadron sent out to hunt him down, but in turn von Spee and four of his cruisers were sunk off the Falkland Islands in the South Atlantic. During the last weeks of 1914 most of the German surface raiders were sunk or captured.

3. Stalemate on the Western Front

The Dardanelles Operation

In October 1914 Turkish naval forces joined a German squadron and shelled several Russian ports on the Black Sea. The Allies declared war on Turkey, but by so doing they denied themselves the ability to use the eastern Mediterranean to supply their ally, Russia, with much-needed military supplies and to get wheat supplies for themselves from Russia. In the winter months Allied supplies would have to make the long sea journey to the Russian port of Vladivostock on the Pacific Ocean, and then travel the 7,000 miles over the single-track Trans-Siberian Railway to the Russian front.

Winston Churchill, then First Lord of the Admiralty, or Secretary of the Navy, decided that Britain's control of the seas gave her the opportunity to attack the Dardanelles. The capture of Constantinople would take Turkey out of the war, open up the Black Sea for supplies to Russia, relieve the pressure on the Balkan ally, Serbia, and threaten Germany from another flank. The Dardanelles plan was well conceived but ineffectively carried out. The British navy gave grudging and insufficient support, and the French generals refused to divert sufficient troops to make the operation decisive. They were fearful of a German breakthrough in France if forces were diverted from the western front.

The navy reduced the outer forts, sailed in to attack the inner defenses but lost ships in a minefield and called off the action. Churchill sent in at Gallipoli British troops and the Anzacs, the Australian and New Zealand Army Corps, to take the Turkish forts by land. The operation was finally abandoned in January 1916, at a cost of 55,000 men. Turkish records found after the war showed that the British naval attack was at the very brink of success. The forts were in ruins, were desperately short of munitions, and the Sultan of Turkey was ready to leave Constantinople before it fell to the British naval forces.

Verdun: Symbol of French Honor

On the western front both the Allies and the Germans determined to force a breakthrough. Ever since the end of 1914 the opposing armies had done little more than attempt limited attacks against each other's lines. Sometimes they broke through and formed salients, or projections, in the enemy lines. These salients were usually of no military value because they could be surrounded and isolated by the enemy, but generals on both sides had to prove some sort of success, however limited and valueless. Commanders on both sides were men of limited perception, dependent upon conventional military tactics, unwilling to experiment with new weapons, and in general were not willing to work with industrialists and inventors. They still thought of war in terms of sheer numbers of men armed with a rifle and bayonet. The objective of each side appeared to be that of killing off large numbers of the enemy, regardless of the cost to one's own troops. As a result, the two offensives of 1916 were contests in sheer numbers of troops.

The Germans decided to attack the famous fortress of Verdun, intending to bleed France white and force her out of the war. On February 21, 1916, they opened the offensive with an artillery preparation of several hundred thousand shells from 1,400 guns during the first twelve hours. French officers knew that Verdun was of very little military value and that its defense would be of no military significance. It formed an awkward salient that extended the French line unnecessarily. But Aristide Briand, the French Prime Minister, fell into the German trap and insisted that French national honor was at stake.

In defense of the slogan, "They shall not pass!" the French poured seventy-eight divisions into incredible slaughter in four months. The German general, Falkenhayn, had intended to slaughter the French army with German artillery, but the German Crown Prince, heir to the throne, eager for a brilliant victory to bolster the prestige of the Imperial throne, ruthlessly sent hundreds of thousands of men to their destruction against the determined French.

By early July, when the fighting died out, the Germans had captured 130 square miles of territory around Verdun, but had not taken the fortress. The campaign cost the French nearly 350,000 casualties, and the Germans 300,000 killed and wounded, an appalling daily average of more than 4,500 men. The defense of Verdun inspired the French nation to resist Germany, but it shattered the morale of the French army, which was on the brink of mutiny before the fighting ended there. General Pétain, who had entered the war as a colonel, became a Marshal of France later, largely because of his reputation as the defender of Verdun.

The Somme Campaign

While the French were fighting at Verdun, the British were building up preparations for an offensive on the Somme River, where Sir Douglas Haig, British commander, believed that the war could be won, an opinion shared by very few of his subordinates. Numerous preliminary raids by British troops led the Germans to strengthen their fortifications. Consequently, when the British opened the offensive in June 1916, they had to attack crests of hills heavily protected with barbed wire behind which the German troops waited in dug-outs forty feet deep and secure from artillery bombardment.

The offensive opened with five days of bombardment from British guns on an 18-mile front, which did nothing but churn up the ground so

World War I, 1915

Night Attack by Artillery

badly that infantry could not advance in traditional orderly fashion. On July 1, thirteen British divisions advanced across No Man's Land between the trenches, in the face of heavy machine-gun fire. By the end of the day nothing had been gained, and the British had lost 20,000 killed and 40,000 wounded.

Month after month the senseless attacks were continued. By mid-November the British front-line had advanced no more than five miles, but in those six months of fighting over 1,000,000 men were killed or wounded. The British and Germans lost over 400,000 each, and the French 200,000.

Verdun and the Somme revealed the stupidity of generals and the incredible waste of manpower.

The War at Sea: British Blockade v. German Submarines

Britain's main weapon was the blockade of Germany by sea. Under international law the blockade of war materials was permitted, but Britain's blockade of non-contraband, or non-war materials, raised a great outcry from neutral nations as well as from Germany. Quite arbitrarily Britain enforced a blockade system on foods and all supplies which could assist the war effort of even the enemy civilian population.

Britain restricted such neutral nations as Holland and Sweden to importing only their normal peace-time supplies. She could operate this system by setting up check-points along the English coast, and by denying coal to ships of nations that attempted to evade the blockade. She could do this in an age of steam because she controlled most of the coaling stations across the world. The United States protested against this interference with her right to trade in non-contraband with neutral nations, but Britain, fighting with her back to the wall, was in no mood to listen to complaints of neutrals.

The problem for Germany was how to break the blockade and impose a counter-blockade on Britain, now the depot of supplies for herself and her allies. The usual means were mines and surface raiders, now implemented by the new submarine which, by international law, was supposed to permit a ship's crew to get off in lifeboats before their ship was torpedoed. When Britain ordered their merchant ships to ram submarines, and hid guns on innocent-looking merchant ships, German submarines had no choice but to sink ships on sight. Germany soon found herself much more bitterly criticized than Britain. The British blockade simply interfered with neutral property, but the German submarine campaign killed neutral civilians.

The sinking of the British liner *Lusitania*, in May 1915, with the loss of nearly 1,200 civilians, including more than 100 American passengers, led to vigorous protests by President Woodrow Wilson. Further sinkings brought more protests from America, until in September 1916 Germany announced the suspension of unlimited submarine warfare against merchantmen.

The War at Sea: The Battle of Jutland

In May 1916 the one naval battle of the war in European waters, off the western coast of Denmark, was fought indecisively between a total of 250 British and German warships. German Admiral Scheer hoped to entice the stronger British fleet into individual actions that would wear it down. But Admiral Jellicoe, commanding the British navy, perhaps remembered the fate of the Russian fleet at Tsushima Straits in the Russo-Japanese war. He did not intend to lose the British fleet, and perhaps the war, in one afternoon. The smaller but newer German navy had superior armor and firepower, and inflicted greater casualties on the British, who lost 14 ships to the German 9. The important result of that naval battle was

Germany's decision to build a large submarine fleet and once again use unrestricted submarine warfare. This could prove to be the decisive weapon, because the Western Allies were now almost entirely dependent upon supplies from overseas.

4. The United States Enters the War

The year 1917 opened with conditions little changed from those of 1916. But 1917, seen in retrospect, proved to be a fateful year. The Russian Czar abdicated in March, and the Lenin-inspired Bolshevik Revolution started in October. In the west the United States joined the Allied cause in mid-year.

In December 1916 Lloyd George became British Prime Minister and immediately marshalled all the nation's resources for the war effort. Labor was virtually conscripted for work in munitions factories, food production was closely supervised, and shipping was placed under government control.

On the western front the Germans were dug in behind their newly-fortified Hindenburg Line, fifty miles back from the Somme battlefield. They had left that area completely deserted, with all railroad lines destroyed, wells poisoned, and mines liberally planted throughout the region.

Unrestricted Submarine Campaign

Germany now made a fateful decision. On January 31, 1917, she announced that as of February she would renew unrestricted submarine warfare on all vessels in a zone around the British Isles and in the Mediterranean. Germany's decision to do this was a calculated gamble. Up to this time Germany had been sinking about 75,000 tons of shipping every week. She calculated that if her submarines could sink 150,000 tons a week for six months, or a total or some 3,750,000 tons, they would reduce Britain's shipping to the point of collapse before any assistance could come. Germany was almost certain that the United States would enter the war on the Allied side, but because of its state of unpreparedness it would not be able to affect the outcome of the war before the fateful six months were up and the Allies forced out of the war.

President Wilson was aghast when he heard the news, for he realized that the United States would probably be forced into the war. He immediately broke off diplomatic relations with Germany because it sank American vessels on sight. Germany then committed the act which precipitated the United States into the war. Zimmerman, the German Foreign Secretary, wrote to the German Ambassador in Mexico to suggest to Mexico that if the United States did declare war on Germany, then Germany would help Mexico to recover all the territory it had lost to the United States in the Mexican War of 1846. The scheme was hare-brained. Germany could obviously not help Mexico, and that country had no intention of fighting the United States. But the incident made magnificent propaganda and outraged American public opinion.

On April 6, 1917, the United States declared war on Germany by a vote of 82 to 6 in the Senate, and 373 to 50 in the House. Since the United States was obviously in no danger from German attack, her intervention had to be justified on other grounds. President Wilson declared that the mission of the United States was to make this a "war to end all wars," a "war to make the world safe for democracy." This was a sincere belief, because the United States did not enter the war with any intention of seeking conquests or rewards.

Although the United States declared that the Germans were the sole aggressors it remained an Associated Power and was never officially a member of the Allied Powers. The United States did not enter the war, however, as a completely disinterested nation. By early 1917 it had made large loans to the Allies and was selling vast quantities of raw materials and food to the Allies. Unrestricted submarine warfare could interfere with the great trade boom being enjoyed in the United States. Defeat of the Allies would result in loss of loans made to them.

Germany's estimate of America's assistance was generally correct. She had limitless resources, but for the future. She had a great navy, but a small army; she had to conscript, train, and equip millions of men; and she had very few and inadequate munitions factories.

The German gamble of unrestricted submarine warfare almost paid off. In the single month of April German submarines sank 1,000,000 tons of Allied and neutral shipping. American and neutral sailors refused to sail for England. The British navy admitted that it could offer no solution to the problem. Suggestions that merchant ships be gathered together in port and then convoyed across the Atlantic by destroyers were flatly rejected as completely unworkable.

Finally Prime Minister Lloyd George ordered the British navy to adopt the convoy system without further argument. The British admirals found that it worked so well that earlier losses of 1 out of every 4 ships not convoyed now dropped to 1 out of every 100 ships convoyed. By the end of 1917 the United States and Great Britain were building ships faster than Germany could sink them, and were sinking German submarines faster than they could be replaced.

The Western Front, 1917

Once again the generals decided to try again what had so disastrously failed before. The British opened an offensive around Arras that was at first successful and then settled down into dreadful trench warfare that brought no results but casualties of 150,000 to the British and 100,000 to the Germans. This was only a preliminary to the main attack by the French under General Nivelle who believed, and convinced others, that he had the secret for success. His campaign resulted only in widespread mutiny in the French army. Nivelle had promised a 6-mile advance the first day. That evening the French troops had managed to advance 600 yards in the face of withering machine-gun fire.

For two weeks more Nivelle persisted in frontal attacks, without any success. Before the mutiny was over, 54 divisions refused to obey orders, over 100,000 soldiers were court-martialed, and 55 of them officially shot. How many were shot without sentence or deliberately obliterated by their own artillery is not generally known. The mutiny was officially called "undiscipline" by the French.

U.S. Gunners, 1918

The Eastern Front

Conditions on the Russian front and in Russian cities became increasingly worse during the winter months of 1916 and 1917. The soldiers were so badly armed that the majority of them had to wait until a companion was killed or wounded before they could get a rifle. At home the government was unable to supply the cities with adequate food and fuel during the bitter cold months, and was severely criticized for incompetence and corruption. The Czar was asked to abdicate by his own generals, who believed that only his abdication could save the monarchy in Russia. Nicholas was expected to abdicate in favor of his young son, around whom all the nation would probably rally. Somebody had to be the scapegoat, and Czar Nicholas was that person. But he realized that abdication would almost certainly mean exile and that he would be parted from his son, who suffered from an incurable blood disease. The Czar therefore passed over his son and appointed his own brother the Grand Duke Michael to be Czar. The Grand Duke refused the crown until the people should have the opportunity to vote on the issue. The country was now without a head of state, and the armed forces had no one to whom they should be loyal.

In St. Petersburg a provisional or temporary government under Prince Lvov was set up but it failed to understand that the nation was tired of war. Prince Lvov was replaced by Alexander Kerensky as head of the provisional government, who continued the error. His June and July offensives against Austria-Hungary and Germany were shattered by a German counter-

World War I, 1916–18. These two maps show the influence on the war made by the internal changes in Russia.

offensive. Russian troops simply walked off the battle lines and started for home. Kerensky wanted to make a separate peace with Germany but hesitated in the face of opposition from the French and British, who feared that German troops would be transferred from the Russian to the French front.

Lenin, the Russian revolutionary, was allowed by Germany to start home from exile in Switzerland through Germany in a sealed train. Germany expected him to lead a radical revolution and take Russia out of the war. Before Christmas 1917 a truce was signed between Russia and Germany, and in March 1918 the two nations signed the Treaty of Brest-Litovsk which ended the war between them (*see* Volume IV, Chapter 2, for the course of the Russian Revolution).

The Italian Front

Italy came into the war on the Allied side in May 1915, claiming that she was no longer bound by the Triple Alliance because Germany had been the aggressor. Italy joined the Allies, partly because she estimated that they would win the war, and partly because she was promised several territories that she wanted. For two years between May 1915 and late 1917 Italy fought eleven battles in an unsuccessful attempt to cross the Isonzo River which barred her way to Istria, one of the desired territories that she wanted. In October 1917 Germans and Austrians inflicted a crushing defeat on the Italians at the battle of Caporetto, in which Italy lost 200,000 men in battle and 400,000 as deserters. The British and French sent 11 divisions to bolster up the Italians, who rallied just north of Venice and finally forced the enemy to retreat.

The War beyond Europe

Apart from the disastrous Gallipoli campaign, the Allies were engaged in a number of small campaigns around the fringes of the Ottoman Empire. The British were heavily dependent for oil upon a British concession in Mesopotamia, between the Tigris and Euphrates Rivers. They decided to occupy this Turkish province.

The Suez Canal was of such strategic value to the Allies that they sent forces to protect it; from Egypt they invaded Turkish Syria, which included Palestine, and finally captured Damascus.

In Africa the Allies occupied all the German colonies and brought to an end the German Empire on that continent.

5. Peace Proposals and the Armistice

By the spring of 1918 Germany realized that her submarine campaign had failed to keep supplies from Britain, and that her airship and airplane raids on civilian populations had not interfered with production or morale.

The Final German Offensive

Ludendorff launched the last German offensive, expecting to suffer large casualties but hoping for a decisive victory. In March three armies advanced on a 50-mile front in the area around Arras and St. Quentin to drive a wedge between the British and French forces. At first the Germans had important successes, and by May they had reached several of their advanced positions of 1914. Then the tide began to turn against them. Between April and July the Americans sent in more than 675,000 men to plug holes in the Allied lines at Soissons, St. Mihiel, and Château-Thierry; by October almost one-fifth of the battle front was manned by United States troops. On August 8 the Allies began to force the Germans back, a day which Ludendorff called the "black day of the German army." The initiative had now passed to the Allies, and by the middle of August Ludendorff admitted that the war would have to end by negotiation and not with a German victory. The German government astutely asked President Wilson for an armistice, or cessation of hostilities, based on his Fourteen Points.

The Four Principles of Peace

In January 1918 Woodrow Wilson had delivered to Congress an address in which he proposed the general principles of a "just peace" to end the war. A lasting peace, he said, could not be one of victors and vanquished, because such a peace could only lead to a desire for revenge and to more war. A just peace must be based upon Four Principles: (1) every section of the peace settlement must be just and fair, for such a settlement would be most likely to bring about permanent peace, (2) racial and colonial groups must not be used as pawns by other nations, (3) every boundary settlement must be based upon the wishes of the people in the area, (4) and wherever possible, racial groups should be allowed to decide how they wished to be governed, and by whom.

The Fourteen Points

The Fourteen Points enunciated by Wilson contained those four principles and also what he regarded as basic causes of war. If these causes could be removed, then the need for war would be removed also. The Fourteen Points can be divided into four main categories: the Causes of War; the Restoration of Conquered and Occupied Territories; Self-Determination; and an International Organization for Peace.

The five Points under the heading of Causes of War were: I. Open diplomacy, without secret treaties between nations; II. Freedom of the seas. No blockades or interference with neutral rights; III. Reduction of tariffs among nations; IV. Disarmament; V. The settlement of colonial claims should take into consideration the wishes of the colonial people. These Five Points were idealistic, scarcely practicable because each nation had its own attitudes toward each of these topics. The second grouping of Points under Restoration of Territories were: VI. Russian territory was to be evacuated; VII, VIII, XI. Belgium, France, Rumania, Serbia and Montenegro were to be evacuated. Under the issue of Self-Determination much of the map of Europe was altered. Points IX, X, XII, XIII concerned racial groups in Austria-Hungary, Turkey, and Polish areas, and encouraged them to ask for independence or at least "home rule" to run their own internal affairs as autonomous, or self-governing groups; Italy's northern

World War I, Allied Victory. This map and the others in this chapter show that at no time did fighting take place on German soil.

boundary was to influence Italian-speaking people not now under Italy. Point XIV was the capstone to the other Points. This was to be the League of Nations which was expected to be able to resolve all disputes peacefully.

The Armistice, November 11, 1918

On October 4, 1918, the German government addressed a Note to President Wilson, not to General Foch, the Commander-in-Chief, requesting an armistice. By agreeing to accept Wilson's Fourteen Points, the German government cleverly suggested that Germany was idealistic in its peace aims. Wilson, who wanted the United States to play a major role as the architect of future world peace, replied directly to the German government without consulting the Allies, stating that Germany must evacuate all occupied territory before he could enter into armistice negotiations. The German government could rightly assume that this was the basic condition of peace, and that Germany would suffer no other punitive measures.

The Allies resented Wilson's failure to consult them because they were afraid that they would be cheated out of the victory to which they felt entitled. Out of the wrangle came Allied agreement to an *armistice* based upon the Fourteen Points, because this would end the fighting and force Germany back to her own frontiers. The actual *peace* negotiations would come later, and Clemenceau of France and Lloyd George of Britain expected to bargain to their own advantage. Wilson thought that he could make peace on the more idealistic terms of the Fourteen Points. He was to be sadly disillusioned.

Inside Germany conditions rapidly deteriorated. Sailors revolted at their Kiel naval base, soldiers mutinied, and the German people made very clear their lack of confidence in the Kaiser and his advisors. The German General Staff very cleverly avoided responsibility for defeat by persuading the Kaiser to flee to exile in Holland on November 8. The next day Prince Max of Baden, the last Chancellor of the short-lived German Empire, announced the abdication of the Kaiser, and turned over the task of government to the leaders of the powerful Socialist Democratic Party.

On November 11 the Germans accepted and signed the terms of the armistice, which required Germany to (1) withdraw her forces from all occupied territory and also from her own territory on the "left bank" or west of the Rhine River, (2) allow the Allies to occupy the three important Rhine River bridgehead towns of Cologne, Coblenz, and Mainz, (3) surrender all her submarines, most of her surface vessels, and large quantities of guns, airplanes, and railroad equipment.

The war was ended, but the problems of keeping the future peace had only just begun.

In 1914 the three nations, Great Britain, France, and Russia, controlled over three-quarters of the Earth's surface, and three nations, Great Britain, France, and Germany, controlled more than half the world's industry and international trade.

In 1914 each of the belligerents set out to defend its particular interests. Before the war ended it was no longer one for particular prizes such as raw materials, markets, or strategic bases but had become a crusade by the Allies to defend democracy against autocracy, a war "to make the world safe for democracy."

World War I was the first "total" war in history, involving civilian populations and the vast resources of the fighting nations. It marked the turning-point of the 20th century, for much of the history of the modern world hinges upon the events and the results of those four fateful years.

Three empires disappeared between 1914 and 1918, and a fourth a few years later. The Russian, Austrian, and German Empires collapsed by the end of 1918, and in 1923 the Sultan of Turkey was deposed. Europe emerged from the war devastated, economically and physically exhausted, with no one the victor.

The losses in killed and wounded were staggering, particularly until the last year of the war, when the deadly war of barbed wire and trenches, whose so-called defenses were almost useless against high explosive shells, was replaced by a war of movement. The new tactics were used by the French; no longer did they leap out of trenches and surge across No Man's Land, but went out in small groups, each with a machine-gun, and approached the enemy from several sides. The Americans used these tactics when they went into combat, and as a consequence their losses were relatively much lighter than the British and French losses in the earlier years of the war.

Over 1,390,000 United States soldiers, marines, and sailors saw active combat service; 49,000 were killed in action or died from wounds; 230,000 more were wounded, and 57,000 died from disease, particularly from the influenza-

The Aftermath. One of the war cemeteries in France.

pneumonia epidemic that swept through American camps.

Losses of other combatants were so terrible that in the World War II years of 1939 to 1945 prime minister Churchill and many of his generals who remembered the horrors of the earlier war resolved that never again should British troops go through such an Armageddon except for national survival. In some battles a single day's casualties rose as high as 60,000 on the Allied side. The French estimated that between August 31, 1914 and February 28, 1917[7] one Frenchman was killed every minute, more than 1,300,000.

Bare statistics cannot convey the horrors of war, but they can give some indication of the costs in lives and suffering:

65,000,000	persons directly involved
9,000,000	killed and died of wounds
22,000,000	wounded
5,000,000	"missing" in action—many simply blown to bits
9,000,000	civilians died of starvation, epidemics, massacres
30,000,000	dead, twice the losses of all the wars of the 19th century.

The dollar costs were almost beyond comprehension, particularly since the buying power of money was over four times its present value:

Allied Powers $126,000,000,000 (1919 value)
Central Powers $60,000,000,000

By 1918 over $10,000,000 was being spent every hour.

Dr. Nicholas Murray Butler, former president of Columbia University, estimated that the total costs of all belligerents was the stupendous sum of $400,000,000,000 in property. He estimated that this amount of money would have built in 1920 an average house, costing then $2,500, with $1000 of furniture on 5 acres of land worth $100 an acre, for every family for the 1920 population of the United States, Canada, Australia, the United Kingdom, France, Belgium, Germany, and Russia, and for each country a $5,000,000 library and a $10,000,000 university, would have endowed salaries for 125,000 teachers and 125,000 nurses—and then could have bought up Belgium and France.

In 1919 men were determined that this must be the "war to end all wars," and that nations must work together in some kind of international organization for future peace.

Review Questions

Sections 1 and 2
1. Although the German armies advanced rapidly through Belgium and France, the Schlieffen Plan broke down. Why?

Section 3
2. What were the objectives of the Dardanelles campaign?
3. Georges Clemenceau of France once said that war was too serious to be left to generals. Would this be a fair comment on the Verdun and Somme campaigns?
4. Why did the United States complain more strongly about German than about British interference with her shipping?

Section 4
5. What actions by Germany caused the United States to declare war on Germany in 1917?
6. Why did Italy join the war on the side of the Allies in 1915, and why did Russia end the war with Germany in early 1918?

Section 5
7. In what ways were the Four Principles of Peace expected to bring about a "just peace"?
8. Of Wilson's Fourteen Points, which of the topics under Causes of War do you think were possibly acceptable to the Allies, and which ones most probably unacceptable?
9. How does an armistice differ from peace negotiations? Did the armistice terms give the Allies any bargaining power when the time came to discuss peace terms?

9

The Search for Peace through Collective Security

The Paris Peace Conference

Terms of the Versailles Treaty and Other Treaties

German Acceptance of the Treaty of Versailles

Evaluation of the Treaty of Versailles

The League of Nations

Collective Security v. The Alliance System

The tragic loss of military and civilian lives, the devastation of northern France and Belgium, and the enormous financial costs of the war lent force to Woodrow Wilson's insistence that this must be "the war to end all wars." Because the alliance system had helped to precipitate the war, people and governments were ready to try out a new method of international relations, the theory of collective action for collective security.

If nations agreed collectively to take immediate action against an aggressor, or potential aggressor, wherever aggression occurred and whether or not they were actually involved, then the aggressor could be quickly subdued. But nations were by no means willing to put aside their own immediate interests for the general common interest, and they were not ready to put into actual operation the theory that any attack, upon any nation, anywhere, was a threat to the long-run security of all nations, because nations were not willing to surrender some independence of decision and action.

Disarmament failed because without an international guarantee of assistance in the event of attack nations had to be ready to defend themselves. International guarantees of assistance were not undertaken because nations were unwilling to commit themselves to responsibility for others.

Terms

1. Mandate
2. Treaty of Versailles
3. Treaty of Sèvres
4. Self-determination
5. Reparations
6. "Honor" Clauses
7. Weimar Republic
8. Polish Corridor
9. Collective Security
10. League Assembly
11. League Council
12. World Court
13. Articles X, XVI of the League Charter
14. Five Power Pact
15. Nine Power Pact
16. Little Entente
17. Locarno Agreements
18. Kellogg–Briand Pact
19. Geneva Protocol
20. London Naval Conference
21. Maginot Line
22. Treaty of Mutual Assistance

People

23. Woodrow Wilson
24. Lloyd George
25. Georges Clemenceau
26. Vittorio Orlando
27. Stanley Baldwin

Places

28. Alsace-Lorraine
29. The Saar
30. Left Bank of the Rhine
31. Poland
32. Danzig
33. Czechoslovakia
34. Yugoslavia
35. Rumania
36. Austria

Events

1919 January	Beginning of Paris Peace Conference	1925	Locarno Agreements
June	Treaty of Versailles signed	1927	Geneva Naval Conference
1921	Peace signed between the United States and Germany	1928	Kellogg–Briand Pact
	Washington Conference	1930	London Naval Conference

1. The Paris Peace Conference

Wilson's Role as Peacemaker

Even before the United States entered the war in April 1917, President Wilson assumed the role of champion of a peace that would eliminate war as a national policy. If the *causes* of war could be eliminated, said Wilson, then war itself could serve no useful purpose. The Fourteen Points called for the end of colonialism and imperialism, the right of self-determination by ethnic groups, easy access to raw materials for all nations, and a policy of no punishment for the defeated nations. If all disputes could be brought before an international body, they could be discussed calmly and solved peaceably.

As the architect of these proposals, Wilson believed that he must attend the Peace Conference in person, and that as spokesman for an international organization he must have the nation's support. He asked the country to return a Democratic Congress in the mid-term elections of November 1918 as an indication of such national support. The country returned a Republican majority to both Houses of Congress, and the result occasioned the prophetic but unwise remark from former President Theodore Roosevelt, "our Allies and our enemies...should all understand that Mr. Wilson has no authority to speak for the American people at this time."

President Wilson announced his intention of attending the Peace Conference in person, despite the advice of political associates that he should remain at home away from the day-to-day details and pressures of the Paris negotiations. It was his task, they advised, to give cool judgment to all the proposals that would come out of the Conference, and this could not be done in the excited atmosphere of Paris. Wilson ignored the advice and delayed his departure only until he had delivered his State of the Union message to Congress in December.

Versailles 1919. Lloyd George of Britain, Orlando of Italy, Clemenceau of France, and Wilson.

He made what many observers considered to be his great political error by taking with him a peace delegation from the United States that included only one Republican, and that an almost unknown person. Leading Republicans denounced this as a deliberate move to give all credit for the peace settlement to the Democratic Party. This failure to appoint prominent Republicans was a surprisingly inept move by the President because he well knew that all treaties must be ratified by a two-thirds vote of the Senate, which now had 49 Republicans and 47 Democrats. Had prominent Republicans been members of the delegation they would later in Congress have supported their decisions at the Peace Conference, and the peace delegation would have been bi-partisan, not simply Democratic.

The Big Four

Paris was Wilson's choice as the site of the Peace Conference, and was an unfortunate one because the French had little sympathy with

Wilson's idealism, and they showed no hesitation in publicly criticizing whatever they opposed. Of the thirty-two nations which had fought against the Central Powers and were now gathered in Paris, only five were expected to make the basic decisions. The Council of Ten consisted of two delegates from the five nations of the United States, Great Britain, France, Italy, and Japan.

Soon, however, the major decisions were made by the Big Four consisting of President Wilson of the United States, Prime Minister Lloyd George of Great Britain, Prime Minister Georges Clemenceau of France, and Prime Minister Orlando of Italy. Wilson's three associates in the Big Four each had personal demands to make on behalf of their countries. Great Britain had had no election since 1910, and Lloyd George wanted the support of his country before he went to the Peace Conference. His election campaign was based upon such slogans as "Hang the Kaiser!" and "squeeze the German lemon until the pips squeak," meaning that Germany should be made to pay the entire costs of the war, a sentiment that flatly contradicted Wilson's sentiments.

Conflicting Interests of the Big Four

Although the four nations had been allies during the war, their interests were decidedly different. Clemenceau cared nothing for idealism and world collaboration. His concern was only for France, a nation which had twice been invaded by Germans, in 1870 and 1914. He had little use for either Wilson or his Fourteen Points. "Ten Commandments were good enough for God," he said, "but Wilson has to have fourteen." His aims were simple and direct. French soil and industries had been ravaged by German troops, while German soil and industries were untouched. He wanted revenge and peace with victory. Germany should be made to pay with huge reparations, the confiscation of her industrial wealth, and the loss of the Rhineland region. He prophesied another invasion of France within twenty-five years unless Germany was crushed. His prophesy was to prove only too true.

Lloyd George wanted to preserve Britain's traditional balance of power position, in which no nation could dominate the continent of Europe. Although he favored defeating Germany, he also wanted to prevent France from becoming too powerful in Europe at the expense of Germany, for that would upset the balance of power. He expected to dismember the German colonial empire and to eliminate Germany as a naval and trade rival of Great Britain.

Vittorio Orlando came to the Peace Conference to get the strategic areas of the Tyrol and South Trentino on her northern border, and the peninsula of Istria with its important port of Trieste.

Woodrow Wilson came to the Conference to insist upon "peace *without* victory," but above all to bring about the establishment of the League of Nations. So determined was he to set up this organization that he allowed himself to compromise on others of the Fourteen Points.

2. Terms of the Versailles Treaty and Other Treaties

The Boundaries of Germany

The Allies agreed without argument that Alsace-Lorraine, which Germany had taken from France in 1871, must be restored to France. A controversial issue was the nearby Saar region, a coal-rich area of 750 square miles around the town of Saarbrucken. This had been historically German territory except for the years 1792 to 1815, when France occupied it. France was given

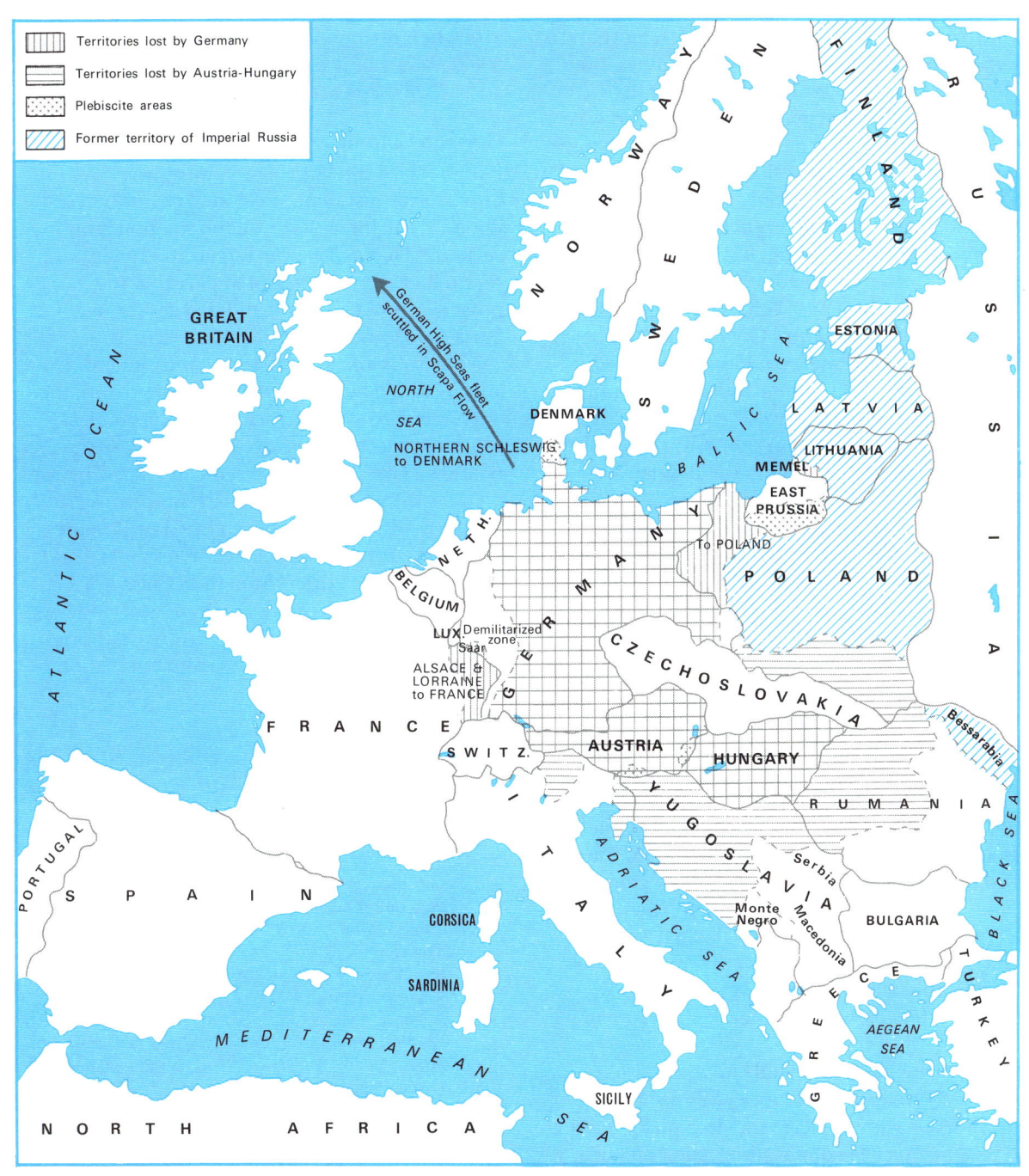

The Search for Peace through Collective Security 171

Europe after Treaty of Versailles

control of the Saar coal mines for fifteen years as payment for damages to French mines, but the actual territory of the Saar technically remained under German sovereignty and was to be administered under the League of Nations. The population of some 600,000, mostly Germans, would be allowed at the end of 15 years to vote to become French or German, or remain under the League of Nations. In 1935 they voted to be reunited with Germany.

France asked for the "left bank" of the Rhine, but the United States and Great Britain opposed it. The best that France could get was Allied military occupation of that area and a 30-mile strip east of the Rhine for 15 years.

Three little pieces of territory, Eupen, Malmédy, and Moresnet, on the Belgian–German border went to Belgium.

On Germany's eastern frontier the controversial issue was Poland, which had disappeared as a nation between 1772 and 1795, when Austria, Prussia, and Russia had, in three consecutive bites each, dismembered it. Briefly it reappeared as the Grand Duchy of Warsaw during Napoleon's era. The Paris Peace Conference decided to set up an independent Poland as a buffer against Bolshevist Russia. Those sections of Germany inhabited by Poles or by a mixture of Poles and Germans were given to Poland as the "corridor" along the Vistula River to the Baltic Sea. This cut off East Prussia from the rest of Germany and became a highly emotional political issue for each successive German government. The port city of Danzig, an old German town with a majority of Germans, was "internationalized" under the League of Nations and belonged neither to Germany nor Poland.

A future source of trouble was a disputed Polish–German area of Upper Silesia at the southeast corner of Germany. In a plebiscite the Germans won 844 communities, the Poles 675, and when the boundary division was settled, 350,000 Germans were transferred to Poland, and 570,000 Poles to Germany.

German Colonies and Turkish Provinces

Number 4 of the Fourteen Points stated "an impartial adjustment of colonial claims based upon . . . the interests of the populations concerned." During the war England, France, and Japan had secretly agreed to partition the possessions of Germany and Turkey, and at Paris they found a face-saving device.

These territories were to become "mandates" administered by a "mandatory" power until they were ready for self-government. For political convenience they were divided into Classes A, B, and C. Class A mandates, mostly non-Turkish peoples within the old Ottoman Empire, were almost ready to rule themselves. Class B mandates were former German colonies in Africa, needing greater supervision than Class A. Class C mandates were assigned to mandatory powers as integral parts of their own empires, although they were answerable to the League of Nations for their administration.*

---

*Mandates

	Mandate	Mandatory Power
Class A	Syria	France
	Lebanon	France
	Palestine, Transjordan, Iraq	Great Britain
Class B	Cameroon	France & Great Britain
	Togoland	France & Great Britain
	East Africa	Great Britain
	Ruanda-Urundi	Belgium
Class C	Southwest Africa	Union of South Africa
	Western Samoa	New Zealand
	Mauru	Great Britain
	Former German Pacific Islands south of the Equator	Australia
	Former German Pacific Islands north of the Equator	Japan

Turkey: Treaties of Sèvres and Lausanne

One of the war-time secret treaties among the Allies proposed that after the war Russia should receive Constantinople and control of the Straits between the eastern Mediterranean and the Black Sea. This agreement indicated that Britain and France needed Russia's support against Germany, because during the 19th century those two nations had consistently opposed Russia's attempts to dominate the Dardanelles. Other secret treaties had arranged to divide most of Turkish territory among Britain, France, and Italy, had vaguely promised independence to Arab people under Turkish control, and in the Balfour Declaration of 1917 had promised a "national home" in Palestine to the Jews.

The Peace Conference was faced with these promises and with requests from Armenians and Kurds that they become independent of Turkey. The situation was somewhat changed when the Peace Conference opened because Bolshevist Russia was much too busy with domestic affairs to be concerned with Turkish territory, and the Allies certainly did not intend to have Russia controlling the Dardanelles.

The Treaty of Sèvres, 1920, signed by Turkey under duress, left her with only a small corner in Europe and the little province of Anatolia. But this treaty was never implemented because the Turks refused to abide by the humiliating terms signed by the Sultan. Under Mustafa Kemal, a military commander who distinguished himself during the war, Turkish nationalism was revived, the Sultan deposed in 1922, and a Turkish Republic set up.

By the Treaty of Lausanne, which the Allies negotiated with Turkey in 1923, Turkey lost her non-Turkish territories but retained Asia Minor, Constantinople, and the Dardanelles, which were to be open to ships of all nations. The basic terms of the Treaty of Lausanne were:

1. Mesopotamia and Palestine became British mandates independent of Turkey. 2. Syria became a French mandate independent of Turkey. 3. Arabia became free and broke into free states. 4. Turkey renounced rights over Libya, Egypt, and the Sudan.

The Treaty of Neuilly ended the war with Bulgaria, while the Treaty of Trianon concluded peace with Hungary. Both these treaties reduced the nations to very minor ones.

Self-Determination

Poland. At the end of the war the Poles who had been subjects of Russia, Austria, and Germany formed the Polish Republic. The Peace Conference recognized the existence of a Polish nation, awarded it the Polish Corridor and set up a temporary eastern frontier suggested by Lord Curzon, and therefore called the Curzon Line. Although it was based on racial lines, this eastern boundary did not suit Poland, and in 1920 it was extended eastward into Russia by force. This area was to be taken back by Russia in 1939 when Germany invaded Poland from the west.

The "Succession States" of Austria-Hungary. By the Treaty of St. Germain with Austria and the Treaty of Trianon with Hungary, the Allies, in applying the principle of self-determination attempted in the Treaty of Versailles, created out of the old Austro-Hungarian Empire, the independent new states of Czechoslovakia, Yugoslavia, Rumania, a small Austria, and an independent Hungary.

The Republic of Czechoslovakia. This new nation was centered on the old semi-independent Kingdom of Bohemia, the home of the Czechs, who now wanted their "historic frontier" of the Sudeten and Erzberg Mountains to the west and north. Such a boundary contra-

174   *Industrialism, Imperialism, and War*

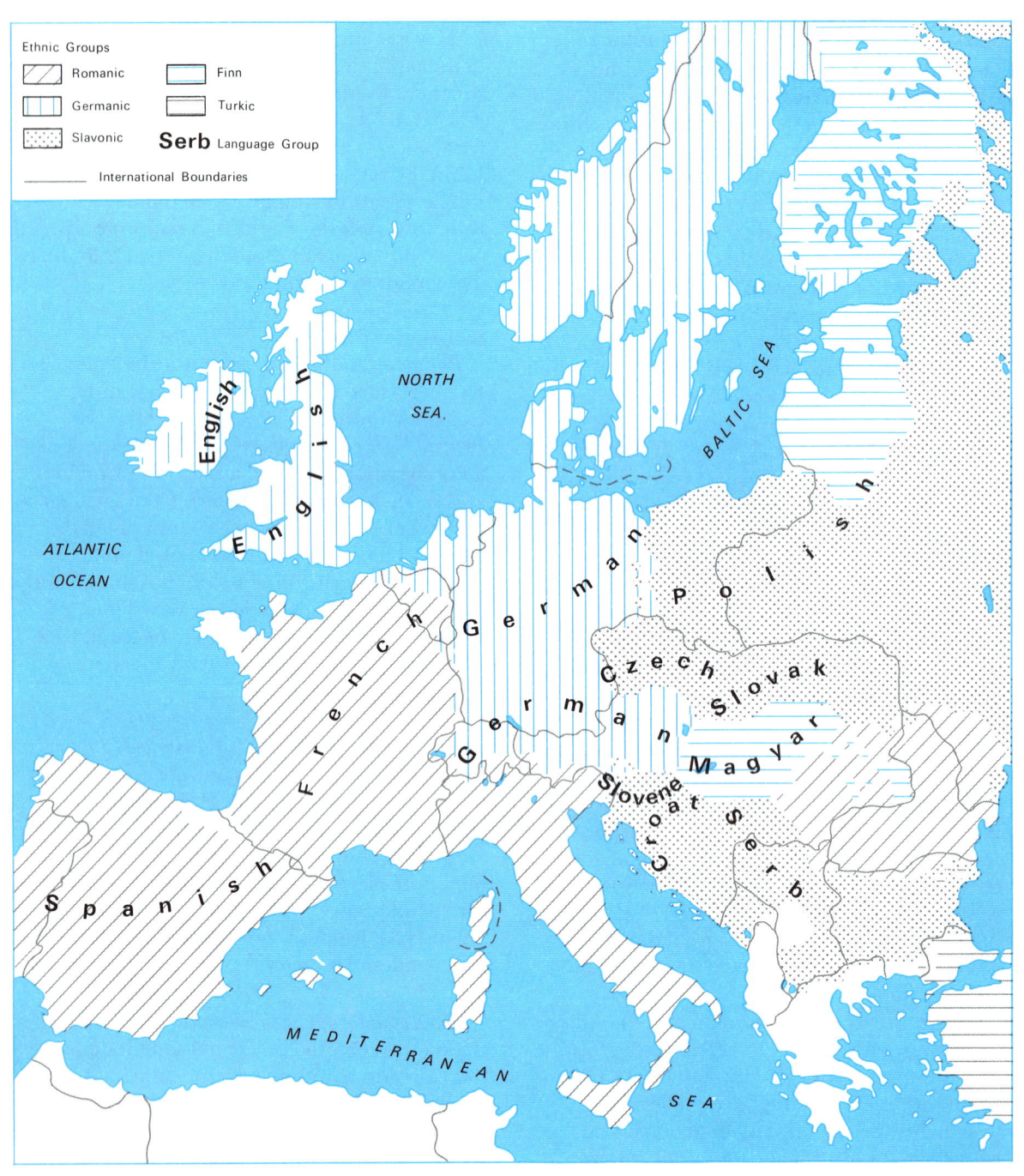

Ethnic and Linguistic, 1914

dicted the principle of self-determination to a certain extent because it included some 3,000,000 Germans who, on a racial basis, should be united with Germany or Austria. But Czechoslovakia demanded this mountain boundary for self-defense. To the east they demanded part of the ancient Kingdom of Hungary inhabited by Slovaks because they were a Slavic people related to the Czechs. They also wanted their frontier on the south extended to the Danube River for access along that water route to the Black Sea. This boundary placed 1,000,000 Ruthenians and Magyars within the Czech nation of 14,000,000 people.

The Kingdom of Yugoslavia had as its core the Kingdom of Serbia, whose expansionist ambitions in 1914 had precipitated the war. Serbia was enlarged to include the little mountain kingdom of Montenegro and the former Austrian provinces of Bosnia-Herzegovina and Croatia inhabited by Slavs. The final boundary included some 1,250,000 Germans, Italians, Rumanians, and Magyars, who were to become a future cause for friction in the new nation of Yugoslavia.

The Kingdom of Rumania had been a small independent country before the war but was dissatisfied because it did not include within its boundaries that part of the Hungarian province of Transylvania inhabited by Rumanians. At the Peace Conference it received that part and also a piece of Hungary inhabited by Magyars. Once again the principle of self-determination was compromised because the Magyars, or Hungarians, resented being ruled by aliens.

The Republic of Austria was reduced to only 6,500,000 people, of whom one-third lived in Vienna, who wanted to be united with the new German Republic. The French refused to permit this because it would strengthen their former enemy Germany.

The Kingdom of Hungary, like Austria, lost territory to Czechoslovakia, Yugoslavia, and Rumania, and was left a small country of 8,000,000 people, largely agricultural, who were obliged to share with Austria the costs of reparations for damage done to Allied civilian property during the war.

There were obviously some injustices done in carrying out the principle of self-determination, and some were inevitable where racial groups overlapped natural frontiers. In fact, absolute self-determination was impossible, because natural boundaries such as rivers, mountains, and coastlines did not coincide with racial boundaries. In balance, however, the European map of 1919 was racially more just than that of 1914.

Reparations

Traditionally victor nations have demanded some sort of indemnity, or payment of war costs, from the vanquished, regardless of who was the aggressor.

At the Paris Peace Conference both France and Great Britain wanted Germany to pay for the total cost of the war, not only for damage caused to civilian property but the military costs as well. The United States refused to agree, so Prime Minister Lloyd George modified his demand by including war pensions as civilian damages. The United States wanted the issue of reparations to be based upon a definite sum, and upon economic ability to pay. The figures suggested by Britain and France were astronomical, $120,000,000,000 and $200,000,000,000.

This far exceeded the prewar total wealth of France and Belgium based on houses, farms, industry, factories and equipment. The figure finally arrived at was $32,000,000,000 in cash and a list of payment in goods: 90,000 cattle, 35,000 horses, 110,000 sheep, all merchant ships over 1,600 tons, 1,000,000 tons of ships to be built over the next ten years and given to the Allies, and 400,000,000 tons of coal over a 10-year period.

Disarmament

The opening paragraph of Part V of the Treaty of Versailles clearly suggests that all nations should disarm, not just Germany alone.

"In order to render possible the initiation of a general limitation of armaments of all nations, Germany undertakes strictly to observe the military, naval, and air clauses which follow."

Germany could not have a conscript army but only one of 100,000 men enlisted for 12 years. This limitation would prevent a rotating series of short-term enlistments to train several hundred thousand men. One unforeseen result was that these 100,000 highly-trained men became the officers and non-commissioned officers of the future German army. Germany was allowed only a specified quantity of guns and munitions produced in factories under Allied supervision. Her navy was restricted to 36 vessels and only 15,000 sailors. She could have neither a military nor a naval air force.

Disarmament was not generally carried out after the war, and one of Germany's future grievances was that she had been treated like an outlaw and singled out for one-sided disarmament.

The "Honor" Clauses

When the Germans received on June 16, 1919, the final peace terms submitted by the Allies, the German cabinet was divided in opinion about signing, and resigned. With great difficulty a new cabinet was formed, and the problem of the peace terms was placed before the German National Assembly, which voted 237 to 138 to

Destruction of German Arms.

sign the Treaty, but with the "honor reservation,"

"The Government of the German Republic is ready to sign the Peace Treaty without thereby acknowledging that the German people are the responsible authors of the World War, and without accepting Articles 227 and 231 (concerning the trial of the Kaiser and of war criminals, and war guilt)."

Germany regarded Article 231 of the Treaty, which she labeled the "war guilt" clause, as the crowning ignominy and the one to which she most violently objected. In it, Germany "accepted the responsibility" for all loss and damage resulting from the war. A further objection to it was the fact that it was the first clause in the section on reparations and therefore seemed to indicate that Germany's "war guilt" was the justification for reparation demands by the Allies. Germans therefore argued that Germany had no moral obligation to pay reparations if she was not solely responsible for the war. She certainly did not think she was, since she had "accepted" responsibility only under duress.

The other "honor" clauses demanded the trial of the Kaiser and "other persons accused of having committed acts in violation of the laws and customs of war." Lloyd George had promised to "hang the Kaiser," but Holland had no extradition treaties with the various Allies regarding political extradition, and thereby saved the Allies the very probable embarrassment of what to do with the Kaiser if they got their hands on him.

3. German Acceptance of the Treaty of Versailles

One important fact to be considered is that on November 9, 1918, the Imperial Government of Germany had ended with the abdication of the Kaiser. The royal family no longer ruled Germany, which now became a republic with an elected head. Since the German General Staff, headed by Hindenburg and Ludendorff, had actually dominated German policy during the war years, they should have been obliged to sign the Treaty and share in whatever disgrace was later to be attached to its acceptance. Unfortunately, the delegates who were obliged to accept the Treaty were representatives of the first republic of Germany, the Weimar Republic, named after the quiet town of Weimar, home of Goethe. In later years democracy in Germany was associated with national humiliation and defeat and with the Weimar Republic. The Allied statesmen responsible for this situation could scarcely have delivered a more effective blow to the success of democracy in Germany.

When the German government was requested to send officials to "receive" the Treaty — not to "consider" or "discuss" it — they sent no one. The Allies then changed the word to "negotiate," and on May 7, 1919, Count Brockdorff-Rantzau arrived with his delegation at Versailles. He refused to stand as though a criminal before a court, and sat facing his accusers as he defended Germany.

"The demand is made that we shall immediately acknowledge that we are guilty of having caused the war. Such a confession in my mouth would be a lie."

He stated that the principles of the Fourteen Points were binding upon both sides, and that *upon this basis* Germany was ready to *examine* the peace terms.

After several communications back and forth Germany agreed to sign all except the "war guilt" and the "war trial" clauses. The Allies threatened to march into Germany unless she signed unconditionally within twenty-four hours. Only one and a half hours before the expiration of that ultimatum, Germany signified her willingness to sign, although under duress.

On June 28, 1919, on the fifth anniversary of the assassination of the Austrian Archduke at Sarajevo, the Treaty of Versailles was signed in the Great Hall of Mirrors at Versailles, where only 48 years earlier William I had been crowned Emperor of the Germans.

The Treaty came into force on January 10, 1920, when Great Britain, France, Italy, and Germany exchanged official ratifications. The next day the Paris Peace Conference officially ended.

United States' Failure to Ratify the Versailles Treaty

In the United States Wilson's political adversaries knew that they could not defeat the basic *principle* of the League of Nations, but they believed that Wilson would accept no "reservations" or modifications of the League constitution. Wilson had fought insistently for the League and had compromised on several of his original Fourteen Points in order to win European support for the League.

In the Senate, Henry Cabot Lodge led a group which added reservations to prevent the League as a body from obliging the United States to become involved in foreign affairs contrary to its own desires and interests. Wilson would tolerate no basic changes in the League charter although had he been willing to accept certain changes in detail he could almost certainly have won American support for the League principles.

Wilson's supporters suggested that once the basic principles were accepted, he could later persuade Congress and the nation to work out the details. The important issue, they said, was to put the tremendous moral force of the United States behind the League. Wilson ignored the advice and ordered his supporters in the Senate to vote against the Treaty if any modifications were attached to the League charter, which was an integral part of the Treaty of Versailles.

In the final vote on the "Treaty with reservations" 49 senators voted to accept it, and 35 voted against acceptance with reservations. Of the 35 voting against the Treaty, 23 were Democrats. Had only 7 of the 23 Democrats changed their vote to "Yea," the final vote would have been 56 to 28, the necessary two-thirds for ratification of the Treaty.

On July 2, 1921, by a joint resolution of both Houses, which required only a simple majority, Congress declared the war at an end. The final treaty of peace between the United States and Germany was signed on August 25, 1921.

4. Evaluation of the Treaty of Versailles

Favorable Aspects

The Treaty of Versailles, a document of some 230 pages, took less than six months to complete, and showed many evidences of decisions made in too great haste or without adequate knowledge. Nevertheless, it did bring peace rapidly to a war-weary Europe, and it did prepare the way for rehabilitating the continent.

It introduced a completely new concept to European politics, the concept that an ethnic or racial group of people should have the right of self-determination, the right to be independent. It was assumed by Wilson that the right of self-determination would remove such causes of war as the assassination of 1914. This concept of self-determination was to appear as "nationalism" in Asia and Africa after the Second World War.

The exhausted nations of Europe, appalled by the senseless slaughter and damage of four years of war, placed their hopes on disarmament and the League of Nations. Disarmament, it was hoped, would lessen the chances of war; the League of Nations would resolve all issues which could lead to war. People assumed that all nations would continue to want peace, and that all nations would work together for the common good of all. Time was to prove that nations would not work together because they were not prepared to accept the consequences of collective action.

Criticisms

There are several valid criticisms of the Treaty of Versailles, and one obvious one is that Paris was not the place in which to work out a peace treaty which was supposed to keep the future peace. Clemenceau, who was certainly the spokesman for France, was adamant on crushing Germany. The French wanted revenge for two invasions. French war veterans, many seriously mutilated, were quite deliberately prominent on the streets as propaganda. Allied delegates to the Conference were very conscious of the demands of their people at home. French newspapers played up French resentment at any suggestion of liberal treatment for Germany. And Woodrow Wilson the idealist was no match for the shrewd and ruthless Clemenceau and Lloyd George in the conference room.

The Treaty of Versailles should have been much harsher or much more lenient. It fell between the two, and was neither one nor the other. It provided Germany with grievances but did not remove from her the ability to seek military revenge for those grievances. The "war guilt" clause and the creation of the Polish Corridor provided Germany with the same desire for revenge that the French loss of Alsace-Lorraine in 1871 gave to the French. Clemenceau, who could appreciate this, predicted that Germany would attack France within 25 years unless she was completely crushed. Wilson predicted future wars unless this one ended in "peace without victory" for the victors. Both men could foresee the future, each from a different viewpoint.

The excellent concept of self-determination, which was expected to remove a cause of war, did not prove to be so effective when put into practice. New nations such as Czechoslovakia, Poland, and Yugoslavia were created on the principle of self-determination, but within each nation there were racial minorities who were unwilling to accept their position. Obviously, no border could be drawn that would completely separate one racial group from another. Hungarians still lived in Czechoslovakia, and Germans lived in Poland. The German minority living in the Sudetenland of Czechoslovakia were to be the excuse for the Munich crisis of 1938 which led to the total absorption of Czechoslovakia into Germany, which was the immediate prelude to World War II.

Another factor of European politics that was not sufficiently considered by the peacemakers was Communist Russia. In the past, nations had certainly fought each other, but they had not customarily incited revolution within each other's borders. But this was precisely what Communist Russia was doing in Germany and Hungary, as part of her policy to encourage world revolution. In Germany the uncompromising Leninist supporters, Karl Liebknecht and Rosa Luxemburg, organized the Spartacist movement and in January 1919 attempted to overthrow the government. In Hungary the radical Bela Kun, a friend of Lenin, proclaimed a Communist republic. And in March 1919, Communist Russia set up in Moscow as the headquarters and guiding hand of Communist parties across the world the Third or Communist International, or Comintern, to plan and encourage world revolution. It was not long before many European statesmen came to regard Communist Russia as a far greater threat than Germany.

One expert with the British delegation to the Peace Conference summed up most succinctly one aspect of the Treaty of Versailles.

"The policy of reducing Germany to servitude for a generation, of degrading the lives of millions of human beings, and of depriving a whole nation of happiness should be abhorrent and detestable ... Some preach it in the name of Justice. In the great events of man's history, in the unwinding of the complex fates of nations Justice is not so simple. And if it were, nations are not authorized, by religion, or by natural morals, to visit on the children of their enemies the misdoings of parents or of rulers."*

---

*J. M. Keynes, *The Economic Consequences of the Peace*, Labour Research Department, London, 1920, pp. 209–210.

5. The League of Nations

Collective Security through Collective Action

The incredible cost of the war in lives and money was convincing evidence that balance of power, alliances, and the stockpiling of armaments were no guarantees of peace. If the alliance system had so tragically failed to keep peace among nations, what method could keep peace? Woodrow Wilson believed he had the answer. And he had, only provided that nations were willing to make an international organization work.

The Covenant or Charter of the League of Nations set up a relatively simple organization that Wilson and other supporters of the League hoped would become world-wide. The League had no precedent in history, and it was something more than a mere coalition or alliance, but it was by no means the "Parliament of Man" that some idealists claimed it to be. It was an international agency *intended* to be permanent and to have the duty of maintaining peace by encouraging nations to act *collectively*, as a group, to prevent the causes of war.

The working parts of the League were the Secretariat, the Assembly, the Council, and supplementary organizations. The Secretariat was simply the necessary clerical staff of some 500 people whose functions were to collect data required by the League, to report and register treaties, and to serve as secretaries to the Assembly and the Council. The Assembly was a world forum that could debate issues but could not legislate. Each member state was entitled to three delegates but only one vote. Its functions were to confer and advise, but not to legislate action, and to admit states to membership. It was to meet at least once a year in Geneva, Switzerland, to deal with any matter affecting the peace of the world, to suggest action to the Council, and to select the rotating, non-permanent members of the Council.

The Council consisted of the three permanent members, Great Britain, France, and Italy, and four, later increased to eleven, members elected by the Assembly for a term of office. The Council had the power to take action if the peace was threatened, with unanimous agreement necessary for important decisions.

Other League agencies included technical organizations such as the Health Organization, and the Economic and Financial Organization, and advisory committees on such subjects as disarmament and mandates. The Permanent Court of International Justice, usually referred to as the World Court, was instituted to settle legal disputes between nations, such as breaches of treaties or interpretations of international law. The Court had neither the power to bring nations before it nor to enforce its decisions. This court should not be confused with The Hague Court set up at The Hague in Holland in 1899 to act as an arbitrator at the request of the nations involved. To The Hague Court each nation appointed a number of judges, and from this list five were to be chosen by the nations wishing to resolve a dispute by arbitration.

The Preservation of Peace

The most important Articles of the League of Nations for the preservation of peace are X and XVI. These Articles could not be enforced, and the League could only "recommend" to member governments what action they should take.

By Article X members of the League undertake "to respect and preserve against external aggression the territorial integrity and existing political independence of all Members of the League." According to Article XVI "should any Member of the League resort to war . . . it shall *ipso facto* be deemed to have committed an act of war against all other Members of the League."

This was the *collective* principle, that an attack on any one League member was an attack on all of them, and they should "undertake immediately" to suspend "all trade and financial relations" with the aggressor. However, the League could only "recommend to the several governments concerned" what pressure they should bring to bear on the aggressor; it could not enforce any action whatever.

Actions of the League

In theory, the League could threaten a possible or an actual aggressor with such overwhelming force that it would not dare to attack another nation. In actual fact the League could be only as effective as its members allowed it to be.

The Åland Islands dispute of 1920 concerned the nationality of islands situated in the Gulf of Bothnia between Finland and Sweden. The islands belonged to Finland but wished to be annexed to Sweden. The League settled the dispute in favor of Finland.

The League was unsuccessful in settling the Vilna controversy between Lithuania and Poland over the city of Vilna; the city had been assigned at the Paris Peace Conference to Lithuania, but it was taken over later by Poland, who refused to negotiate.

Another typical controversy was the 1923 controversy over the boundary between Albania and Greece. A boundary commission of four Italians and one Albanian was killed on Greek soil. Italy immediately demanded a large indemnity payment, and an inquiry to be conducted in Greece. When Greece objected, Italy bombarded and occupied the Greek island of Corfu. Greece was finally ordered by the League to pay the indemnity, and Italy was ordered to

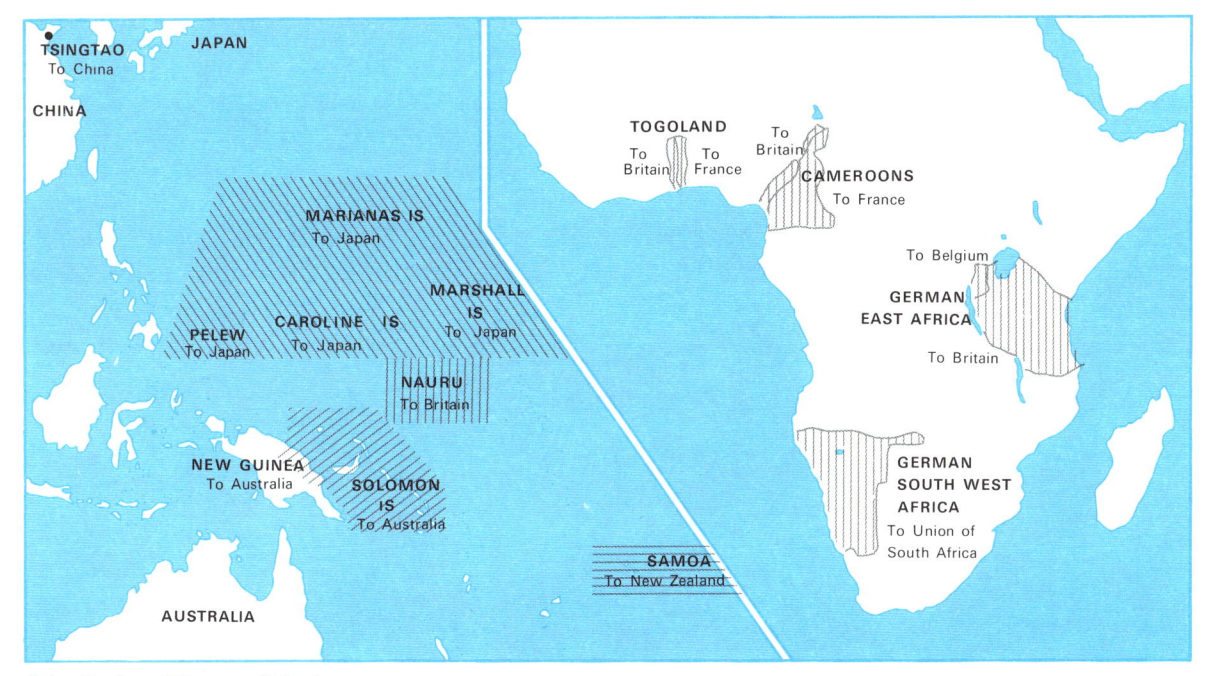

Distribution of German Colonies

evacuate the island, but she was not censured by the League for the use of force.

Reasons for the Weakness of the League

The League could settle incidents between small nations without much difficulty, but had less success where large nations were involved. It was unable to prevent aggression or punish the aggression in the Manchurian Incident when Japan took Manchuria from China in 1932, when Italy conquered Ethiopia in 1936 and made it part of the Italian Empire, and when Germany occupied and absorbed Austria in 1936.

One fatal weakness of the League was that it never included at any one time all the Great Powers. The United States was never a member; Germany joined in 1926 but left in 1934; Japan pulled out in 1933; the Soviet Union was not admitted until 1934.

Another weakness was that the League never had any real military strength to enforce decisions against aggressors.

The Illusion of Internationalism

Perhaps the greatest reason for the League's failure to be really effective was the growing belief in pacificism and internationalism as principles, but with little to back them up. A natural reaction after a costly war was to be

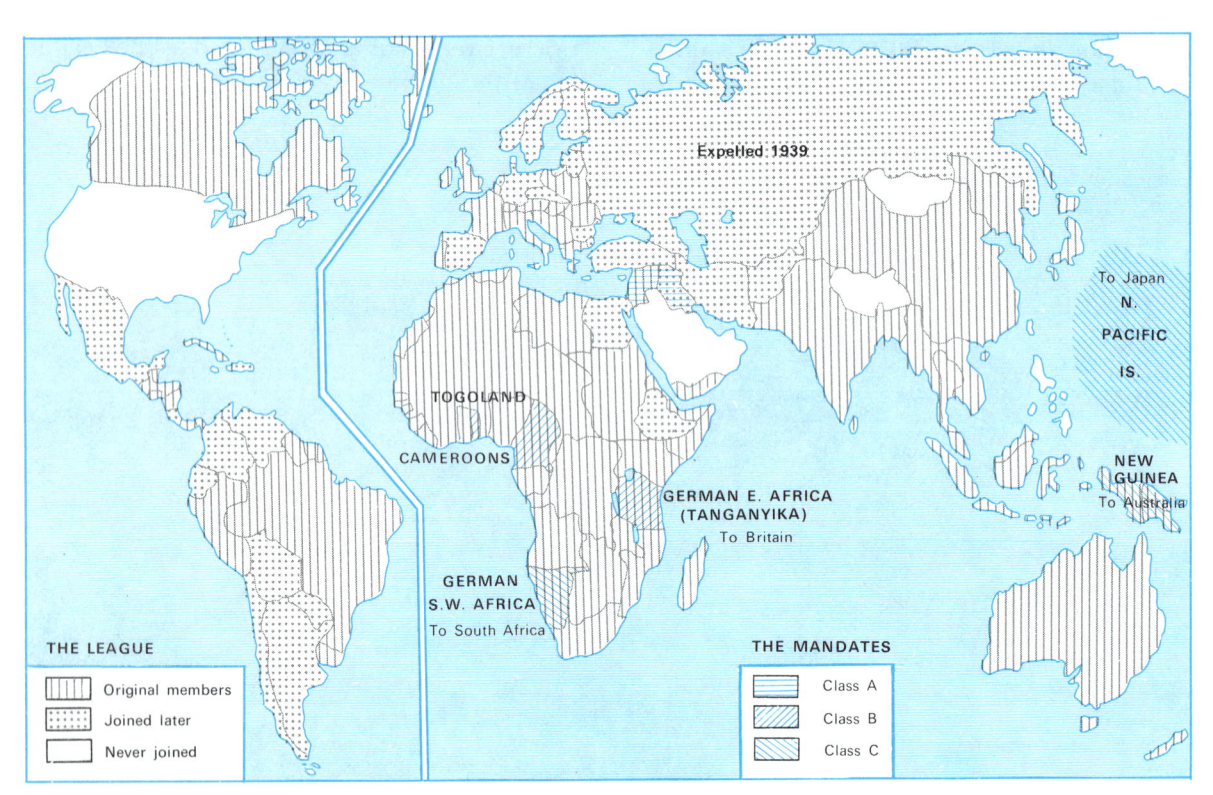

The League of Nations and the Mandates

against war of any kind and a conviction that another war would be the end of civilization.

Instead of setting up an organization with power to stop an aggressor, some people favored disarmament and pacificism, which was a demand for peace and a refusal to fight under any circumstances and regardless of the consequences. If only nations would disarm, argued pacifists, there could be no war. In theory, this argument sounds reasonable. But if some nations did not disarm, what was to prevent them from attacking a weak or disarmed nation?

Some people believed that the League of Nations was the answer, and they were ready to leave all issues to the League. But could the League prevent war if member nations did not act immediately and forcefully against an aggressor? If nations regarded war as the greatest threat to their interests, then, paradoxically, they must be ready to fight collectively against an aggressor. A nation which wished to be neutral could continue to be so only as long as other nations decided not to interfere with it, unless, of course, to attack it would be too costly for the aggressor.

France became a prime example of a pacifist attitude because it had suffered the loss of one half of its 1914 male population between the ages of 20 and 32 in the first world war. As defense against a possible future attack it built an elaborate system of fortifications, called the Maginot Line, along its eastern frontier between the Belgian and Swiss frontiers, assuming that such defenses were impregnable against attack, and would therefore prevent serious loss of troops defending them. This "Maginot Line Mentality" was one reason for the collapse of French resistance when Germany attacked France in 1940. The Maginot Line proved to be useless because German troops simply by-passed the line by advancing through Belgium and getting in behind the French defenses.

6. Collective Security v. The Alliance System

The Washington Conference, 1921

The first positive attempt at general disarmament came in 1921 when the United States called a conference in Washington. When the war ended in 1918 Great Britain, the United States, and Japan ranked in that order as the world's largest naval powers, and naval building programs indicated that Japan would become the dominant naval power in the Far East. Great Britain, Japan, France, and Italy were invited to the conference to consider naval limitation.

Agreements were reached in the Five-Power Pact setting a ratio of $5:5:3:1.67:1.67$ for the United States, Great Britain, Japan, France, and Italy, in that order, for battleships, on a basis of 500,000 tons. The signatories agreed to this limitation, and in addition Great Britain agreed to build no fortifications east of Singapore, and the United States agreed to build none west of Hawaii. North of the equator, within that unfortified area, lay the German Pacific Islands which Japan acquired at the end of the war, and which Japan agreed not to fortify. Japan also signed a Nine-Power Pact in which the members agreed to respect China's independence and existing boundaries.

The Washington Agreements on naval limitations made Japan the strongest one-ocean navy in the world, because the United States and Great Britain had two or more oceans in which their interests had to be defended, while Japan had only one limited area of interests. Furthermore, no machinery was set up to enforce Japan's agreement not to fortify her Pacific Islands.

France and Italy were not interested in the conference because they were more afraid of land attacks across their frontiers, and nothing about military and air forces was discussed at the conference. The Washington Conference was only the beginning of disarmament, but it was also virtually the end, because further attempts at disarmament proved to be fruitless.

In 1927 at Geneva and in London in 1930 further reductions in naval disarmament were attempted. At Geneva Japan was largely a spectator, France and Italy refused to attend because they wanted military limitations applied, and the United States and Great Britain could not agree on the issue of cruiser size and strength.

At the London Conference France and Italy refused to accept any agreement, and Britain insisted upon an "escalator clause" which permitted the signatory powers to increase their building programs if the "national security" demanded it, and provided they notified each other of their intentions. Disarmament was finally killed at a conference in 1932 when Germany walked out because she was not allowed under the Versailles Treaty to have equality in armaments. In October 1933, Hitler withdrew his nation from the League and thus increased its ineffectiveness.

The French Alliance System

In 1919 France indicated her early reluctance to rely upon the League of Nations by negotiating, with the United States and Great Britain, treaties to guarantee her frontier against future aggression by Germany. When the United States Senate refused to ratify such a treaty, Great Britain refused to commit herself alone. France then looked for allies on the Continent. Between 1920 and 1927 she made alliances with Belgium and Poland guaranteeing mutual protection in a defensive war, and with the Little Entente of Czechoslovakia, Yugoslavia, and Rumania guaranteeing support for each other if any of the three was attacked by Hungary, which resented its loss of territory in the Versailles Treaty.

These alliances between France and Poland and the Little Entente were designed as defensive agreements primarily against Russian Communism and resurgent German nationalism. Unfortunately they were in contradiction to the idea of "collective security by collective action" and were a return to the former alliance system which had not been able to prevent war.

The Locarno Agreements, 1925

The passing years indicated that if collective security was to work, then it needed to be clearly defined. Herriot of France and MacDonald of Great Britain suggested at the Fifth Assembly of the League in Geneva that the word "aggressor" be clearly and automatically defined as a nation that resorted to war before using peaceful means to settle a dispute. The League should then be obliged to take action against the aggressor. The smaller nations favored the Geneva Protocol, as it was called, but the larger powers wanted no responsibility for its enforcement. Once again, collective action was side-stepped by the very nations that could give it muscle.

The occupation of the German industrial district of the Ruhr by French troops in 1923 because Germany was in default in reparations payments, and the attempt of France to set up an independent Rhineland state emphasized the seriousness of the Rhineland problem in international relations. In October 1925, France, Great Britain, and Germany called a conference in Locarno, Switzerland and invited Belgium, Poland, Czechoslovakia, and Italy to attend.

The results of the conference were hailed by statesmen as a great step forward in international relations, as the "Spirit of Locarno" to settle all issues peacefully. However, a close look at the agreements shows that the Locarno pact was really a return to the alliance system rather than real collective action. The main agreements were (1) two arbitration treaties by Germany with Belgium and France guaranteeing their common frontiers unconditionally, (2) two treaties by Germany with Poland and Czechoslovakia agreeing that any frontier change must be by peaceful means only, (3) a guarantee by Great Britain and Italy of the Franco-German and Belgo-German frontiers, and (4) two mutual defense pacts by France with Poland and Czechoslovakia.

The basic and very serious weaknesses of these treaties were three in number. First, Great Britain and Italy guaranteed military aid to protect the frontiers between France and Germany, and Belgium and Germany, but did not guarantee Poland or Czechoslovakia against German invasion. This was certainly not collective action. Second, the French felt obliged to make alliances promising military aid to Poland and Czechoslovakia, another example of the failure of collective action. Third, the Soviet Union was antagonized because she suspected that some of the Western nations were willing to allow Germany to expand eastward, and were perhaps even tacitly encouraging her to do so.

The Kellogg-Briand Pact, 1928

One of the most extraordinary and futile attempts at collective action was the Kellogg-Briand Pact, or Pact of Paris, in which nations believed or pretended to believe that they had eliminated war. The idea of the pact began with Aristide Briand, who was Premier of France in the early months of 1917. He wished to commemorate the entry of the United States into the war in April 1917, and suggested in April 1927 that the two nations renounce war as an instrument of national policy. The expression "to outlaw war" came into popular use, although politically the concept made little sense.

The term came from the medieval word of "outlaw," by which a person was literally put outside the protection of the law, and could be killed by any man without danger of punishment for the deed. But to "outlaw" war was impossible. If one nation attacked another, then war resulted. However, in December 1927, United States Secretary of State Frank Kellogg proposed that the treaty between France and the United States be extended to more nations. Eventually 63 nations ratified what was one of the shortest treaties on record, containing only 78 words in which the signatory nations condemned "recourse to war for the solution of international controversies and renounced it as an instrument of national policy."

However, although these nations "outlawed" war as "national policy," they reserved the right to "defensive war" which was not outlawed. History frequently shows that nations claimed that although they struck the first blow, it was a "defensive" blow before the enemy could strike first. The essential futility of the Kellogg-Briand Pact was that it failed to include either a method of preventing aggressive attack by one nation or to set up a practicable and effective plan of action by signatory powers against an aggressor. Public reaction to the Pact was optimistic because people believed that it had ended war forever. The victor nations of World War I assumed that the vengeful phase of the early peace years was over, and that disputes would be settled peacefully, that there would be no more wars, and that collective security was finally achieved.

Shrewd observers of the international scene were very doubtful of these high hopes because there had already been particular examples of the unwillingness of nations to support real collective action.

Disarmament, which would have greatly reduced the chances of war, never got beyond the very limited agreements of the Washington Conference. France had only grudgingly supported the agreements because she feared land or air attack. Twice in forty-five years she had been invaded, and the Washington agreements included nothing about reductions in armies or limitations on the new air weapon. France refused to disarm until she received an iron-clad guarantee of security against attack, but neither Great Britain nor the United States would guarantee to protect France's borders.

Treaty of Mutual Assistance
In 1923 a commission appointed by the League of Nations to study the question of armaments reduction submitted a Treaty of Mutual Assistance which would have provided the guarantee that France demanded. It would oblige every member of the League to go to the defense of any member that was attacked, if that member had reduced armaments according to whatever plan the League should adopt. The treaty also required the League Council to decide who the aggressor was within four days of receiving a complaint of aggression.

Several nations were willing to commit themselves, but Great Britain and the United States were concerned only with their immediate security, and were not ready to do precisely what "collective action" meant, to take action against any aggressor, wherever the aggression, and whoever the victim was.

The Geneva Protocol
Great Britain and the United States were not willing to commit themselves partly because the definition of "aggressor" was left to the League. Nations said that if they disarmed and were attacked, and the League stalled in defining the aggressor, they could be overwhelmed by the aggressor before help came.

So, in 1924 Great Britain and France supported the Geneva Protocol, which defined war as a "criminal act," clearly defined an aggressor as a nation which resorted to war, and imposed all the penalties of the covenant of the League. British Prime Minister Stanley Baldwin and Foreign Secretary Austen Chamberlain of the Conservative government which replaced MacDonald's Labour government in 1924, killed the proposal. Individual nations clearly had to depend upon themselves and upon regional alliances.

London Naval Conference
One more effort at disarmament was made with the London Naval Conference of 1930, where limitations on warships other than aircraft carriers and battleships, limited earlier by the Washington Conference, were discussed. France and Italy refused to agree to vital clauses of the Treaty because of their rivalry in the Mediterranean. The limitation on cruisers, destroyers, and submarines was agreed to by the United States and Great Britain. But the effectiveness of the limitation was nullified by the "escalation" clause which stated that if new naval construction by other nations threatened any signer of the Treaty, then that nation could increase its naval forces if it notified the other signatory powers.

The final blows to disarmament were Japan's notice in 1934 to terminate the Washington Naval Treaty of 1922 because the greater ratio for the United States and Great Britain was humiliating to Tokyo, and Italy's refusal to sign.

Behind the facade of the "spirit of Locarno" and the "outlawing" of war by the Kellogg-Briand Pact, power politics were still operating. The realistic French were building a ring of alliances with Czechoslovakia, Rumania, and Yugoslavia around Germany, and constructing the immense fortifications known as the Maginot Line from Switzerland to the Belgian border, but not beyond because the Ardennes region, according to the French, was impregnable against attack. Two contradictory methods, the old alliance system and the "new order" of collective action, were both in operation, but neither was sufficiently supported to be effective.

Review Questions

Section 1
1. Was President Wilson justly criticized for attending the Peace Conference in person, and for the membership of the American delegation to Paris?
2. How did the interests of the Big Four differ?

Section 2
3. Do you think that the boundary settlements of Germany could be a cause for future difficulties in Europe?
4. Why did President Wilson favor "self-determination"? What new nations were created by self-determination?
5. Why could Germans believe that each of the following was unfair to them: Reparations, Disarmament, the Honor Clauses?

Section 3
6. Were the Allies politically unwise to make the representatives of the Weimar Republic sign the Treaty of Versailles?
7. Why did the United States refuse to sign the Treaty of Versailles?

Sections 4 and 5
8. What were some of the arrangements in the Treaty of Versailles which could threaten to lead to future trouble?
9. What is "collective security"? Was the League of Nations able to make collective security work? What did its chances of success depend upon?

Section 6
10. Why was each of the following an effective or an ineffective way to prevent war: the Washington Conference Agreements, the Locarno Agreements, the Kellogg-Briand Pact?
11. What measures for collective action had failed by 1930? For what reasons had they failed?

Glossary*

Abolitionist. One who wanted immediate freedom for slaves, usually without compensation to the owner. The Anti-Slavery Society, founded in 1833, was a coalition of groups dedicated to emancipation of slaves.

Aboriginal. A person who is native to a particular region. Used in reference to natives using Stone Age methods.

Alliance. An agreement among two or more nations to act together for a common purpose.

Anti-Clericalism. A political philosophy which believes in subordinating the Church to the State.

Anti-Trust. Usually refers to legislation to prevent the growth of, or to break up, business monopolies.

Armistice. A suspension of fighting by agreement among the nations or groups at war.

Associated Territories. In 1967 the Caribbean islands of Antigua, St. Christopher–Nevis–Anguilla, Dominica, Grenada, and St. Lucia organized a new form of association with Great Britain. Each controls its own internal affairs and retains the right to declare its independence. Great Britain is still responsible for external affairs and defense.

Augsleich. Means "compromise." A particular agreement between Austrians and Hungarians in 1867 providing for the Dual Monarchy of Austria-Hungary, with a common monarch, joint foreign relations, military forces, but each with a separate parliament for domestic affairs.

Autonomy. Literally it means self-rule, but historically it refers to a measure of self-rule, usually in domestic affairs. The term "home rule" is often associated with autonomy.

Balance of Power. The foreign policy of two or more nations acting together to prevent one nation or group from becoming predominant over all others. Not a permanent alliance.

Belligerent. A nation at war; in a more limited sense, a member of the military forces of a nation at war.

Blockade. A method by which a nation prevents another nation from getting supplies. Usually enforced by naval ships.

---

*From the Latin *glossa*, an explanation.

Bourgeois. Marxists used the word to designate the middle class, the bourgeoisie, who supported capitalism and the profit motive. Used by Marxists in a derogatory sense.

British Commonwealth of Nations. This is the name given to a loose association of former British colonies which are now sovereign, independent nations. There are 28 members of the Commonwealth (The word British was dropped from the title in the 1960's.)

British Empire. Since the Statute of Westminster in 1931 the term refers to the various non-Commonwealth territories of the United Kingdom, and includes Associated States, Dependent Territories, Protectorates, and Protected States.

Collective Action. The policy by which nations jointly use restrictive measures, and force if necessary, against any aggressor anywhere, even though some of those nations may not be immediately threatened. The policy is based upon the belief that war anywhere can in turn threaten every nation. Such collective action is expected to maintain collective security or safety.

Colonialism. The policy of a nation of taking control over a territory but not making it an integral part of its own land. (*See* **Colony**.)

Colony. An area of land which is completely subject to the rule of an independent state, but is not part of that state.

Communism. Basically this is communal or society ownership of the means of production and distribution, as distinct from private ownership in a capitalist society. Economically Communism and Socialism do not differ. Politically Communism differs in that it does not allow the existence of opposition parties (cf. **Socialism**).

Concessions. After the Anglo-Chinese (Opium) War of 1840–42, China was obliged to grant special rights to European nations. There were several kinds of concessions: (1) outright cession of territory, (2) warships of European nations were allowed to call in at any Chinese port, and even to sail up the Yangtze River, (3) the sixteen "treaty" ports were operated under the laws of the European nations, not China's, (4) low import duties were established on foreign goods and could not be raised except by consent of the European powers. These rights are also called "extra-territorial" rights, meaning outside of, or freedom from, local legal restrictions.

Co-operative. A group of consumers or producers who organize their production, selling, buying jointly, to save costs. Most co-operatives sell at market price and distribute their profits to the members in proportion to the amount the members purchase.

Corn Laws. Since the late 17th century English landowners were protected against foreign food grains (collectively called "corn" in England) that could undersell them. In 1846, after a severe famine in Ireland caused deaths from starvation, the middle class was able to repeal the Corn Laws, and so reduce the price of wheat and other grains for their workers.

Corporation. A business unit owned by shareholders which is legally regarded as an artificial person, able to take decisions, operate, and function as a person.

Dependent Territories. Territories dependent upon the United Kingdom, which include a dependent territory, protectorates and protected states. A Dependent Territory is one which has by settlement or conquest been annexed to the British Crown. Hong Kong, Gibraltar, and Bermuda are examples.

Dialectical Materialism. Dialectic means the art of logical argument. Materialism as used here is the belief that essential changes in history have been caused by economic factors. According to Marx, all human history has developed in a dielectical process, according to a pattern. For example, the Class Struggle is demonstrated in the clash between the Bourgeoisie (the thesis) with its opposite the Proletariat (the antithesis), resulting in the Socialist Revolution (the synthesis).

Dialectics. A process of reason based upon change, as reasoned by the German philosopher Hegel. German mid-19th century disunity (thesis) in conflict with its opposite unity (antithesis) would result in the ideal German state (synthesis).

Direct Primary. A party election in which the voters directly (not through representatives) elect a candidate who will run in a general election.

Dominion. As used by Great Britain, the term referred to a colony which received self-government in domestic affairs. By the British North America Act of 1867 (commemorated by Expo 67 in Canada in 1967) Great Britain initiated this policy. With the enactment of the Statute of Westminster in 1931 the "dominions" became completely independent, sovereign nations.

Dreikaiserbund. The League of Three Emperors of Germany, Austria, and Russia, initiated by Bismarck, Chancellor of the German Empire, in 1873, was an "understanding" that the three nations should act together in their common interest.

Dual Monarchy. *See* **Augsleich**.

Dyarchy. Rule or government by two independent authorities.

Dynasty. A succession of rulers of the same family, usually governing by hereditary right.

Economic Determinism. According to Karl Marx, history was so powerfully affected by economic factors that it was determined or changed by these factors.

Emancipist. One who favors freedom from slavery or other control.

Enclosure Acts. In the 16th century many small farms were combined into large ones by Acts of Parliament for the purpose of profitable sheep-raising. In later times small farms were "closed down" and expanded into large ones for wheat-raising to meet increased demands for food. Small farmers were forced to become farm laborers.

Entente. A diplomatic "understanding" between two or more nations. The French and British in 1904 had such an "understanding" about their common interests, the Entente Cordiale.

Extra-Territoriality. *See* **Concessions**.

Federal Reserve System. A banking system created by Congress to influence the amount of money in circulation. It attempts to control inflation and avoid recessions.

Feminist. One who advocates the same rights for women as for men.

Fourteen Points. The terms suggested by President Woodrow Wilson for ending World War I "justly," so that the defeated nations, particularly Germany, would not later seek revenge.

Free Silver. Owners of silver mines who wanted high prices for their silver, and people who wanted more money in circulation, urged the U.S. government to buy up all the silver produced at a fixed price, higher than the competitive market price, and convert it into coin money.

Grange. The National Grange is a farm group organized by the Patrons of Husbandry (raising of livestock; farming) in the 1860's to circulate information among farmers and act as their spokesman. Local farmers met in their local Grange.

Greenbackers. Americans who advocated larger amounts of paper money to be printed by the government and circulated. So named from the green ink used on the paper money.

Home Rule. The management of domestic affairs by a people. The British North America Act of 1867 granted "home rule," in internal affairs to Canada, and later to other dominions.

Honor Clause. A clause in the Treaty of Versailles, 1919, which the defeated Germans were obliged to sign, stating that the Germans "accepted full responsibility" for all losses resulting from the first world war. The Germans felt that their honor had been falsely slandered.

Ideology. A set of ideas about social or political issues, usually the program of a group or a party which it wants to put into operation.

Imperialism. Historically the term refers to the 19th century acquisition by nations of undeveloped areas for use as strategic bases, for sources of raw materials, and for development for the benefit of the "mother" country.

Initiative. The process which allows voters to start or initiate legislation, or to instruct legislators to introduce legislation for discussion.

Internationalism. A belief that all nations could work together for a common purpose without resorting to war.

Irredentism. The demand of a people for the recovery of what they consider to be "lost" territory which they claim rightfully belongs to them. In the late 19th century the Italians regarded Trieste, Nice, and Savoy as "unredeemed," as *Italia Irredenta*, which must some day become part of Italy.

Interstate Commerce. The U.S. Constitution gives Congress the power to regulate all commerce with foreign nations and across state lines. This prevents one state from charging customs duties on goods from other states, and from foreign countries.

Internationals. The three International Associations of workingmen to organize on a world-wide basis to achieve socialism. The first two were organized by Karl Marx in 1864 and 1889, the Third by Lenin in 1919, known as the Communist International or Comintern.

Kulturkampf. "Conflict of Ideas," a term describing the conflict between Bismarck and the Roman Catholic Church. Bismarck believed that the Church was attempting to gain influence over German citizens. The Catholic Center Party was anti-Prussian, and Bismarck replied to this by denying the right of priests to refer to politics in their sermons.

Laissez-faire. The economic doctrine of individualism, of the complete absence of restrictions, by government or any other agency, on any aspect of the economy. Literally, "leave alone," colloquially, "hands off."

Mandates. Territories which were formerly German colonies, and non-Turkish regions of the Turkish Empire, were by the treaties after World War I given to Allied nations to administer until they were ready for self-government. The League of Nations was given supervisory power over the operation of mandates.

Muckraker. An unfortunate term used by President Theodore Roosevelt to describe journalists and authors such as Ida Tarbell, Lincoln Steffens, and Upton Sinclair who exposed the monopolistic practices of the Standard Oil Company, corruption in city government, and the disgusting conditions in Chicago's meat-packing plants.

Nation. A group of people who live in clearly defined bounaries, who are bound together by common ties of culture, customs, usually by language, with a belief in their own identity as an independent people.

Open Door Policy. The policy adopted by the United States in 1899 advocating and supporting equal economic opportunity for all nations in China, where many nations had concessions. Later, the policy included support for China's independence.

Pacifism. The belief that disputes between nations can be peacefully settled; opposition to war and the refusal to participate in war.

Phalanx. François Fourier believed that society must be organized for the betterment of mankind. He advocated groups of 1,600 persons to work together as units. Each person was to receive a minimum for subsistence, with the remainder to be divided five-twelfths, four-twelfths, and three-twelfths for labor, capital, and talent.

Pocket Borough. Before the Reform Act of 1832 about 75 landowning families controlled the House of Commons because they appointed members to parliament. The Duke of Norfolk controlled eleven seats in districts where there were no voters. Landowners had these seats "in their pockets."

Political Party. People with the same political ideas, who organize to put their candidates into office in order to get laws passed in their interests. A political party, in the Western meaning, always acknowledges the right of the minority to become the majority *by peaceful means*. Such dictatorial "parties" as the Fascists, Nazis, and Communists, are not political parties in the historical sense because they have not permitted the existence of opposition political parties.

Populists. The People's or Populist Party represented farmers' interests in the election of 1892, on a platform of more money in circulation, government ownership of railroads, and a graduated income tax.

Progressives. These were reformers in the early 20th century who demanded political, social, and economic reforms to remedy the unethical practices of business, the exploitation of women and child labor, factory conditions, food adulteration, and other abuses.

Prohibition. The forbidding by law of the manufacture, possession, sale, and transportation of alcoholic beverages, by the 18th Amendment. The period 1920–1933 when that law operated.

Proletariat. According to Karl Marx, they formed the

propertyless class of workers, who sold their labor to people who owned the means of production.

Protected State. This is a territory under its own ruler and operating its own internal affairs, but is protected by Great Britain for its foreign affairs. (*See* **British Empire**.)

Protectorate. A protectorate is a territory not formally annexed but in which by agreement Great Britain has power and jurisdiction over it. The British Solomon Islands are a protectorate (*See* **British Empire**.)

Recall. The political process by which voters may remove public officials from office before their term expires.

Referendum. The process of referring a piece of legislation, or a proposal, to the voters for their approval or disapproval.

Reparations. Compensation in goods, money, or labor for damage done. Traditionally used in regard to the payment by a defeated nation for war damage.

Risorgimento. An Italian word meaning literally "resurrection." It was used in 19th century Italy as a slogan for unification of all territory claimed to be Italian.

Rotten Borough. A parliamentary district with so few voters that the seat in parliament could be bought by bribery.

Salient. The term was used in World War I to describe an angle of a trench jutting out from a main trench. A piece of territory held by troops out in front of their main line.

Samurai. The military aristocracy of feudal Japan.

Schlieffen Plan. The plan for Germany's attack on France, developed by General von Schlieffen, to avoid the French forts facing Germany by outflanking them through Belgium and Luxembourg.

Scientific Socialism. The theory by Karl Marx that economic classes are always in conflict, that in a capitalist society the workers will take over from middle class factory owners, abolish private property, and establish a socialist society. This process, said Marx, was inevitable and "scientific."

Self-Determination. The ability or right of a racial, or ethnic group to decide whether it wishes to rule itself or to be ruled as part of another nation. After World War I several racial groups in the former Austro-Hungarian Empire became independent.

Social Darwinism. Darwin's theory was that the "fittest," that is the most adaptable, survived in nature. Businessmen and generals used the term to mean the strongest, and justified the "survival" of the strongest men and nations over the weaker.

Socialism. Both an economic and a political belief. It is (1) an *economic* theory and practice that the means of production be owned by the State, and is (2) a *political* belief that such an economic process should be done by democratic means, by the free choice of the voters who may remove at an election the socialist government. The economic belief is common to both Socialists and Communists; the political belief is not accepted by Communists, who refuse to permit the existence of opposition political parties.

Sphere of Influence. Countries or parts of countries in which a foreign nation exercises great influence without actual annexation. China in the early 20th century illustrates this influence, or interference, by foreign nations.

Succession States. Those ethnic groups in pre-World War I Austria-Hungary which became independent nations such as Czechoslovakia and Yugoslavia.

Tariff. A tax or duty on imported or exported products.

Temperance. Although the general meaning of temperance is moderation, when the word is associated with liquor it means total abstinence or non-use.

Trialism. A suggested three-way system of government, giving the Slavs in the Austro-Hungarian Empire the same rights of government as the Austrians and Hungarians. (*See* **Augsleich**.)

Uitlanders. The Boer word for foreigners or outsiders, mostly from Great Britain, who came into the Transvaal Republic after the discovery of gold and diamonds. They were not welcome.

Ultimatum. A final statement of terms. Usually accompanied by the threat of serious consequences if the terms are not accepted.

Utopian Socialism. An ideal socialist society—usually impossibly ideal. It was the objective of social reformers of the 19th century, in protest at the materialism, the slums, and the exploitation resulting from the Industrial Revolution. Saint-Simon, Fourier, and Robert Owen were Utopian Socialists.

White Man's Burden. The title of a poem by Rudyard Kipling romanticizing colonialism. A convenient phrase used by colonial nations to suggest that they were sacrificing time and effort for the benefit of the natives in their colonies.

General Index

Abdication of Kaiser William II of Germany, 162, 177
Abolition of Slave-trading, by Great Britain, 81
Act of Union, Great Britain and Ireland, 77
Adkins v. Children's Hospital, 64
Africa, 105
   Europe in Africa, 105
   Fashoda Incident, 134
Agricultural Revolution, 6–8
Åland Islands dispute, 181
Algeciras Conference, 139
Alsace-Lorraine, 32, 34, 58, 170
American Federation of Labor, 119
Amiens, Treaty of, 81
Anthracite Strike, 121
Anti-Corn Law League, 49
Anti-slavery societies, 62
Arkwright, Richard, 4
Armistice, 162, 189 (glossary)
Asquith, Herbert, 53
Australia, 72–75
   Commonwealth of Australia, 74
   Convict settlement in New South Wales, 73
Austria, 175
   Dual monarchy, 31

Babeuf, Gracchus, 15
Bakewell, Robert, 7
Balfour Declaration, 173
Balkan League, 140
Balkan Wars, 140
Belgium: colonies in Africa, 109
Bessemer, Henry, 22
Big Four, Paris Peace Conference, 169
Bismarck, Age of, 33
Bismarck, Count Otto von, 29, 133
"Black and Tans," 79
Black Hand Society, 142
Bleriot, Louis, 24
"Blood and Iron," 29
Boer War, 135
Boers, 82

Bosnia Crisis, 140
Bosnia-Herzogovina, 140, 142
Boulanger, General, 59
Boxer Rebellion, 98
Brest-Litovsk, 160
Briand, Aristide, 185
Britain, *see* Great Britain
British Empire and Commonwealth, 83, 189 (glossary)
Bryan, William Jennings, 121
Butt, Isaac, 78

Canada
   British North America Act, 71
   Canada Act, 1791, 69
   Durham Report, 70
   Rebellions, 69
Cape of Good Hope, 80, 107
Caporetto, battle of, 160
Carbonari, 38
Carleton, Sir Guy, 69
Carnegie, Andrew, 115
Carnegie Steel Company, 115
Carson, Sir Edward, 78
Catholic Center Party, Germany, 35
Catholic Emancipation, Ireland, 78
Cavour, Count Camillo di, 38, 40
Chamberlain, Joseph, 83
Chartists, 49
China, 91
   Boxer Rebellion, 98
   Confucianism, 91
   Opium War, 92
   Partitioning by European nations, 98
   Sino-Japanese War, 97
   Taiping Rebellion, 93
   Treaty of Tientsin, 95
   United States in, 93
   United States Open Door Policy, 100
Christian Socialists, 22
Clayton Anti-Trust Act, 124
Clemenceau, Georges, 170, 178
Collective Security, 180
Colt revolver, 115

Comintern, 22
Commonwealth of Australia, 74
Communist Manifesto, 18
Confucianism, 91
Congo Free State, 109
Conservatives, Germany, 35
Convoy System, 158
Cook, Captain James, 72
Corn Laws, 48, 189, (glossary)
Cotton Gin, 5
Cuba, 124
Cushing, Caleb, 93
Czechoslovakia, 173

Danzig, 172
Dardanelles Operation, 154
Darwin, Charles, 89
Das Kapital, 19
De Beers Consolidated Mines, 109
Decatur, Stephen, 105
Democratic Party, 121
Descent of Man, 90
Dialectical Materialism, 19, 190 (glossary)
Diesel engine, 24
Disarmament, 176
Disraeli, Benjamin, 52
Dominion of New Zealand, 76
Dreikaiserbund, 36, 133, 190 (glossary)
Dreyfus, Captain Alfred, 59
Dual Alliance, 133
Dual Entente, 134
Durham Report, 70
Dutch East India Company, 80
Dutch East Indies, 102
Dynasties, 91, 190 (glossary)

East India Company, 85
East Prussia, 172
Easter Rebellion, 79
Economic and Financial Organization, 180
Economic Determinism, 19
Economic interpretation of history, 19
Education Act, Great Britain, 51

193

Eighteenth Amendment, 65
Eire, 80
Electricity, production of, 24
Ems Dispatch, 52
Enclosure Movement, 7, 190 (glossary)
Engels, Friedrich, 18
Entente Cordiale, 136, 190 (glossary)
Esterhazy, Major Charles, 59

Fabian Society of Socialists, 22
Factory Act, 1833, 14
Factory Acts, 51
Factory System, 8, 12
Fashoda Incident, 106, 134
Federal Reserve System, 123, 190 (glossary)
Ferdinand, Archduke Francis, 141
Fifteenth Amendment, 62
Five-Power Pact, 183
Flying Shuttle, 4
France
  Boulanger Affair, 59
  Colonies in Africa, 109
  Dreyfus, 59
  Dual Entente, 134
  Entente Cordiale, 136
  Franco-Prussian War, 58
  Second Republic, 56
  Third Republic, 58
  Triple Entente, 136
Franco-Prussian War, 32
Free Silver Movement, 120
French Alliance System, 184
Fourier, Charles, 16
Four Principles of Peace, 161
Fourteen Points, 161, 190 (glossary)
Fourteenth Amendment, 62

Garibaldi, Guiseppe, 38, 41
Garibaldi's Red Shirts, 38, 41
Geneva Conference, 184
Geneva Protocol, 186
German Empire
  Beginning of, 33
  Dreikaiserbund, 36
  Dual Alliance, 36
  Political Parties, 34
  Triple Alliance, 36
German Naval Laws, 136
Germany
  Abdication of Kaiser William II, 177
  Age of Bismarck, 33
  Austrian or Seven Weeks' War, 30
  Colonies in Africa, 109
  Dual Alliance, 133
  Ems Dispatch, 32
  Franco-Prussian War, 32

Naval Laws, 136
North German Confederation, 31
Treaty of Brest-Litovsk, 160
Triple Alliance, 133
Unification of, 29
War with Denmark, 30
Weimar Republic, 177
Gladstone, William, 52
Government of Ireland Act, 79
Grange, the, 120, 190 (glossary)
Great Britain, 23
  Colonies in Africa, 107-9
  Entente Cordiale, 136
  Parliamentary Reform, 47, 52, 54
  Social reforms, 55
  Triple Entente, 136
Great Trek, 82
Greenback Movement, 120, 190 (glossary)
Grey, Earl Charles, 47

Hague Court, 180
Haldane Mission, 140
Hammer v. Dagenhart, 63
Hargreaves, James, 4
Hawaii, 104
Hay, John, 100
Health Organization, 180
Hegel, Georg W. F., 19
Hepburn Act, 122
Hindenberg Line, 157
Hindenberg, General Paul von, 151
History of the Standard Oil Company, 122
Home Rule Bill, 78-79
Home Rule issue in Ireland, 78
"Honor" Clauses, 176, 190 (glossary)
Hottentots, 81
Hudson's Bay Company, 71
Hungary, 175

Ireland
  Act of Union, 77
  Catholic Emancipation, 78
  Easter Rebellion, 79
  Eire and the Republic of Ireland, 80
  Government of Ireland Act, 79
  Home Rule Issue, 78
  Irish Free State, 80
  The Pale, 77
  Ulster Plantation, 77
Irish Free State, 80
Irish Republican Army, 80
"Iron Law of Wages," 11
Imperial Conference, 83-84
Imperialism, 87-111, 191 (glossary)
India, 84
Industrial Revolution, 3-6

Industrial Revolution, Second, 22
Industrialization, 1-25
Internal Combustion Engine, 24
International
  First, 21
  Second, 21
  Third, 21
International Congo Association, 107
Internationalism, 182
Interstate Commerce Act, 1887, 117, 190 (glossary)
Ishmail Pasha, Khedive of Egypt, 106
Italy
  Independence movement, 38
  Kingdom of, 42
  Revolts of, 39
  Unification of, 37
  United Kingdom of, 41
  World War I, 160

***J'Accuse*, 59**
Jameson, Sir Leander, 82
Japan, 95
  Russo-Japanese War, 101
Jungle, The, 122
Junkers, 35
Jutland, battle of, 156

Kay, John, 4
Keating-Owen Act, 63
Kellogg, Frank, 185
Kellogg-Briand Pact, 185
Kerensky, Alexander, 159
Kitchener, General, 83, 106, 135
Korea, 97
Kruger, Paul, 82
Kulturkampf, 35, 191 (glossary)
Kun, Bela, 179

Labour Exchanges Act, 56
Labour Party, 55
Laissez-faire, 9, 50, 191 (glossary)
Lausanne, Treaty of, 173
League of Nations, 83, 162, 170, 172, 178, 180-83
Lease, Mary Ellen, 120
Lenin, Nikolai, 160
Liebknecht, Karl, 179
Little Entente, 184
Livingstone, David, 89, 107
Lloyd George, David, 53, 170
Locarno Agreements, 184
Lodge, Henry Cabot, 178
London Naval Conference, 1930, 184, 186
Louis-Napoleon, 56
Luxemburg, Rosa, 179

General Index

MacKenzie, William, 70
Maginot Line, 183, 186
Malthus, Thomas, 11, 90
Manchurian Incident, 182
"Mandates," 172, 191 (glossary)
Mann, Horace, 62
Maoris, 75
Marchand, Captain Jean-Baptiste, 106, 135
Marne, battle of the, 150
Marxist Doctrine, 20
Marx, Karl, 17, 18, 59
   contribution of, 21
Mazzini, Guiseppe, 38
McCormick Reaper, 115
McKinley, William, 121
Mill, John Stuart, 11
Missionaries, 89
Monroe Doctrine, 126
Morgan, J. Pierpont, 115
Moroccan Crisis, 137
Mutual Assistance, Treaty of, 186

Nanking, Treaty of, 92
Napoleon III, 32, 57
National Insurance Act, 56
National Liberals, Germany, 35
Navigation Acts repealed, 50
Neuilly, Treaty of, 173
New Caledonia, 59
Newcomen, Thomas, 5
New Harmony, 17, 61
New Lanark, 17
"New Liberals," 15
New Zealand, 72, 75
   Dominion of New Zealand, 76
Nine-Power Pact, 183
Nineteenth Amendment, 63
Northern Ireland, 80
Northern Securities Case, 121

Old Age Pensions Act, 53, 55
Open Door Policy, 100, 125, 191 (glossary)
Opium War, 92
Orange Free State, 82
Origin of Species, 90
Orlando, Vittoria, 170
Owen, Robert, 16, 51, 61

Pacific Railroad Act, 115
Pact of Paris, 185
Panama Canal, 126
Papineau, Louis, 70
Paris Commune, 58
Paris Peace Conference, 169
Parliament Bill, 54

Parnell, Charles, 78
Pennsylvania Railroad Company, 115
Permanent Court of International Justice, 180
"People's Charter," 49
Perry, Commander Matthew, 96
Philippines, 124
Poland, 173
Populist Party, 120, 121, 191 (glossary)
Portsmouth, Treaty of, 102, 126
Portugal
   colonies in Africa, 109
Poynings' Laws, 77
Princep, Gavrilo, 142
Principles of Political Economy, 12
Principles of Population, 11
Progressive Movement, 121
Prohibition, 64, 191 (glossary)
Pullman Strike, 119
Pure Food and Drugs Act, 122

Quebec Act, 69

Radicals, 47
Realpolitik, 30
Red Shirts, 38, 41
Reform Acts, 48, 53
Reform Bills, 47, 52
Re-Insurance Treaty, 133
Reparations, 175
Republic of Ireland, 80
Rhineland problem, 184
Rhodes, Cecil, 82, 109
Rhodesia, 82, 109
Ricardo, David, 11
Rockefeller, John D., 115
Roosevelt Corollary, 126
Roosevelt, President Theodore, 121
"Rotten Boroughs," 47, 192 (glossary)
Rumania, 175
Russia
   Abdication of Czar Nicholas, 159
   Dual Entente, 134
   Russo-Japanese War, 101
   Treaty of Brest-Litovsk, 160
   Triple Entente, 136
Russian Front, World War I, 151

Saar, 170
Sadler Report, 13
Sadowa, battle of, 30, 58
St. Germain, Treaty of, 173
Saint-Simon, Comte de, 16
Samoan Islands, 104
Samurai, 97
Sarajevo Crisis, 141

Savery, Thomas, 5
Schleswig-Holstein, 30
Schlieffen Plan, 149, 192 (glossary)
"Scientific Socialism" of Karl Marx, 17, 192 (glossary)
Scientific Socialism, 15
Second Empire, 57
Second Moroccan Crisis, 139
Sedan, Battle of, 33, 58
Seventeenth Amendment, 63
Sèvres, Treaty of, 173
Shaftesbury, Lord Anthony, 51
Shame of the Cities, 122
Shaw, Bernard, 22
Sherman Anti-Trust Act, 118
Shimonoseki, Treaty of, 98
Siemens, Sir William, 23
Singapore, 104
Sinn Fein, 79
Sino-Japanese War, 97
Smith, Adam, 10
Social Darwinism, 89, 192 (glossary)
Social Democrat Party, Germany, 34
Socialist Democratic Party, Germany, 162
Social Security Legislation of Bismarck, 36
Society of Equals, 15
Somme, battle of the, 155
South Africa, 80–83
   Boer War, 82, 135
   Union of South Africa, 83
Southeast Asia, 102–105
Spain; colonies in Africa, 109
Spanish-American War, 100, 124
Spartacist Movement, 179
Spinning Jenny, 4
"Spirit of Locarno," 184
Standard Oil Company, 115
Stanley, Henry M., 107
Statute of Westminster, 84
Steam Engine, 5, 25
Submarines, 156, 157
"*Succession States*," 173
Sudetenland, 179
Suez Canal, 106

Taft, William Howard, 123
Taiping Rebellion, 93
Tannenberg, battle of, 152
Test Act, repeal, 78
Third Communist International, 179
Thirteenth Amendment, 62
Three Emperors' League, 36
Tientsin, Treaty of, 95
Tory Party, 47
Townshend, Sir Charles V., 7
Trades Disputes Act, 52

Trade Unions, 51
Transvaal republic, 82
Treaty
  Amiens, 81
  Brest-Litovsk, 160
  Lausanne, 173
  Mutual Assistance, 186
  Nanking, 92
  Neuilly, 173
  Portsmouth, 102, 126
  Re-Insurance, 133
  St. Germain, 173
  Sèvres 173
  Shimonoseki, 98
  Tientsin, 95
  Trianon, 173
  Versailles, 170, 177, 178
  Wang-hsia, 93
  Washington Naval, 186
Trianon, Treaty of, 173
Triple Alliance, 133, 136
Tull, Jethro, 7
Turkey
  Treaty of Lausanne, 173
  Treaty of Sèvres, 173
Twenty-First Amendment, 65

Uitlanders, 82, 192,(glossary)
Ulster Plantation, 77
Uncle Tom's Cabin, 62
Union of South Africa, 1910, 83
United Empire Loyalists, 69
United States of America
  Agrarian protests, 120

United States of America *cont'd*
  Cuba and the Philippines, 124
  Emergence as a world power, 124
  Failure to ratify the Treaty of Versailles, 177
  Growth of corporations and railroads, 115
  Growth of Labor movement, 118
  Industrialization, 113
  Immigration, 61
  Kellogg-Briand Pact, 185
  Open Door Policy, 125
  Panama Canal, 126
  Populist Party, 120
  Political, social, and economic reforms, 60
  Progressive Movement, 121
  Pullman Strike, 119
  Roosevelt Corollary, 126
  Spanish-American War, 124
  Treaty of Portsmouth, 102
  World War I, 126, 157
United States v. E. C. Knight Co., 118
Upper Silesia, 172
Utopian Socialists, 15, 16, 192 (glossary)

Valera, Eamonn de, 79
Vanderbilt, Cornelius, 115
Verdun, battle of, 154
Versailles, Treaty of, 170, 177, 178
Victor Emmanuel I, 37
Victor Emmanuel II, 38
Vilna dispute, 181

Wabash, St. Louis and Pacific Railway v. Illinois, 117
Wang-hsia, Treaty of, 93
Washington Conference, 183
Washington Naval Treaty, 186
Watt, James, 6
Wealth of Nations, 10
Weaver, James B., 121
Weimar Republic, 177
Wells, H. G., 22
West Coast Hotel Company v. Parrish, 1937, 64
Whig Party, 47
Whitney, Eli, 5
Wilson, President Woodrow, 123, 157, 169, 178
World War I, 131–146
  Alliance System, 133, 144
  Austrian Ultimatum to Serbia, 142
  Background and origins, 131
  Balkan Wars, 140
  Blunders by European powers, 143
  Bosnia Crisis, 140
  Major events, 148
  Moroccan Crisis, 137
  Peace Proposals and Armistice, 160
  Sarajevo Crisis, 141
  War at Sea, 152, 156
Women's suffrage, U.S.A., 63
Workmen's Compensation Act, 55
World Court, 180
Wright Brothers, 24

Yugoslavia, 175

Zola, Émile, 59

Map Index

Abyssinia, 108
Adelaide, 75
Aden, 84
Afghanistan, 103
Agadir, 138
Algeciras, 138
Algeria, 108, 138
Algiers, 108
Alsace-Lorraine, 31, 171
Amoy, 94
Anglo-Egyptian Sudan, 84, 108
Angola, 94, 108
Arras, 161
Armistice, 159
Ascension Is., 84
Atlanta, Georgia, 116
Auckland, 75
Australia, 75, 84, 153, 181
Austria, 38, 171
Austria-Hungary, 31, 33, 41, 138, 149, 150, 155 159, 161

Bahamas 84, 125
Barbados, 84
Basutoland, 108
Battle fronts, 150, 153, 155, 159, 161
Bavaria, 31
Bechuanaland, 81, 84, 108
Belfast, 76
Belgium, 31, 33, 149, 171
Belgium Congo, 108
Belgrade, 150, 155, 161
Berlin, 31, 33, 155, 159, 161
Bermuda, 84
Birmingham, 48
Bloemfontein, 81
Bombay, 103
Borneo, 94
Bosnia, 41, 138
Bosnia-Herzegovina, 138
Boston, 116
Brest Litovsk, 159
Brisbane, 75
British Columbia, 71

British Guiana, 84, 125
British Honduras, 84, 125
British India, 84, 103
British Somaliland, 84, 103
Brussels, 161
Brunei, 84
Bucharest, 159
Bulgaria, 155, 159, 161
Burma, 94, 103
Butte, Montana, 116

Cairo, 108
Calcutta, 103
Calgary, 71
Cambodia, 94
Cambrai, 159
Cameroons, 84, 153, 181
Canada, 71, 84, 153
Canal Zone, 125
Canberra, 75
Canton, 94
Cape Breton Is., 71
Cape Colony, 81, 108
Cape Town, 81, 108, 153
Caporetto, 159
Caribbean, 125
Caroline Is., 94, 181
Ceylon, 84, 103
Château-Thierry, 161
China, 103
Chinese Eastern Railroad, 94
Christchurch, 75
Cochin China, 94
Cocos Is., 84
Colombia, 125
Congress of Vienna, 38
Constantinople, 150, 155
Coronel, battle of, 153
Corsica, 38, 41, 171
Costa Rica, 125
Cuxhaven, 159
Czechoslovakia, 171

Dairen, 94

Dakar, 108
Dardanelles, 155
Darwin, 75
Delhi, 103
Denmark, 31, 33, 149, 161, 171
Denver, Colorado, 116
Disenfranchised Boroughs, 48
Dominican Republic, 125
Dover, 161
Drogheda, 76
Dublin, 76
Durban, 81, 153
Dutch East Indies, 94
Dutch Guiana (Surinam), 125

East Africa, 108
East Prussia, 171
Edmonton, 71
Egypt, 84, 108, 138
Eire, 76
El Salvador, 125
Ems, 31
England, *see* Great Britain
Eritrea, 108
Estonia, 161, 171
Ethnic and Linguistic, 174
Europe after Treaty of Versailles, 171

Falkland Is., 84, 153
Finland, 171
Florence, 38
Foochow, 94
France, 31, 38, 41, 138, 149, 150, 155, 159, 161, 171
French Guiana, 125

Galicia, 150
Gambia, 84, 108
Garibaldi's Route, 41
German colonies, distribution 1919, 182
German East Africa, 108, 153, 181
German Southwest Africa, 181
German Unification, 31, 33
Germany, 138

Industrialism, Imperialism, and War

Gibraltar, 84, 153
Gilbert Is., 84
Gold Coast, 84, 108
Gorlice, 155
Great Britain, 48, 84, 138, 149, 150, 155, 161, 171
Greece, 159, 171
Guyana, 84, see British Guiana

Haiti, 125
Halifax, 71
Holland, 31, 33, 149; see Netherlands
Honduras, 125
Hong Kong, 84, 94
Hungary, 171, see Austria-Hungary

Ifni, 108
Immigration, U.S., 60
India, 84, 103, 153
Iraq, 84
Ireland, 76
Irish Free State, 76
Italian Somaliland, 108
Italian States, 31, 33, 38, 41
Italy, 38, 41, 138, 149, 155, 159, 161, 171

Jamaica, 84, 125
Japan, 153
Johannesburg, 81
Jutland, 153, 159

Kamerun, 153
Kansas City, 116
Kenya, 84
Kiaochow Bay, 84
Kiev, 161
Kingdom of the Two Sicilies, 38
Kowloon Bay, 94
Kwangchow, 94

Lagos, 108
Laos, 94
Latvia, 171
Leeds, 48
Liaotung Penninsula, 94, 108
Liberia, 108
Liège, 150
Limerick, 76
Limpopo, 81
Lithuania, 171
Lodz, 150
Lombardy, 38, 41
London, 48, 150, 155, 159
Londonderry, 76
Lorraine, 31, 171
Los Angeles, 116

Lower Canada, 71
Lutsk, 155, 171

Madagascar, 108
Malaya, 84, 94
Malta, 84, 153
Manchester, 48
Manchuria, 182
Manitoba, 71
Marianas Is., 94, 181
Marne, 150
Marsala, 41
Marshall Is., 94, 181
Mauritius, 84
Melbourne, 75
Memel, 171
Metz, 33
Mexico, 133
Milan, 38
Minsk, 155, 159
Modena, 38, 41
Mongolia, 84
Montenegro, 171
Morocco, 108, 138
Mozambique, 108
Mukden, 94
Munich, 31, 33

Napier, 75
Naples, 38, 41
Nauru, 181
Nepal, 103
Netherlands, 149, 161, 171, see Holland
New Boroughs, 48
New Brunswick, 71
New Guinea, 84, 153, 182
New Hebrides, 84
New Munster, 75
New Orleans, 116
New South Wales, 75
New Ulster, 75
New York, 116
New Zealand, 75, 84, 153
Newcastle on Tyne, 48
Newfoundland, 153
Nicaragua, 125
Nice, 38, 41
Nigeria, 84, 108
Ning-po, 94
North Borneo, 84
North German Federation, 33
North Island, N.Z., 75
Northern Ireland, 76
Northern Territory, 75
Norway, 161
Nova Scotia, 71

Nyasaland, 108

Omaha, Nebraska, 116
Ontario, 71
Orange Free State, 81, 108
Ottawa, 71

Palatinate, 31
Pale, the, 76
Palestine, 84
Panama, 125
Papal States, 38, 41
Paris, 150, 155, 159
Parliament Act, 1832, 48
Parma, 38
Peleu, 181
Persia, 103
Perth, 75
Pescadores, 94
Petrograd, 150, 159, 161
Philippines, 94
Piedmont, 38, 41
Pinsk, 155, 159
Poland, 171
Port Arthur, Canada, 71
Port Arthur, Lushan, 94
Portugal, 171
Portuguese East Africa, 81
Portuguese Guinea, 108
Prince Edward Is., 71
Prince Rupert, 71
Prussia, 31
Puerto Rico, 125

Quebec, 71
Queensland, 75

Railroads in U.S. to 1900, 116
Republic of Ireland, 76
Rhodesia, 81, 84, 108
Riga, 159, 161
Rio de Oro, 108
Rio Muni, 108
Romagna, 38, 41
Rosyth, 159
Rome, 41, 159, 161
Russia, 138, 149, 150, 155, 159, 161, 171
Rumania, 159, 161, 171

Saar, 171
Sadowa, 31
Saint John, 71
Saint Lawrence River, 71
Salisbury, Rhodesia 108
Salt Lake City, 116
Samoa, 153, 181

Santa Fe, 116
Sarawak, 84
Sardinia, 171
Sardinia, Kingdom of, 38, 41
Savoy, 38, 41
Scapa Flow, 153, 171
Schleswig-Holstein, 31, 171
Schlieffen Plan, 149
Sea Power, 1914, 153
Seattle, Washington, 116
Sedan, 33
Serbia, 138, 150, 155, 159
Shanghai, 94
Sheffield, 48
Sicily, 38, 171
Sierra Leone, 84, 108
Singapore, 94, 153
Sofia, 155
Soissons, 161
Solferino, 41
Solomon Is., 181
Somme, 159
South Africa, 84
South Australia, 75
South Island, N.Z., 75
Southwest Africa, 84, 153
Suez, 108
Sumatra, 94
Surinam, 125
Swaziland, 108
Sweden, 161
Switzerland, 31, 33, 41, 149, 161, 171
Sydney, 75

Tanganyika, 84
Tangier, 138
Tannenberg, 150
Tasmania, 75, 84
Territories lost by Germany, 1919, 171
Tibet, 103
Togo, 108
Togoland, 153, 181
Toronto, 71
Trans-Siberian Railroad, 94
Transvaal, 81, 108
Trench warfare lines, 1914–18, 153
Triple Alliance, 138
Triple Entente, 138
Tripoli, 108, 138
Tsingtao, 153, 181
Tsushima Straits, 94
Tunisia, 108, 138
Turkey, 150, 155, 159
Tuscany, 38, 41
Two Sicilies, Kingdom, 38, 41

U-Boat Activities, 1914–1918, 153
Uganda, 84, 108
Ulster, 76
Union of South Africa, 108
United Kingdom, *see* Great Britain
Upper Canada, 71
Upper Volta, 108

Vaal River, 81
Van Dieman's Land, 75
Venetia, 38, 41

Venezuela, 125
Venice, 38
Verdun, 155, 159
Versailles, Treaty settlements, 171
Victoria, Australia, 75
Victoria, Canada, 71
Vienna, 150, 155, 159, 161
Vilna, 155
Virgin Is., 125
Vittorio Veneto, 161

Walvis Bay, 108
Warsaw, 150, 161
Wei-Hai-Wei, 94
Wellington, 75
Western Australia, 75
Westport, N.Z., 75
Wexford, 76
Wilhelmshaven, 150
Winnipeg, 71
Wolverhampton, 48
Württemberg, 31

Ypres, 159
Yucatan, 125
Yugoslavia, 171

Zanzibar, 84

Picture Credits

Photographs were supplied by courtesy of the following: Historical Pictures Service: 5 (top right), 18 (bottom left and right), 39 (top left and right), 73, 79, 90, 92, 98, 99, 119, 126, 141 (top left), 153, 176; Brown Brothers: 61, 63, 64, 65, 96, 117, 127, 158, 169; Mansell Collection: 6, 9, 13, 17, 49; Radio Times Hulton Picture Library: 29, 40, 57, 101, 134, 135, 139; Imperial War Museum: 151, 152, 155, 162; Merrimack Valley Textile Museum: 4, 5 (top left), 8; John Dent: 32, 58, 106; John Freeman: 141 (bottom right); *Punch*: 41; Southwest Picture Agency, Bristol: 23; Australian News and Information Bureau: 74; New Zealand News and Information Bureau: 76.